SHONEN JUMP'S

Yu-Gi-Oh!™ TRADING CARD GAME

Master Duelist's Guide

Prima's Official Card Catalog

Prima Games
A Division of Random House, Inc.

3000 Lava Ridge Court
Roseville, CA 95661
(800) 733-3000
www.primagames.com

Product Manager: Jill Hinckley
Project Editor: Teli Hernandez
Design and Layout: Melissa Francis and Sherry Macias

ISBN: 0-7615-4514-X
Library of Congress Catalog Card Number: 2002103848
Printed in the United States of America

03 04 05 06 GG 10 9 8 7 6 5 4 3 2 1

Contents

Official Rules

This is an introduction to the Official Rules for the *Yu-Gi-Oh! TRADING CARD GAME.* For complete rules, see the Official Rulebook included with all Starter Decks.

Preparing Your Deck

Your Starter Deck contains all the cards you'll need to challenge an opponent to a Duel. In the following list you'll find basic rules for preparing your Deck.

- **The Deck used for Dueling should contain a minimum of 40 cards. Aside from this minimum limit, your Deck can contain as many cards as you'd like.**
- **In addition to your Dueling Deck, you can also have 15 additional cards in a separate pile, known as the Side Deck. The Side Deck allows you to modify your Deck to better suit your strategy during a Match.**

Between Duels, you can exchange any card from your Side Deck with any card in your Deck—as long as you end up with the same number of cards that your Deck began the Match with.

The Side Deck you create must contain exactly 15 cards at the beginning of a Match. In other words, if you don't have enough cards to create a 15-card Side Deck, you cannot use one at all.

In any Match, the Deck and Side Deck combined cannot contain more than three copies of the same card. Also, be aware of Forbidden and Limited Cards.

Preparing to Fight

You need the following items to start:

- **Deck of *Yu-Gi-Oh! TCG* cards (made up of at least 40 cards)**
- **Game Mat**

Game Mat

While battling, lay cards that you play and throw away onto the Game Mat.

Gameplay

In accordance with the Official Rules, a Duel is conducted in the following manner:

- **Before you start a Duel, greet your opponent with a friendly handshake.**
- **Both players shuffle their respective Decks and hand them to their opponent to shuffle (this is called Cutting the Deck). The Decks are then returned to their owners and placed face-down in their respective Deck Zones on the Game Mat.**
- **When using Fusion Monster Cards, place the cards face-down on the Fusion Deck Zone of the Game Mat. A Fusion Deck is a card or a group of cards consisting only of Fusion Monsters formed by fusing two or more monsters during a Duel.**
- **Show your opponent that your Side Deck contains exactly 15 cards (the cards may be counted face-down). When your Side Deck cards are exchanged with those in your Deck, count the cards in your Side Deck again to verify that the Deck still contains the same number of cards.**
- **For the first Duel in a Match, decide who starts first with a coin toss. Whoever wins the coin toss, can decide to go first or second. For subsequent Duels in the Match, the loser of the previous Duel decides who starts first. If the previous Duel ended in a tie, re-toss a coin to determine who starts first in the next Duel.**
- **Finally, each player draws five cards from the top of their respective Decks. Once both players have five cards in their hand, the Duel begins.**

Manners in Dueling

Remember the following codes of conduct when facing an opponent:

- **Always declare each move in a loud, clear voice before you execute any play.**
- **Your opponent is entitled to know the content of your Graveyard and the number of cards in your hand. If asked, you are obliged to answer truthfully.**
- **Never touch an opponent's cards without asking permission.**

Objective of the Game

Follow these Official Rules when waging battle:

- **The objective of the *Yu-Gi-Oh! TCG* is to win a Match against your opponent.**
- **A single Match consists of three Duels. Each card battle against an opponent in which a win, loss, or draw is determined is referred to as a Duel.**
- **The first person to win two Duels or has one win and two draws in a Match wins that Match.**
- **A Match with Duels that result in one win, one loss, and one draw or three draws is a draw Match, and no one wins or loses.**

Winning a Duel

The outcome of a Duel is decided according to the following Official Rules:

- **Each player begins a Duel with 8000 Life Points.**
- **Life Points decrease as a result of damage calculation after battle. You win a Duel if you reduce your opponent's Life Points to zero. If your opponent reduces your Life Points to zero, YOU lose!**
- **If you and your opponent both reach zero Life Points at the same time, the Duel is declared a draw.**
- **If either player's Deck runs out of cards during a Duel, the first player unable to draw a card is declared the loser. Bearing this in mind, a good Duelist should make every card count.**
- **If at any time during the Duel you hold the following cards in your hand, you instantly win the Duel:**
  "Right Leg of the Forbidden One"
  "Left Leg of the Forbidden One"
  "Right Arm of the Forbidden One"
  "Left Arm of the Forbidden One"
  "Exodia the Forbidden One"

Phases of Gameplay

Draw Phase

Draw one card from the top of your Deck on your turn.

Standby Phase

If there are any cards in play on the field that specifically state that certain actions must be taken during this phase, these must be dealt with prior to entering the Main Phase. Refer to the cards for specific details regarding the actions to be taken. If there are no such cards in play, proceed to Main Phase 1.

Main Phase 1

During this phase, you may: (1) Normal Summon or Set one Monster Card, (2) activate and/or Set Spell Cards, and (3) Set Trap Cards. Keep in mind that you may not exceed the five-card limit for the Monster Card Zone or the Spell & Trap Card Zone.

During this phase, you may also change the Attack or Defense Position of cards placed on the field during a previous turn. The postion of each card can be changed only once in a single turn, during either Main Phase 1 or 2. However, remember that once a monster attacks, it cannot be changed to Defense Position in the same turn.

IMPORTANT! You CANNOT change the Battle Position (Attack to Defense Position or vice-vesa) of a Monster Card during the same turn in which it has been summoned or Set.

At the end of the Main Phase 1, you can choose to enter the Battle Phase or proceed to the End Phase (the starting player cannot conduct a Battle Phase in their first turn).

Battle Phase

The Battle Phase consists of the following four steps:

Start Step: **Declare that you are entering the Battle Phase. You and your opponent may both play Quick-Play Spell and/or Trap Cards.**

Battle Step: **Select and announce one monster to attack with, and declare one of your opponent's monsters your target (the monster you wish to attack). You and your opponent may both play Quick-Play Spell and/or Trap Cards.**

Damage Step: **Calculate the damage points of the designated monsters. If a monster has a Flip Effect, apply it immediately after damage calculation. However, a Flip Effect does not affect monsters that have already been destroyed as a result of damage calculation.**

End Step: **Resolve all battles by repeating the Battle and Damage Steps as many times as necessary, then declare an end to your Battle Phase. You and your opponent may both play Quick-Play Spell and/or Trap Cards.**

Determining Damage

When the Opponent's Monster is in Attack Position

When the monster you attack is also in the Attack Position, determine the damage by comparing the ATK of the two monsters.

If the ATK of your attacking monster are greater than the ATK of your opponent's monster, your opponent's monster is destroyed. Subtract the value of the ATK of your opponent's monster from the ATK of your monster. Deduct the result from your opponent's Life Points.

If the ATK of your monster are the same as your opponent's monster, the battle is a draw, and both monsters are destroyed. Neither player receives damage, resulting in no change in Life Points.

If the ATK of your monster are less than the ATK of your opponent's monster, your monster is destroyed. Subtract the value of the ATK of your monster from the ATK of your opponent's monster. Deduct the result from your Life Points.

When the Opponent's Monster Is in Defense Position

When the monster you attack is in the Defense Position, determine the damage by comparing the ATK of your monster with the DEF of the monster you are attacking.

If the ATK of your attacking monster are greater than the DEF of your opponent's monster, destroy your opponent's monster. Neither player receives damage, resulting in no change in Life Points.

If the ATK of your monster are the same as the DEF of your opponent's monster, neither monster is destroyed. Neither player receives damage, resulting in no change in Life Points.

If the ATK of your monster are less than the DEF of your opponent's monster, neither monster is destroyed. Subtract the value of the ATK of your monster from the DEF of your opponent's monster. Deduct the result from your Life Points.

When the Opponent Has No Monsters on the Field

If no enemy Monster Cards exist on the field, your opponent receives Direct Damage. Deduct the attacking monster's ATK from your opponent's Life Points.

Main Phase 2

When the Battle Phase is over, the turn proceeds to Main Phase 2. As in Main Phase 1, you may Set or play Monster, Spell, and/or Trap Cards. Remember that you are allowed to change the Attack or Defense Position of each monster or perform a Normal Summon only ONCE PER TURN. Remember that if a monster attacks in the Battle Phase, it may not be changed to Defense Position in the same turn. Also keep in mind that you may not exceed the five-card limit for the Monster Card Zone or the Spell & Trap Card Zone.

End Phase

Announce the end of your turn. If your hand contains more than six cards, discard to the Graveyard until only six cards remain in your hand. The opposing player then begins his/her turn with the Draw Phase.

Concluding a Duel

Continue the steps from the Draw Phase to the End Phase until a winner is decided. This happens when one player's points reach zero, can no longer draw a card from his Deck when required to draw, or holds all five Exodia cards in his hand, and the Duel comes to an end.

Game Cards

Three main card types are used in *Yu-Gi-Oh! TCG:* Monster Cards, Spell Cards, and Trap Cards. Additionally, each type of card is divided into further sub-categories. For now, just read the card descriptions. After familiarizing yourself with the "Phases of Gameplay" section, you will understand the special role of each of the cards.

Monster Cards

A Monster Card is the basic card used to attack your opponent. Monster Cards are categorized by type and attribute. There are 20 different types and six different atttributes. Type and attribute affect each monster's ability to attack and defend.

The overall strength of a monster is indicated by its Level (the number of stars at the upper right of the Monster Card). Also note that the italicized text in the card description box is descriptive text only, and has NO effect on gameplay.

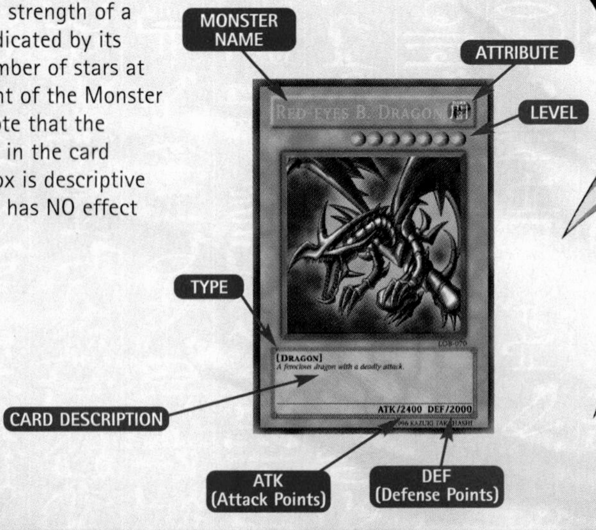

Other than Normal Monster Cards, there are also Fusion Monster Cards, Ritual Monster Cards, Effect Monster Cards, and Monster Tokens. Please refer to the Official Rulebook for more details.

Spell Cards

There are several types of Spell Cards. Spell Cards can only be activated or Set during Main Phases. The only exception to the rule are Quick-Play Spell Cards.

Spell Cards types are indentified by card icons. Spell Cards are color-coded GREEN.

There are Normal Spell Cards, Continuous Spell Cards, Equip Spell Cards, Field Spell Cards, Quick-Play Spell Cards, and Ritual Spell Cards. Please refer to the Official Rulebook for more details.

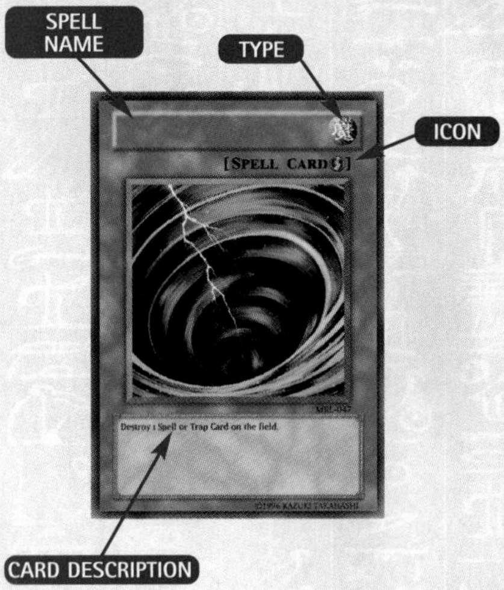

Trap Cards

You can Set these cards on the field and activate them at any time after the start of the next turn providing the requirements for activating the Trap Card have been met. Trap Card types are identified by card icons. Trap Cards are color-coded PURPLE.

There are Normal Trap Cards, Counter Trap Cards, and Continuous Trap Cards. Please refer to the Official Rulebook for more details.

Starter Deck Yugi

SDY-001 Mystical Elf

Card Type: Normal Monster
Monster Type: Spellcaster
Attribute: Light
Level: 4
ATK: 800
DEF: 2000
Rarity: Common

Rely on "Mystical Elf" for defense. However, since she has low ATK, she's easy prey for "Fissure...."

SDY-002 Feral Imp

Card Type: Normal Monster
Monster Type: Fiend
Attribute: Dark
Level: 4
ATK: 1300
DEF: 1400
Rarity: Common

This small Fiend's entire body is colored green. Its love of practical jokes makes it troublesome to deal with.

SDY-003 Winged Dragon, Guardian of the Fortress #1

Card Type: Normal Monster
Monster Type: Dragon
Attribute: Wind
Level: 4
ATK: 1400
DEF: 1200
Rarity: Common

Mountain battles are this Dragon's specialty. It frustrates enemies with sneak attacks!

SDY-004 Summoned Skull

Card Type: Normal Monster
Monster Type: Fiend
Attribute: Dark
Level: 6
ATK: 2500
DEF: 1200
Rarity: Common

Though "Summoned Skull" is a high-level Fiend, it's easy to summon and extremely useful.

SDY-005 Beaver Warrior

Card Type: Normal Monster
Monster Type: Beast-Warrior
Attribute: Earth
Level: 4
ATK: 1200
DEF: 1500
Rarity: Common

"Beaver Warrior" is one of Yugi's favorite Beast-Warriors. Set this monster first in Defense Position, then switch it to Attack Position when you see an opening!

SDY-006 Dark Magician

Card Type: Normal Monster
Monster Type: Spellcaster
Attribute: Dark
Level: 7
ATK: 2500
DEF: 2100
Rarity: Ultra Rare

A high-ranking magician of the Spellcaster-Type, the "Dark Magician" is very dangerous unless you destroy him as soon as your opponent places him on the field.

SDY-007 Gaia The Fierce Knight

Card Type: Normal Monster
Monster Type: Warrior
Attribute: Earth
Level: 7
ATK: 2300
DEF: 2100
Rarity: Common

Yugi uses this top-class Warrior. Don't fail to include this card in a Warrior-Type Deck!

SDY-008 Curse of Dragon

Card Type: Normal Monster
Monster Type: Dragon
Attribute: Dark
Level: 5
ATK: 2000
DEF: 1500
Rarity: Common

This cursed Dragon chars everything with its breath of flame. Instead of Setting it in Defense Position, attack!

SDY-009 Celtic Guardian

Card Type: Normal Monster
Monster Type: Warrior
Attribute: Earth
Level: 4
ATK: 1400
DEF: 1200
Rarity: Common

With high ATK, "Celtic Guardian" is an elite Warrior. He slices his enemies with his skilled techniques!

SDY-010 Mammoth Graveyard

Card Type: Normal Monster
Monster Type: Dinosaur
Attribute: Earth
Level: 3
ATK: 1200
DEF: 800
Rarity: Common

Even Yugi uses this Dinosaur-Type card. It has balanced ATK!

SDY-011 Great White

Card Type: Normal Monster
Monster Type: Fish
Attribute: Water
Level: 4
ATK: 1600
DEF: 800
Rarity: Common

The main monster of Fish-Type Monsters, its high ATK rivals "Rogue Doll's!"

SDY-012 Silver Fang

Card Type: Normal Monster
Monster Type: Beast
Attribute: Earth
Level: 3
ATK: 1200
DEF: 800
Rarity: Common

Yugi often uses this feral wolf in Duels. Power it up and defeat your opponent!

SDY-013 Giant Soldier of Stone

Card Type: Normal Monster
Monster Type: Rock
Attribute: Earth
Level: 3
ATK: 1300
DEF: 2000
Rarity: Common

This card will be the main monster in a Rock-Type Deck. For a Level 3 monster, the ATK and DEF are amazing!

SDY-014 Dragon Zombie

Card Type: Normal Monster
Monster Type: Zombie
Attribute: Dark
Level: 3
ATK: 1600
DEF: 0
Rarity: Common

Magical powers revived this Zombie from the grave. It used to be a Dragon, but no one knows which one.

SDY-015 Doma The Angel of Silence

Card Type: Normal Monster
Monster Type: Fairy
Attribute: Dark
Level: 5
ATK: 1600
DEF: 1400
Rarity: Common

A Fairy with DARK, this creature is full of mystery. You must offer one monster as a Tribute to summon this monster.

SDY-016 Ansatsu

Card Type: Normal Monster
Monster Type: Warrior
Attribute: Earth
Level: 5
ATK: 1700
DEF: 1200
Rarity: Common

When powered up by "Invigoration," this high-level Warrior can even defeat the "Mystical Elf!"

SDY-017 Witty Phantom

Card Type: Normal Monster
Monster Type: Fiend
Attribute: Dark
Level: 4
ATK: 1400
DEF: 1300
Rarity: Common

This Fiend is a hard-working nice guy and is quite popular with the ladies of the underworld.

SDY-018 Claw Reacher

Card Type: Normal Monster
Monster Type: Fiend
Attribute: Dark
Level: 3
ATK: 1000
DEF: 800
Rarity: Common

This Fiend can instantly extend its arms like a machine, but its abilities are low.

SDY-019 Mystic Clown

Card Type: Normal Monster
Monster Type: Fiend
Attribute: Dark
Level: 4
ATK: 1500
DEF: 1000
Rarity: Common

Though not as powerful as "Rogue Doll," this low-level monster has high ATK, making it a dangerous force!

SDY-020 Sword of Dark Destruction

Card Type: Spell
Monster Type: –
Attribute: Spell
Level: –
ATK: –
DEF: –
Rarity: Common

This Equip Spell Card can be equipped on any type of monster as long as it has DARK. You'll want this card in your Deck!

Starter Deck Yugi

SDY-021 Book of Secret Arts

Card Type: Spell
Monster Type: —
Attribute: Spell
Level: —
ATK: —
DEF: —
Rarity: Common

Use this book on "Dark Magician" to easily destroy every Monster Card, except "Blue-Eyes White Dragon!"

SDY-022 Dark Hole

Card Type: Spell
Monster Type: —
Attribute: Spell
Level: —
ATK: —
DEF: —
Rarity: Common

"Dark Hole" is very effective when the Duel is deadlocked against an opponent who is using monsters with high DEF!

SDY-023 Dian Keto the Cure Master

Card Type: Spell
Monster Type: —
Attribute: Spell
Level: —
ATK: —
DEF: —
Rarity: Common

This motherly goddess will refill 1000 Life Points. If you have three of this card in your Deck, you can regain 3000 Life Points.

SDY-024 Ancient Elf

Card Type: Normal Monster
Monster Type: Spellcaster
Attribute: Light
Level: 4
ATK: 1450
DEF: 1200
Rarity: Common

Rumors say this elf has lived for millenniums.

SDY-025 Magical Ghost

Card Type: Normal Monster
Monster Type: Zombie
Attribute: Dark
Level: 4
ATK: 1300
DEF: 1400
Rarity: Common

A magician combined with a ghost to revive herself from the afterlife. She attacks with spells that attack her opponent's confidence.

SDY-026 Fissure

Card Type: Spell
Monster Type: —
Attribute: Spell
Level: —
ATK: —
DEF: —
Rarity: Common

This card affects face-up Monster Cards. Even the mightiest Monster Cards cannot escape this effect!

SDY-027 Trap Hole

Card Type: Trap
Monster Type: —
Attribute: Trap
Level: —
ATK: —
DEF: —
Rarity: Common

Activate "Trap Hole" when your opponent Normal Summons or Flip Summons a monster!

SDY-028 Two-Pronged Attack

Card Type: Trap
Monster Type: —
Attribute: Trap
Level: —
ATK: —
DEF: —
Rarity: Common

"Two-Pronged Attack" is very useful when you have many monsters on your field. Use it as soon as your opponent summons a powerful monster!

SDY-029 De-Spell

Card Type: Spell
Monster Type: —
Attribute: Spell
Level: —
ATK: —
DEF: —
Rarity: Common

This Spell Card can even destroy face-down Spell Cards. If the chosen face-down card is a Trap Card, then return the Trap Card back to normal.

SDY-030 Monster Reborn

Card Type: Spell
Monster Type: —
Attribute: Spell
Level: —
ATK: —
DEF: —
Rarity: Common

If there's a Monster Card in the Graveyard, use this Spell Card to resurrect it and make it part of your team! This is an extremely important card!

SDY-031 Reinforcements

Card Type: Trap
Monster Type: —
Attribute: Trap
Level: —
ATK: —
DEF: —
Rarity: Common

Put a weak monster in Attack Position, and use this Trap Card when your opponent attacks. It's a counterattack!

SDY-032 Change of Heart

Card Type: Spell
Monster Type: —
Attribute: Spell
Level: —
ATK: —
DEF: —
Rarity: Common

The heart is a transient thing, and this is true for monsters' hearts as well—so much that monsters at times forget who their masters are. The monster you worked so hard to summon suddenly defects to your opponent. This effect lasts only the turn "Change of Heart" is activated, so the monster is often offered as a Tribute.

SDY-033 The Stern Mystic

Card Type: Effect Monster
Monster Type: Spellcaster
Attribute: Light
Level: 4
ATK: 1500
DEF: 1200
Rarity: Common

This card allows you to see all face-down Monster, Spell, and Trap Cards. If you know what cards your opponent is playing, you can easily prepare countermeasures.

SDY-034 Wall of Illusion

Card Type: Effect Monster
Monster Type: Fiend
Attribute: Dark
Level: 4
ATK: 1000
DEF: 1850
Rarity: Common

There are few Level 4 and below monsters that can defeat 1850 DEF. The monsters that can defeat "Wall of Illusion" are usually Tribute Summoned monsters, but they will be returned to your opponent's hand if they attack "Wall of Illusion."

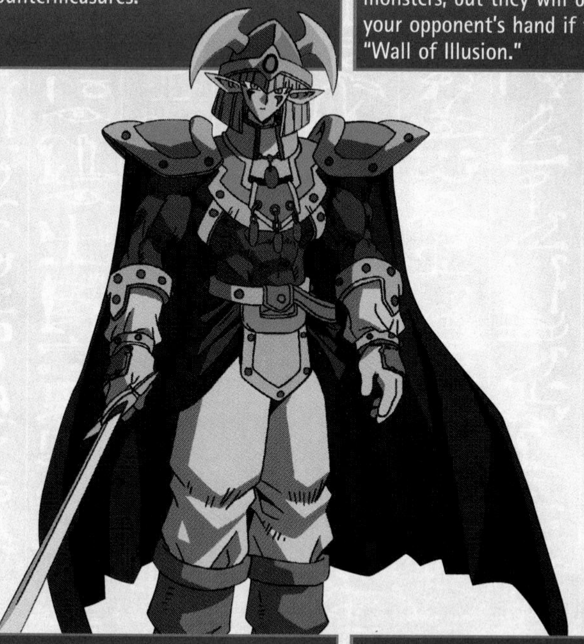

SDY-035 Neo the Magic Swordsman

Card Type: Normal Monster
Monster Type: Spellcaster
Attribute: Light
Level: 4
ATK: 1700
DEF: 1000
Rarity: Common

This monster has the LIGHT, but since it is also a Spellcaster, it will be powered up by the Yami Field Spell Card.

SDY-036 Baron of the Fiend Sword

Card Type: Normal Monster
Monster Type: Fiend
Attribute: Dark
Level: 4
ATK: 1550
DEF: 800
Rarity: Common

This card will power up in the Yami field.

SDY-037 Man-Eating Treasure Chest

Card Type: Normal Monster
Monster Type: Fiend
Attribute: Dark
Level: 4
ATK: 1600
DEF: 1000
Rarity: Common

This monster has 1600 ATK, but it will power up even further in the Yami field.

SDY-038 Sorcerer of the Doomed

Card Type: Normal Monster
Monster Type: Spellcaster
Attribute: Dark
Level: 4
ATK: 1450
DEF: 1200
Rarity: Common

This Spellcaster is an expert in extermination spells, but its ATK and DEF may not help save his own life.

SDY-039 Last Will

Card Type: Spell
Monster Type: —
Attribute: Spell
Level: —
ATK: —
DEF: —
Rarity: Common

Don't make the mistake of thinking this card is useless because you can only summon monsters 1500 ATK and below. With this card, you can summon Effect Monster Cards that hold the key to a combo.

SDY-040 Waboku

Card Type: Trap
Monster Type: —
Attribute: Trap
Level: —
ATK: —
DEF: —
Rarity: Common

Zero battle damage means that the effects of "White Magical Hat" or "Robbin' Goblin" disappear. However, "Waboku's" effect lasts for only one turn.

Starter Deck Yugi

SDY-041 Soul Exchange

Card Type:	Spell
Monster Type:	—
Attribute:	Spell
Level:	—
ATK:	—
DEF:	—
Rarity:	Super Rare

You cannot attack this turn, but you will use your opponent's monster for a Tribute Summon.

SDY-042 Card Destruction

Card Type:	Spell
Monster Type:	—
Attribute:	Spell
Level:	—
ATK:	—
DEF:	—
Rarity:	Super Rare

This card is especially useful when you have no useful cards in your hand while your opponent has many powerful cards in his or her hand.

SDY-043 Trap Master

Card Type:	Effect Monster
Monster Type:	Warrior
Attribute:	Earth
Level:	3
ATK:	500
DEF:	1100
Rarity:	Common

You can destroy your opponent's Trap Card without it activating. It may be fun to Set this monster on your first turn. It will baffle your opponent and throw his or her game off-track.

SDY-044 Dragon Capture Jar

Card Type:	Trap
Monster Type:	—
Attribute:	Trap
Level:	—
ATK:	—
DEF:	—
Rarity:	Common

Dragon-Types should be wary of this Trap Card. Even the "Stop Defense" Spell Card can't affect "Dragon Capture Jar!"

SDY-045 Yami

Card Type:	Spell
Monster Type:	—
Attribute:	Spell
Level:	—
ATK:	—
DEF:	—
Rarity:	Common

Since Fairy-Type monsters crave the light, they're weak in Yami terrain. However, this terrain strengthens Fiend- and Spellcaster-Type monsters who thrive on magical powers!

SDY-046 Man-Eater Bug

Card Type:	Effect Monster
Monster Type:	Insect
Attribute:	Earth
Level:	2
ATK:	450
DEF:	600
Rarity:	Common

If "Man-Eater Bug" is the only monster on the field, its effect will destroy the "Man-Eater Bug" itself....

SDY-047 Reverse Trap

Card Type:	Trap
Monster Type:	—
Attribute:	Trap
Level:	—
ATK:	—
DEF:	—
Rarity:	Common

This card counteracts all the Spell Cards and the like that are powering up monsters. This is a scary Trap Card!

SDY-048 Remove Trap

Card Type:	Spell
Monster Type:	—
Attribute:	Spell
Level:	—
ATK:	—
DEF:	—
Rarity:	Common

This Spell Card destroys one face-up Trap Card on the field. It cannot destroy face-down Trap Cards.

SDY-049 Castle Walls

Card Type:	Trap
Monster Type:	—
Attribute:	Trap
Level:	—
ATK:	—
DEF:	—
Rarity:	Common

Similar to "Reinforcements," use this card on monsters in Defense Position. Send back the damage!

SDY-050 Ultimate Offering

Card Type:	Trap
Monster Type:	—
Attribute:	Trap
Level:	—
ATK:	—
DEF:	—
Rarity:	Common

As long as this card is face-up on the field, you can freely Normal Summon or Set the monster in your hand during your Main Phase or your opponent's Battle Phase.

Starter Deck Kaiba

SDK-001 Blue-Eyes White Dragon

Card Type: Normal Monster
Monster Type: Dragon
Attribute: Light
Level: 8
ATK: 3000
DEF: 2500
Rarity: Ultra Rare

Kaiba's favorite monster is the most powerful Normal Monster Card. Destroying "Blue-Eyes" without a Spell Card will be difficult!

SDK-002 Hitotsu-Me Giant

Card Type: Normal Monster
Monster Type: Beast-Warrior
Attribute: Earth
Level: 4
ATK: 1200
DEF: 1000
Rarity: Common

Even Kaiba uses this Beast-Warrior-Type monster. Be sure to put its high ATK to use!

SDK-003 Ryu-Kishin

Card Type: Normal Monster
Monster Type: Fiend
Attribute: Dark
Level: 3
ATK: 1000
DEF: 500
Rarity: Common

A mysterious new fiendish statue stands among ruins.... This must be "Ryu-Kishin!" Destroy it from afar!

SDK-004 The Wicked Worm Beast

Card Type: Effect Monster
Monster Type: Beast
Attribute: Earth
Level: 3
ATK: 1400
DEF: 700
Rarity: Common

If this monster is destroyed during the Battle Phase, it will not return to your hand.

SDK-005 Battle Ox

Card Type: Normal Monster
Monster Type: Beast-Warrior
Attribute: Earth
Level: 4
ATK: 1700
DEF: 1000
Rarity: Common

This ox wears armor and wields a large axe, making it as strong as it looks. You don't need to offer another monster for a Tribute to summon "Battle Ox," making this monster extremely useful.

SDK-006 Koumori Dragon

Card Type: Normal Monster
Monster Type: Dragon
Attribute: Dark
Level: 4
ATK: 1500
DEF: 1200
Rarity: Common

Even Yugi uses this black Dragon. It fires flames from its mouth and throws down enemies with its large tail. The souls of anyone who looks at this monster becomes corrupted.

SDK-007 Judge Man

Card Type: Normal Monster
Monster Type: Warrior
Attribute: Earth
Level: 6
ATK: 2200
DEF: 1500
Rarity: Common

One of the most powerful Level 6 monsters was also used in Kaiba's Deck.

SDK-008 Rogue Doll

Card Type: Normal Monster
Monster Type: Spellcaster
Attribute: Light
Level: 4
ATK: 1600
DEF: 1000
Rarity: Common

It has high ATK, but you can summon this monster without having to offer another monster for a Tribute! However, its DEF is low.

SDK-009 Kojikocy

Card Type: Normal Monster
Monster Type: Warrior
Attribute: Earth
Level: 4
ATK: 1500
DEF: 1200
Rarity: Common

This Warrior has extremely powerful destructive powers! It will definitely be a core force in Warrior-Type Decks.

SDK-010 Uraby

Card Type: Normal Monster
Monster Type: Dinosaur
Attribute: Earth
Level: 4
ATK: 1500
DEF: 800
Rarity: Common

This powerful Dinosaur has overwhelming strength and will eat and swallow anyone it sets its sights on.

Starter Deck Kaiba

SDK-011 Gyakutenno Megami

Card Type: Normal Monster
Monster Type: Fairy
Attribute: Light
Level: 6
ATK: 1800
DEF: 2000
Rarity: Common

One of the strongest goddesses, "Gyakutenno Megami" has higher DEF than ATK.

SDK-012 Mystic Horseman

Card Type: Normal Monster
Monster Type: Beast
Attribute: Earth
Level: 4
ATK: 1300
DEF: 1550
Rarity: Common

A legendary half-man/half-horse creature, "Mystic Horseman" runs extremely fast, and its speedy attacks are truly horrifying.

SDK-013 Terra the Terrible

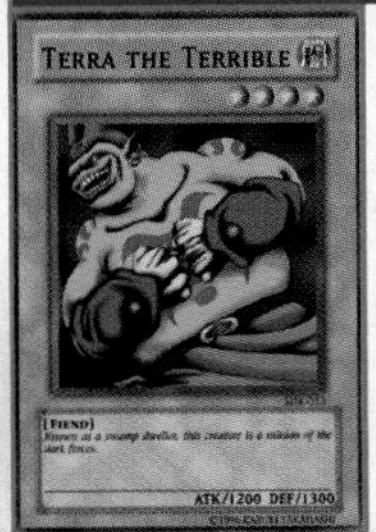

Card Type: Normal Monster
Monster Type: Fiend
Attribute: Dark
Level: 4
ATK: 1200
DEF: 1300
Rarity: Common

"Terra the Terrible" has average abilities, so you can entrust it with both attack and defense.

SDK-014 Dark Titan of Terror

Card Type: Normal Monster
Monster Type: Fiend
Attribute: Dark
Level: 4
ATK: 1300
DEF: 1100
Rarity: Common

This monster enters your dreams and turns them into nightmares. He enjoys watching your horror.

SDK-015 Dark Assailant

Card Type: Normal Monster
Monster Type: Zombie
Attribute: Dark
Level: 4
ATK: 1200
DEF: 1200
Rarity: Common

Due to his popularity, he hasn't received any jobs recently.... It's hard to be famous.

SDK-016 Master & Expert

Card Type: Normal Monster
Monster Type: Beast
Attribute: Earth
Level: 4
ATK: 1200
DEF: 1000
Rarity: Common

The duo fight in perfect sync both offensively and defensively. However, their low ATK is their biggest weakness.

SDK-017 Unknown Warrior of Fiend

Card Type: Normal Monster
Monster Type: Warrior
Attribute: Dark
Level: 3
ATK: 1000
DEF: 500
Rarity: Common

"Unknown Warrior of Fiend" slices enemies by wielding a sword at supersonic speed. This is one of the fastest Warriors.

SDK-018 Mystic Clown

Card Type: Normal Monster
Monster Type: Fiend
Attribute: Dark
Level: 4
ATK: 1500
DEF: 1000
Rarity: Common

Though not as powerful as "Rogue Doll," this low-level monster has high ATK, making it a dangerous force!

SDK-019 Ogre of the Black Shadow

Card Type: Normal Monster
Monster Type: Beast-Warrior
Attribute: Earth
Level: 4
ATK: 1200
DEF: 1400
Rarity: Common

It can only move in straight lines, so you may think this monster is easy to destroy. However, since it moves so fast, it evades many attacks.

SDK-020 Dark Energy

Card Type: Spell
Monster Type: –
Attribute: Spell
Level: –
ATK: –
DEF: –
Rarity: Common

This energy source for Fiend-Type monsters was created by compressing air from the underworld. Fiends use this energy to power-up!

SDK-021 Invigoration

- **Card Type:** Spell
- **Monster Type:** —
- **Attribute:** Spell
- **Level:** —
- **ATK:** —
- **DEF:** —
- **Rarity:** Common

This card affects many Warrior- and Plant-Type monsters. Use this card with "Legendary Sword!"

SDK-022 Dark Hole

- **Card Type:** Spell
- **Monster Type:** —
- **Attribute:** Spell
- **Level:** —
- **ATK:** —
- **DEF:** —
- **Rarity:** Common

"Dark Hole" is very effective when the Duel is deadlocked against an opponent who is using monsters with high DEF!

SDK-023 Ookazi

- **Card Type:** Spell
- **Monster Type:** —
- **Attribute:** Spell
- **Level:** —
- **ATK:** —
- **DEF:** —
- **Rarity:** Common

During meals, there's flames on the stove. If it turns into a fire.... Be careful to avoid disasters!

SDK-024 Ryu-Kishin Powered

- **Card Type:** Normal Monster
- **Monster Type:** Fiend
- **Attribute:** Dark
- **Level:** 4
- **ATK:** 1600
- **DEF:** 1200
- **Rarity:** Common

Kaiba uses this beefed-up version of "Ryu-Kishin." Its armorlike body and huge sharp claws power up its abilities.

SDK-025 Swordstalker

- **Card Type:** Normal Monster
- **Monster Type:** Warrior
- **Attribute:** Dark
- **Level:** 6
- **ATK:** 2000
- **DEF:** 1600
- **Rarity:** Common

"Swordstalker's" sword is said to be powered by the spirits of defeated monsters.

SDK-026 La Jinn the Mystical Genie of the Lamp

- **Card Type:** Normal Monster
- **Monster Type:** Fiend
- **Attribute:** Dark
- **Level:** 4
- **ATK:** 1800
- **DEF:** 1000
- **Rarity:** Common

If you ask this Fiend for crazy wishes, he'll be upset....

SDK-027 Rude Kaiser

- **Card Type:** Normal Monster
- **Monster Type:** Beast-Warrior
- **Attribute:** Earth
- **Level:** 5
- **ATK:** 1800
- **DEF:** 1600
- **Rarity:** Common

The huge axes connected to both arms can cleave a rock in a single slice. Beast-Warriors have high ATK, and "Rude Kaiser" is one of the strongest among them.

SDK-028 Destroyer Golem

- **Card Type:** Normal Monster
- **Monster Type:** Rock
- **Attribute:** Earth
- **Level:** 4
- **ATK:** 1500
- **DEF:** 1000
- **Rarity:** Common

You can count on "Destroyer Golem's" high ATK in combat, but beware—its DEF is surprisingly low!

SDK-029 Skull Red Bird

- **Card Type:** Normal Monster
- **Monster Type:** Winged Beast
- **Attribute:** Wind
- **Level:** 4
- **ATK:** 1550
- **DEF:** 1200
- **Rarity:** Common

"Skull Red Bird" is not as strong as "Rogue Doll," it's a decently powerful Winged Beast. Power it up with the Mountain Field Spell Card!

SDK-030 D. Human

- **Card Type:** Normal Monster
- **Monster Type:** Warrior
- **Attribute:** Earth
- **Level:** 4
- **ATK:** 1300
- **DEF:** 1100
- **Rarity:** Common

"D. Human" wields a weapon created from a Dragon, so Dragons sometime attack him for vengeance!

Starter Deck Kaiba

SDK-031 Pale Beast

Card Type: Normal Monster
Monster Type: Beast
Attribute: Earth
Level: 4
ATK: 1500
DEF: 1200
Rarity: Common

Living deep in the shadows of a forest, the pair of eyes on "Pale Beast's" chin help it find prey.

SDK-032 Fissure

Card Type: Spell
Monster Type: —
Attribute: Spell
Level: —
ATK: —
DEF: —
Rarity: Common

This card affects face-up Monster Cards. Even the mightiest Monster Cards cannot escape this effect!

SDK-033 Trap Hole

Card Type: Trap
Monster Type: —
Attribute: Trap
Level: —
ATK: —
DEF: —
Rarity: Common

Activate "Trap Hole" when your opponent Normal Summons or Flip Summons a monster!

SDK-034 Two-Pronged Attack

Card Type: Trap
Monster Type: —
Attribute: Trap
Level: —
ATK: —
DEF: —
Rarity: Common

"Two-Pronged Attack" is very useful when you have many monsters on your field. Use it as soon as your opponent summons a powerful monster!

SDK-035 De-Spell

Card Type: Spell
Monster Type: —
Attribute: Spell
Level: —
ATK: —
DEF: —
Rarity: Common

This Spell Card can even destroy face-down Spell Cards. If the chosen face-down card is a Trap Card, then return the Trap Card back to normal.

SDK-036 Monster Reborn

Card Type: Spell
Monster Type: —
Attribute: Spell
Level: —
ATK: —
DEF: —
Rarity: Common

If there's a Monster Card in the Graveyard, use this Spell Card to resurrect it and make it part of your team! This is an extremely important card!

SDK-037 The Inexperienced Spy

Card Type: Spell
Monster Type: —
Attribute: Spell
Level: —
ATK: —
DEF: —
Rarity: Common

Since he's still in training, he can only see one card in your opponent's hand. Choose a card that looks suspicious.

SDK-038 Reinforcements

Card Type: Trap
Monster Type: —
Attribute: Trap
Level: —
ATK: —
DEF: —
Rarity: Common

Put a weak monster in Attack Position, and use this Trap Card when your opponent attacks. It's a counterattack!

SDK-039 Ancient Telescope

Card Type: Spell
Monster Type: —
Attribute: Spell
Level: —
ATK: —
DEF: —
Rarity: Common

This very useful card lets you see your opponent's cards and prepare your strategy for the next five turns.

SDK-040 Just Desserts

Card Type: Trap
Monster Type: —
Attribute: Trap
Level: —
ATK: —
DEF: —
Rarity: Common

If your opponent has five monsters on the field, then you can deal 2500 points of damage, but this is easier said than done. It should be good to activate this Trap Card when your opponent has three Monster Cards on the field.

SDK-041 Lord of D.

Card Type: Effect Monster
Monster Type: Spellcaster
Attribute: Dark
Level: 4
ATK: 1200
DEF: 1100
Rarity: Super Rare

"Lord of D." can protect all Dragons, but that's not all! Using "Lord of D." with "The Flute of Summoning Dragon" forms a devastating combo!

SDK-042 The Flute of Summoning Dragon

Card Type: Spell
Monster Type: —
Attribute: Spell
Level: —
ATK: —
DEF: —
Rarity: Super Rare

You can Special Summon not one, but two "Blue-Eyes White Dragons" on the same turn! Your opponent will be dealt a crippling blow instantly. This card seems unfair....

SDK-043 Mysterious Puppeteer

Card Type: Effect Monster
Monster Type: Warrior
Attribute: Earth
Level: 4
ATK: 1000
DEF: 1500
Rarity: Common

This useful card allows you to regain Life Points even when your opponent summons a monster. Combo: When "Mysterious Puppeteer" is face-up on the field, use "Ultimate Offering" and summon your monsters.

SDK-044 Trap Master

Card Type: Effect Monster
Monster Type: Warrior
Attribute: Earth
Level: 3
ATK: 500
DEF: 1100
Rarity: Common

You can destroy your opponent's Trap Card without it activating. It may be fun to Set this monster on your first turn. It will baffle your opponent and throw his or her game off-track.

SDK-045 Sogen

Card Type: Spell
Monster Type: —
Attribute: Spell
Level: —
ATK: —
DEF: —
Rarity: Common

This Spell Card transforms the field into a scenic vast grassland. "Sogen" gives Warrior-and Beast-Warrior-Type monster an advantage in battle!

SDK-046 Hane-Hane

Card Type: Effect Monster
Monster Type: Beast
Attribute: Earth
Level: 2
ATK: 450
DEF: 500
Rarity: Common

Even if face-down "Hane-Hane" is destroyed in battle, you return one monster on the field, but please remember that you can not return "Hane-Hane" itself if it is destroyed.

SDK-047 Reverse Trap

Card Type: Trap
Monster Type: —
Attribute: Trap
Level: —
ATK: —
DEF: —
Rarity: Common

This card counteracts all the Spell Cards and the like that are powering up monsters. This is a scary Trap Card!

SDK-048 Remove Trap

Card Type: Spell
Monster Type: —
Attribute: Spell
Level: —
ATK: —
DEF: —
Rarity: Common

This Spell Card destroys one face-up Trap Card on the field. It cannot destroy face-down Trap Cards.

SDK-049 Castle Walls

Card Type: Trap
Monster Type: —
Attribute: Trap
Level: —
ATK: —
DEF: —
Rarity: Common

Similar to "Reinforcements," use this card on monsters in Defense Position. Send back the damage!

SDK-050 Ultimate Offering

Card Type: Trap
Monster Type: —
Attribute: Trap
Level: —
ATK: —
DEF: —
Rarity: Common

As long as this card is face-up on the field, you can freely Normal Summon or Set the monster in your hand during your Main Phase or your opponent's Battle Phase.

Starter Deck Joey

SDJ-001 Red-Eyes B. Dragon

Card Type: Normal Monster
Monster Type: Dragon
Attribute: Dark
Level: 7
ATK: 2400
DEF: 2000
Rarity: Ultra Rare

Joey received this rare card by defeating "Rex Raptor." This monster can become even stronger if it fuses with another monster by "Polymerization!"

SDJ-002 Swordsman of Landstar

Card Type: Normal Monster
Monster Type: Warrior
Attribute: Earth
Level: 3
ATK: 500
DEF: 1200
Rarity: Common

Joey uses this monster, but it has low ATK and DEF.

SDJ-003 Baby Dragon

Card Type: Normal Monster
Monster Type: Dragon
Attribute: Wind
Level: 3
ATK: 1200
DEF: 700
Rarity: Common

Though "Baby Dragon" is still a baby, it has huge potential for power. Fuse "Baby Dragon" with "Time Wizard" to summon "Thousand Dragon!"

SDJ-004 Spirit of the Harp

Card Type: Normal Monster
Monster Type: Fairy
Attribute: Light
Level: 4
ATK: 800
DEF: 2000
Rarity: Common

This female monster has very high DEF. If you use Yami Field Spell Card, "Spirit of the Harp" will power down.

SDJ-005 Island Turtle

Card Type: Normal Monster
Monster Type: Aqua
Attribute: Water
Level: 4
ATK: 1100
DEF: 2000
Rarity: Common

This large turtle is the size of a small island. Trees and animals live on its back because "Island Turtle" never dives underwater.

SDJ-006 Flame Manipulator

Card Type: Normal Monster
Monster Type: Spellcaster
Attribute: Fire
Level: 3
ATK: 900
DEF: 1000
Rarity: Common

When fused, this Spellcaster transforms into "Flame Swordsman." He's better at defending than he is at attacking!

SDJ-007 Masaki the Legendary Swordsman

Card Type: Normal Monster
Monster Type: Warrior
Attribute: Earth
Level: 4
ATK: 1100
DEF: 1100
Rarity: Common

The legendary Warrior has revived in present times. Dressed in the same armor during battle, he strikes his enemy with his favorite sword.

SDJ-008 7 Colored Fish

Card Type: Normal Monster
Monster Type: Fish
Attribute: Water
Level: 4
ATK: 1800
DEF: 800
Rarity: Common

"7 Colored Fish" is extremely powerful for a monster that does not have to be a Tribute Summon.

SDJ-009 Armored Lizard

Card Type: Normal Monster
Monster Type: Reptile
Attribute: Earth
Level: 4
ATK: 1500
DEF: 1200
Rarity: Common

An offense card of the Reptile-Type monsters, "Armored Lizard's" strength is that it is good to go in any terrain!

SDJ-010 Darkfire Soldier #1

Card Type: Normal Monster
Monster Type: Pyro
Attribute: Fire
Level: 4
ATK: 1700
DEF: 1150
Rarity: Common

This burning soldier is an expert in explosives.

SDJ-011 Harpie's Brother

Card Type: Normal Monster
Monster Type: Winged Beast
Attribute: Wind
Level: 4
ATK: 1800
DEF: 600
Rarity: Common

This birdman flies at incredible speed and can see into great distances with eyes more perceptive than an eagle's.

SDJ-012 Gearfried the Iron Knight

Card Type: Effect Monster
Monster Type: Warrior
Attribute: Earth
Level: 4
ATK: 1800
DEF: 1600
Rarity: Common

"Gearfried the Iron Knight" has high ATK for a Level 4 monster. Though you can't use Equip Spell Cards on "Gearfried the Iron Knight," neither can your opponent!

SDJ-013 Karate Man

Card Type: Effect Monster
Monster Type: Warrior
Attribute: Earth
Level: 3
ATK: 1000
DEF: 1000
Rarity: Common

You can double the ATK of "Karate Man" for one turn, but it will be destroyed at the end of the turn. Know when to use this effect. Remember, this is NOT a Multi-Trigger Effect.

SDJ-014 Milus Radiant

Card Type: Effect Monster
Monster Type: Beast
Attribute: Earth
Level: 1
ATK: 300
DEF: 250
Rarity: Common

When you use this card, all EARTH monsters gain 500 ATK while all WIND monsters lose 400 ATK. This effect affects "Milus Radiant" itself.

SDJ-015 Time Wizard

Card Type: Effect Monster
Monster Type: Spellcaster
Attribute: Light
Level: 2
ATK: 500
DEF: 400
Rarity: Common

This Spellcaster has the ability to control time. Fuse "Time Wizard" with "Baby Dragon" to summon "Thousand Dragon."

SDJ-016 Maha Vailo

Card Type: Effect Monster
Monster Type: Spellcaster
Attribute: Light
Level: 4
ATK: 1550
DEF: 1400
Rarity: Common

"Maha Vailo" looks cool, and its effect is just as cool! Construct a Deck that will increase its ATK and DEF quickly.

SDJ-017 Magician of Faith

Card Type: Effect Monster
Monster Type: Spellcaster
Attribute: Light
Level: 1
ATK: 300
DEF: 400
Rarity: Common

Similar to "Mask of Darkness," "Magician of Faith" can resurrect Spell Cards. Use "Magician of Faith" after using a powerful Spell Card.

SDJ-018 Big Eye

Card Type: Effect Monster
Monster Type: Fiend
Attribute: Dark
Level: 4
ATK: 1200
DEF: 1000
Rarity: Common

See the 5 cards from the top of your deck, arrange them in any order desired, and replace them on top of the deck.

SDJ-019 Sangan

Card Type: Effect Monster
Monster Type: Fiend
Attribute: Dark
Level: 3
ATK: 1000
DEF: 600
Rarity: Common

Similar to "Witch of the Black Forest," you cannot draw a monster with high ATK, but there are many Effect Monsters that are useful.

SDJ-020 Princess of Tsurugi

Card Type: Effect Monster
Monster Type: Warrior
Attribute: Wind
Level: 3
ATK: 900
DEF: 700
Rarity: Common

"Princess of Tsurugi" is very effective against opponents who use many Spell and Trap Cards. If used correctly, you can eliminate almost half your opponent's Life Points.

Starter Deck Joey

SDJ-021 White Magical Hat

Card Type: Effect Monster
Monster Type: Spellcaster
Attribute: Light
Level: 3
ATK: 1000
DEF: 700
Rarity: Common

When this card inflicts damage to your opponent's Life Points, 1 card must be discarded randomly from your opponent's hand to the Graveyard.

SDJ-022 Penguin Soldier

Card Type: Effect Monster
Monster Type: Aqua
Attribute: Water
Level: 2
ATK: 750
DEF: 500
Rarity: Super Rare

No matter how powerful your opponent's monster is, you're safe if you have this card. If you have Set this card earlier, then it's ready to go. However, be careful of Spell Cards that destroy monsters. "Penguin Soldier's" effect can be used on both you and your opponent's monsters.

SDJ-023 Thousand Dragon

Card Type: Fusion Monster
Monster Type: Dragon
Attribute: Wind
Level: 7
ATK: 2400
DEF: 2000
Rarity: Common

"Thousand Dragon" gathers much strength and wisdom through the passage of time. You cannot summon this monster until a Dragon matures.

SDJ-024 Flame Swordsman

Card Type: Fusion Monster
Monster Type: Warrior
Attribute: Fire
Level: 5
ATK: 1800
DEF: 1600
Rarity: Common

This expert swordsman wields a sword enveloped by flames. Joey uses "Flame Swordsman" as his trump card to get out of jams!

SDJ-025 Malevolent Nuzzler

Card Type: Spell
Monster Type: –
Attribute: Spell
Level: –
ATK: –
DEF: –
Rarity: Common

This card is better than "Black Pendant" if you want to use this card over and over. If your monster's ATK increases by 700, it can destroy monsters quite a bit stronger than yours.

SDJ-026 Dark Hole

Card Type: Spell
Monster Type: –
Attribute: Spell
Level: –
ATK: –
DEF: –
Rarity: Common

"Dark Hole" is very effective when the Duel is deadlocked against an opponent who is using monsters with high DEF!

SDJ-027 Dian Keto the Cure Master

Card Type: Spell
Monster Type: –
Attribute: Spell
Level: –
ATK: –
DEF: –
Rarity: Common

This motherly goddess will refill 1000 Life Points. If you have three of this card in your Deck, you can regain 3000 Life Points.

SDJ-028 Fissure

Card Type: Spell
Monster Type: –
Attribute: Spell
Level: –
ATK: –
DEF: –
Rarity: Common

This card affects face-up Monster Cards. If your opponent has only one monster on his field, "Fissure" will destroy it, no matter how high its ATK is!

SDJ-029 De-Spell

Card Type: Spell
Monster Type: –
Attribute: Spell
Level: –
ATK: –
DEF: –
Rarity: Common

This Spell Card can even destroy face-down Spell Cards. If the chosen face-down card is a Trap Card, then return the Trap Card back to normal.

SDJ-030 Change of Heart

Card Type: Spell
Monster Type: –
Attribute: Spell
Level: –
ATK: –
DEF: –
Rarity: Common

The heart is a transient thing, and this is true for monsters' hearts as well—so much that monsters at times forget who their masters are. The monster you worked so hard to summon suddenly defects to the opponent. This effect lasts only on the turn "Change of Heart" is activated, so the monster is often offered as a Tribute.

SDJ-031 Block Attack

Card Type: Spell
Monster Type: —
Attribute: Spell
Level: —
ATK: —
DEF: —
Rarity: Common

Select 1 of your opponent's monsters and shift it to Defense Position.

SDJ-032 Giant Trunade

Card Type: Spell
Monster Type: —
Attribute: Spell
Level: —
ATK: —
DEF: —
Rarity: Common

This card helps against your opponent's Spell and Trap Cards that are hindering your strategy. Also, it can return Spell and Trap Cards regardless of their position.

SDJ-033 The Reliable Guardian

Card Type: Spell
Monster Type: —
Attribute: Spell
Level: —
ATK: —
DEF: —
Rarity: Common

Similar to "Rush Recklessly," "The Reliable Guardian" is a Quick-Play Spell Card and can be used during your opponent's Battle Phase. You can use this to protect Flip Effect Monsters that you do not want destroyed.

SDJ-034 Remove Trap

Card Type: Spell
Monster Type: —
Attribute: Spell
Level: —
ATK: —
DEF: —
Rarity: Common

This Spell Card destroys one face-up Trap Card on the field. It cannot destroy face-down Trap Cards.

SDJ-035 Monster Reborn

Card Type: Spell
Monster Type: —
Attribute: Spell
Level: —
ATK: —
DEF: —
Rarity: Common

If there's a Monster Card in the Graveyard, use this Spell Card to resurrect it and make it part of your team! This is an extremely important card!

SDJ-036 Polymerization

Card Type: Spell
Monster Type: —
Attribute: Spell
Level: —
ATK: —
DEF: —
Rarity: Common

This Spell Card combines various monsters to transform them into a new and powerful Monster Card. This increases your chances for victory!

SDJ-037 Mountain

Card Type: Spell
Monster Type: —
Attribute: Spell
Level: —
ATK: —
DEF: —
Rarity: Common

This Spell Card creates terrain that helps Dragon, Winged Beast, and Thunder-Types.

SDJ-038 Dragon Treasure

Card Type: Spell
Monster Type: —
Attribute: Spell
Level: —
ATK: —
DEF: —
Rarity: Common

Dragons are already powerful to begin with, but this card powers them up even more. This card seems to have no weaknesses!

SDJ-039 Eternal Rest

Card Type: Spell
Monster Type: —
Attribute: Spell
Level: —
ATK: —
DEF: —
Rarity: Common

You can destroy all monsters with Equip Spell Cards.

SDJ-040 Shield & Sword

Card Type: Spell
Monster Type: —
Attribute: Spell
Level: —
ATK: —
DEF: —
Rarity: Common

Line up Level 4 monsters with 2000 DEF and use "Shield & Sword" to flip ATK and DEF. This simple combo inflicts significant damage to your opponent!

Starter Deck Joey

SDJ-041 Scapegoat

Card Type: Spell
Monster Type: —
Attribute: Spell
Level: —
ATK: —
DEF: —
Rarity: Super Rare

You can create four tokens at once. You can either use them in Defense Position to protect your Life Points, or you can offer them as a Tribute to "Cannon Soldier."

SDJ-042 Just Desserts

Card Type: Trap
Monster Type: —
Attribute: Trap
Level: —
ATK: —
DEF: —
Rarity: Common

If your opponent has five monsters on the field, then you can deal 2500 points of damage, but this is easier said than done. It should be good to activate this Trap Card when your opponent has three Monster Cards on the field.

SDJ-043 Trap Hole

Card Type: Trap
Monster Type: —
Attribute: Trap
Level: —
ATK: —
DEF: —
Rarity: Common

Activate "Trap Hole" when your opponent Normal Summons or Flip Summons a monster!

SDJ-044 Reinforcements

Card Type: Trap
Monster Type: —
Attribute: Trap
Level: —
ATK: —
DEF: —
Rarity: Common

Put a weak monster in Attack Position, and use this Trap Card when your opponent attacks. It's a counterattack!

SDJ-045 Castle Walls

Card Type: Trap
Monster Type: —
Attribute: Trap
Level: —
ATK: —
DEF: —
Rarity: Common

Similar to "Reinforcements," use this card on monsters in Defense Position. Send back the damage!

SDJ-046 Waboku

Card Type: Trap
Monster Type: —
Attribute: Trap
Level: —
ATK: —
DEF: —
Rarity: Common

Zero battle damage means that the effects of "White Magical Hat" or "Robbin' Goblin" disappear. However, "Waboku's" effect lasts for only one turn.

SDJ-047 Ultimate Offering

Card Type: Trap
Monster Type: —
Attribute: Trap
Level: —
ATK: —
DEF: —
Rarity: Common

As long as this card is face-up on the field, you can freely Normal Summon or Set the monster in your hand during your Main Phase or your opponent's Battle Phase.

SDJ-048 Seven Tools of the Bandit

Card Type: Trap
Monster Type: —
Attribute: Trap
Level: —
ATK: —
DEF: —
Rarity: Common

Trap Cards can be important cards in your opponent's combo or can seriously damage your strategy. Therefore, paying 1000 Life Points isn't a big deal in comparison!

SDJ-049 Fake Trap

Card Type: Trap
Monster Type: —
Attribute: Trap
Level: —
ATK: —
DEF: —
Rarity: Common

Use this Trap Card to fool your opponent. It's fun to watch your opponent squirm while he or she thinks this card's a Trap Card. However, this card is useless by itself. Fake Trap can protect all your other Trap Cards, making this card indispensable.

SDJ-050 Reverse Trap

Card Type: Trap
Monster Type: —
Attribute: Trap
Level: —
ATK: —
DEF: —
Rarity: Common

This card counteracts all the Spell Cards and the like that are powering up monsters. This is a scary Trap Card!

Starter Deck Pegasus

SDP-001 Relinquished

Card Type: Ritual/Effect Monster
Monster Type: Spellcaster
Attribute: Dark
Level: 1
ATK: 0
DEF: 0
Rarity: Ultra Rare

"Relinquished" is basically a permanent "Change of Heart." Notice that the monsters that "Relinquished" absorbs become Equip Spell Cards. Try to think how to use this fact to your advantage.

SDP-002 Red Archery Girl

Card Type: Normal Monster
Monster Type: Aqua
Attribute: Water
Level: 4
ATK: 1400
DEF: 1500
Rarity: Common

Pegasus punished Yugi with "Red Archery Girl." Its abilities are average, but if you take her lightly, you'd be in bigger trouble than Yugi.

SDP-003 Ryu-Ran

Card Type: Normal Monster
Monster Type: Dragon
Attribute: Fire
Level: 7
ATK: 2200
DEF: 2600
Rarity: Common

This Dragon may wear an egg shell, but you'll be in big trouble if you treat it with kiddie gloves!

SDP-004 Illusionist Faceless Mage

Card Type: Normal Monster
Monster Type: Spellcaster
Attribute: Dark
Level: 5
ATK: 1200
DEF: 2200
Rarity: Common

You won't regret offering a monster as a Tribute to summon this Spellcaster with high DEF. As long as you have its defenses, you're in good health.

SDP-005 Rogue Doll

Card Type: Normal Monster
Monster Type: Spellcaster
Attribute: Light
Level: 4
ATK: 1600
DEF: 1000
Rarity: Common

It has decent ATK, and you can summon this monster without having to offer another monster as a Tribute! However, its DEF is low.

SDP-006 Uraby

Card Type: Normal Monster
Monster Type: Dinosaur
Attribute: Earth
Level: 4
ATK: 1500
DEF: 800
Rarity: Common

This powerful Dinosaur has overwhelming strength and will eat and swallow anyone it sets its sights on.

SDP-007 Giant Soldier of Stone

Card Type: Normal Monster
Monster Type: Rock
Attribute: Earth
Level: 3
ATK: 1300
DEF: 2000
Rarity: Common

This card will be the main monster in a Rock-Type Deck. For a Level 3 monster, the ATK and DEF are amazing!

SDP-008 Aqua Madoor

Card Type: Normal Monster
Monster Type: Spellcaster
Attribute: Water
Level: 4
ATK: 1200
DEF: 2000
Rarity: Common

"Aqua Madoor" has high DEF, and its ATK is not bad either!

SDP-009 Toon Alligator

Card Type: Normal Monster
Monster Type: Reptile
Attribute: Water
Level: 4
ATK: 800
DEF: 1600
Rarity: Common

This is a very cute alligator that appeared in comic books. It has low ATK, but it has decent DEF.

SDP-010 Hane-Hane

Card Type: Effect Monster
Monster Type: Beast
Attribute: Earth
Level: 2
ATK: 450
DEF: 500
Rarity: Common

Even if face-down "Hane-Hane" is destroyed in battle, you return one monster on the field, but please remember that you cannot return "Hane-Hane" itself if it is destroyed.

Starter Deck Pegasus

SDP-011 Sonic Bird

Card Type:	Effect Monster
Monster Type:	Winged Beast
Attribute:	Wind
Level:	4
ATK:	1400
DEF:	1000
Rarity:	Common

This card allows you to search your Deck for the Ritual Spell Card that you need.

SDP-012 Jigen Bakudan

Card Type:	Effect Monster
Monster Type:	Pyro
Attribute:	Fire
Level:	2
ATK:	200
DEF:	1000
Rarity:	Common

"Jigen Bakudan" allows you to deal Direct Damage to your opponent's Life Points. If your opponent's Life Points are low, this can be the finishing blow!

SDP-013 Mask of Darkness

Card Type:	Effect Monster
Monster Type:	Fiend
Attribute:	Dark
Level:	2
ATK:	900
DEF:	400
Rarity:	Common

While "Mask of Darkness" can resrrect Trap Cards from the Graveyard, if there are no Trap Cards in the Graveyard, then you cannot recover anything.

SDP-014 Witch of the Black Forest

Card Type:	Effect Monster
Monster Type:	Spellcaster
Attribute:	Dark
Level:	4
ATK:	1100
DEF:	1200
Rarity:	Common

You can draw most Effect Monster Cards from your Deck while thinning out your Deck at the same time. Also, less than 1500 DEF means that you can add "Summoned Skull" from your Deck!

SDP-015 Man-Eater Bug

Card Type:	Effect Monster
Monster Type:	Insect
Attribute:	Earth
Level:	2
ATK:	450
DEF:	600
Rarity:	Common

If "Man-Eater Bug" is the only monster on the field, its effect will destroy the "Man-Eater Bug" itself....

SDP-016 Muka Muka

Card Type:	Effect Monster
Monster Type:	Rock
Attribute:	Earth
Level:	2
ATK:	600
DEF:	300
Rarity:	Common

If you summon "Muka Muka" on your first turn, you just summoned a monster with 2100 ATK! Afterwards, try to keep as many cards in your hand. If you need to use a card, then attack first.

SDP-017 Dream Clown

Card Type:	Effect Monster
Monster Type:	Warrior
Attribute:	Earth
Level:	3
ATK:	1200
DEF:	900
Rarity:	Common

Since its ATK is low, "Dream Clown" can be easily destroyed before it can activate its effect. However, the effect is very useful. Try using this in a Deck with "Swords of Revealing Light."

SDP-018 Armed Ninja

Card Type:	Effect Monster
Monster Type:	Warrior
Attribute:	Earth
Level:	1
ATK:	300
DEF:	300
Rarity:	Common

Use "Armed Ninja" when you do not have enough "De-Spell" cards in your Deck. It's surprisingly useful for a low-level card.

SDP-019 Hiro's Shadow Scout

Card Type:	Effect Monster
Monster Type:	Fiend
Attribute:	Dark
Level:	2
ATK:	650
DEF:	500
Rarity:	Common

Spell Cards are important in every Deck, especially in setting up combos. By getting rid of your opponent's Spell Cards, you can disrupt his or her strategy.

SDP-020 Blue-Eyes Toon Dragon

Card Type:	Toon Monster
Monster Type:	Dragon
Attribute:	Light
Level:	8
ATK:	3000
DEF:	2500
Rarity:	Common

Similar to the other Toons, you can attack your opponent directly for a devastating 3000 points of damage to his or her Life Points! However, you must have "Toon World" on your side of the field to Special Summon it.

SDP-021 Toon Summoned Skull

Card Type: Toon Monster
Monster Type: Fiend
Attribute: Dark
Level: 6
ATK: 2500
DEF: 1200
Rarity: Common

Similar to the other Toons, you can attack your opponent directly. However, you must have "Toon World" on your side of the field to Special Summon it.

SDP-022 Manga Ryu-Ran

Card Type: Toon Monster
Monster Type: Dragon
Attribute: Fire
Level: 7
ATK: 2200
DEF: 2600
Rarity: Common

Similar to the other Toons, you can attack your opponent directly. However, you must have "Toon World" on your side of the field to Special Summon it.

SDP-023 Toon Mermaid

Card Type: Toon Monster
Monster Type: Aqua
Attribute: Water
Level: 4
ATK: 1400
DEF: 1500
Rarity: Common

Similar to the other Toons, you can attack your opponent directly. However, you must have "Toon World" on your side of the field to Special Summon it.

SDP-024 Toon World

Card Type: Spell
Monster Type: —
Attribute: Spell
Level: —
ATK: —
DEF: —
Rarity: Common

Though you must pay 1000 Life Points, you are now able to Special Summon Toon Monsters that can deal Direct Damage to your opponent!

SDP-025 Black Pendant

Card Type: Spell
Monster Type: —
Attribute: Spell
Level: —
ATK: —
DEF: —
Rarity: Common

This is not the strongest Equip Spell Card, but it's useful for defeating monsters that are slightly stronger than yours. Even if your Monster is destroyed, there's still a bonus!

SDP-026 Dark Hole

Card Type: Spell
Monster Type: —
Attribute: Spell
Level: —
ATK: —
DEF: —
Rarity: Common

Dark Hole is very effective when the Duel is deadlocked against an opponent who is using monsters with high DEF!

SDP-027 Dian Keto the Cure Master

Card Type: Spell
Monster Type: —
Attribute: Spell
Level: —
ATK: —
DEF: —
Rarity: Common

This motherly goddess will refill 1000 Life Points. If you have three of this card in your Deck, you can regain 3000 Life Points.

SDP-028 Fissure

Card Type: Spell
Monster Type: —
Attribute: Spell
Level: —
ATK: —
DEF: —
Rarity: Common

This card affects face-up Monster Cards. If your opponent has only one monster on his field, "Fissure" will destroy it, no matter how high its ATK is!

SDP-029 De-Spell

Card Type: Spell
Monster Type: —
Attribute: Spell
Level: —
ATK: —
DEF: —
Rarity: Common

This Spell Card can even destroy face-down Spell Cards. If the chosen face-down card is a Trap Card, then return the Trap Card back to normal.

SDP-030 Change of Heart

Card Type: Spell
Monster Type: —
Attribute: Spell
Level: —
ATK: —
DEF: —
Rarity: Common

The heart is a transient thing, and this is true for monsters' hearts as well—so much that monsters at times forget who their masters are. The monster you worked so hard to summon suddenly defects to the opponent. This effect lasts only on the turn "Change of Heart" is activated, so the monster is often offered as a Tribute.

Starter Deck Pegasus

SDP-031 Stop Defense

Card Type: Spell
Monster Type: —
Attribute: Spell
Level: —
ATK: —
DEF: —
Rarity: Common

Use "Stop Defense" on monsters that have high DEF that are in Defense Position. Force it to switch to Attack Position.

SDP-032 Mystical Space Typhoon

Card Type: Spell
Monster Type: —
Attribute: Spell
Level: —
ATK: —
DEF: —
Rarity: Common

Unlike "Remove Trap," you can now destroy face-down Trap Cards. To counter against "Mystical Space Typhoon," your opponent may now have to place less-useful Spell Cards on the field.

SDP-033 Rush Recklessly

Card Type: Spell
Monster Type: —
Attribute: Spell
Level: —
ATK: —
DEF: —
Rarity: Common

Your opponent may think his or her monster is destroying one of your weak monsters, but with this Spell Card, your opponent is in for a surprise! Your opponent will worry about attacking if his or her monster's ATK is only 700 more than yours.

SDP-034 Remove Trap

Card Type: Spell
Monster Type: —
Attribute: Spell
Level: —
ATK: —
DEF: —
Rarity: Common

This Spell Card destroys one face-up Trap Card on the field. It cannot destroy face-down Trap Cards.

SDP-035 Monster Reborn

Card Type: Spell
Monster Type: —
Attribute: Spell
Level: —
ATK: —
DEF: —
Rarity: Common

If there's a Monster Card in the Graveyard, use this Spell Card to resurrect it and make it part of your team! This is an extremely important card!

SDP-036 Soul Release

Card Type: Spell
Monster Type: —
Attribute: Spell
Level: —
ATK: —
DEF: —
Rarity: Common

Select up to 5 cards from either you or your opponent's Graveyard and remove them from the current Duel.

SDP-037 Yami

Card Type: Spell
Monster Type: —
Attribute: Spell
Level: —
ATK: —
DEF: —
Rarity: Common

Since Fairy-Type monsters crave the Light, they're weak in "Yami" terrain. However, this terrain strengthens Fiend and Spellcaster-Types who thrive on magical powers.

SDP-038 Black Illusion Ritual

Card Type: Spell
Monster Type: —
Attribute: Spell
Level: —
ATK: —
DEF: —
Rarity: Common

You need this card to Ritual Summon the Ritual Monster "Relinquished." This card is useless by itself, so make sure you have both cards!

SDP-039 Ring of Magnetism

Card Type: Spell
Monster Type: —
Attribute: Spell
Level: —
ATK: —
DEF: —
Rarity: Common

It's best to equip "Ring of Magnetism" on an Effect Monster Card. For example, if you equip it on "Wall of Illusion," your opponent's monsters will return to his or her hand.

SDP-040 Graceful Charity

Card Type: Spell
Monster Type: —
Attribute: Spell
Level: —
ATK: —
DEF: —
Rarity: Super Rare

If you use this card with, for example, "Cockroach Knight," then you can increase the number of cards in your hand with little risk!

SDP-041 Trap Hole

Card Type: Trap
Monster Type: —
Attribute: Trap
Level: —
ATK: —
DEF: —
Rarity: Common

Activate "Trap Hole" when your opponent Normal Summons or Flip Summons a monster!

SDP-042 Reinforcements

Card Type: Trap
Monster Type: —
Attribute: Trap
Level: —
ATK: —
DEF: —
Rarity: Common

Put a weak monster in Attack Position, and use this Trap Card when your opponent attacks. It's a counterattack!

SDP-043 Castle Walls

Card Type: Trap
Monster Type: —
Attribute: Trap
Level: —
ATK: —
DEF: —
Rarity: Common

Similar to "Reinforcements," use this card on monsters in Defense Position. Send back the damage!

SDP-044 Waboku

Card Type: Trap
Monster Type: —
Attribute: Trap
Level: —
ATK: —
DEF: —
Rarity: Common

Zero battle damage means that the effects of "White Magical Hat" or "Robbin' Goblin" disappear. However, "Waboku's" effect lasts for only one turn.

SDP-045 Seven Tools of the Bandit

Card Type: Trap
Monster Type: —
Attribute: Trap
Level: —
ATK: —
DEF: —
Rarity: Common

Trap Cards can be important cards in your opponent's combo or can seriously damage your strategy. Therefore, paying 1000 Life Points isn't a big deal in comparison!

SDP-046 Ultimate Offering

Card Type: Trap
Monster Type: —
Attribute: Trap
Level: —
ATK: —
DEF: —
Rarity: Common

As long as this card is face-up on the field, you can freely Normal Summon or Set the monster in your hand during your Main Phase or your opponent's Battle Phase.

SDP-047 Robbin' Goblin

Card Type: Trap
Monster Type: —
Attribute: Trap
Level: —
ATK: —
DEF: —
Rarity: Common

This card is made for combos. You can use this card with Monsters that can directly attack your opponent, or you can pair it with "White Magical Hat" to make your opponent discard two cards. This card is a real nuisance.

SDP-048 Magic Jammer

Card Type: Trap
Monster Type: —
Attribute: Trap
Level: —
ATK: —
DEF: —
Rarity: Common

Once you Set "Magic Jammer," make sure to have one card that you are willing to discard in your hand. Try not to use "Magic Jammer" until your opponent activates a Spell Card that can seriously cripple you.

SDP-049 Enchanted Javelin

Card Type: Trap
Monster Type: —
Attribute: Trap
Level: —
ATK: —
DEF: —
Rarity: Common

If used correctly, you can negate the damage frome ven the strongest monster.

SDP-050 Gryphon Wing

Card Type: Trap
Monster Type: —
Attribute: Trap
Level: —
ATK: —
DEF: —
Rarity: Super Rare

This is similar to "Anti-Raigeki" for "Raigeki." The extremely powerful "Harpie's Feather Duster" will not be able to be used as easily if you have "Gryphon Wing."

Legend of Blue-Eyes White Dragon

LOB-001 Blue-Eyes White Dragon

Card Type: Normal Monster
Monster Type: Dragon
Attribute: Light
Level: 8
ATK: 3000
DEF: 2500
Rarity: Ultra Rare

Kaiba's favorite monster is the most powerful Normal Monster Card. Destroying "Blue-Eyes" without a Spell Card will be difficult!

LOB-002 Hitotsu-Me Giant

Card Type: Normal Monster
Monster Type: Beast-Warrior
Attribute: Earth
Level: 4
ATK: 1200
DEF: 1000
Rarity: Common

Even Kaiba uses this Beast-Warrior-Type monster. Be sure to put its high ATK to use!

LOB-003 Flame Swordsman

Card Type: Fusion Monster
Monster Type: Warrior
Attribute: Fire
Level: 5
ATK: 1800
DEF: 1600
Rarity: Super Rare

This expert swordsman wields a sword enveloped by flames. Joey uses "Flame Swordsman" as his trump card to get out of jams!

LOB-004 Skull Servant

Card Type: Normal Monster
Monster Type: Zombie
Attribute: Dark
Level: 1
ATK: 300
DEF: 200
Rarity: Common

Find one of these skeleton servants, and it feels as if thirty more are lurking behind. "Skull Servant" transforms into various things when fused.

LOB-005 Dark Magician

Card Type: Normal Monster
Monster Type: Spellcaster
Attribute: Dark
Level: 7
ATK: 2500
DEF: 2100
Rarity: Ultra Rare

A high-ranking magician of the Spellcaster-Type, the "Dark Magician" is very dangerous unless you destroy him as soon as your opponent places him on the field.

LOB-006 Gaia The Fierce Knight

Card Type: Normal Monster
Monster Type: Warrior
Attribute: Earth
Level: 7
ATK: 2300
DEF: 2100
Rarity: Ultra Rare

Yugi uses this top-class Warrior. Don't fail to include this card in a Warrior-Type Deck!

LOB-007 Celtic Guardian

Card Type: Normal Monster
Monster Type: Warrior
Attribute: Earth
Level: 4
ATK: 1400
DEF: 1200
Rarity: Super Rare

With high ATK, "Celtic Guardian" is an elite Warrior. He slices his enemies with his skilled techniques!

LOB-008 Basic Insect

Card Type: Normal Monster
Monster Type: Insect
Attribute: Earth
Level: 2
ATK: 500
DEF: 700
Rarity: Common

This Insect is basically not very strong, but it likes to frolic in the Forest Field.

LOB-009 Mammoth Graveyard

Card Type: Normal Monster
Monster Type: Dinosaur
Attribute: Earth
Level: 3
ATK: 1200
DEF: 800
Rarity: Common

Even Yugi uses this Dinosaur-Type card. It has balanced ATK!

LOB-010 Silver Fang

Card Type: Normal Monster
Monster Type: Beast
Attribute: Earth
Level: 3
ATK: 1200
DEF: 800
Rarity: Common

Yugi often uses this feral wolf in Duels. Power it up and defeat your opponent!

LOB-011 Dark Gray

Card Type: Normal Monster
Monster Type: Beast
Attribute: Earth
Level: 3
ATK: 800
DEF: 900
Rarity: Common

This rare creature's ATK and DEF are well-balanced. If you ever get a chance to see "Dark Gray," you're extremely lucky!

LOB-012 Trial of Nightmare

Card Type: Normal Monster
Monster Type: Fiend
Attribute: Dark
Level: 4
ATK: 1300
DEF: 900
Rarity: Common

This mid-level monster has high ATK.

LOB-013 Nemuriko

Card Type: Normal Monster
Monster Type: Spellcaster
Attribute: Dark
Level: 3
ATK: 800
DEF: 700
Rarity: Common

"Nemuriko" is a Spellcaster that lures people into eternal sleep! Whether "Nemuriko" is a girl or a boy remains a mystery.

LOB-014 The 13th Grave

Card Type: Normal Monster
Monster Type: Zombie
Attribute: Dark
Level: 3
ATK: 1200
DEF: 900
Rarity: Common

This Zombie appeared from grave #13—which was supposedly empty!

LOB-015 Charubin the Fire Knight

Card Type: Fusion Monster
Monster Type: Pyro
Attribute: Fire
Level: 3
ATK: 1100
DEF: 800
Rarity: Rare

Using the Spell Card "Polymerization," this Warrior comes to life when an egg is cooked at high temperature. Beware of its spiked mace!

LOB-016 Flame Manipulator

Card Type: Normal Monster
Monster Type: Spellcaster
Attribute: Fire
Level: 3
ATK: 900
DEF: 1000
Rarity: Common

When fused, this Spellcaster transforms into "Flame Swordsman." He's better at defending than he is at attacking!

LOB-017 Monster Egg

Card Type: Normal Monster
Monster Type: Warrior
Attribute: Earth
Level: 3
ATK: 600
DEF: 900
Rarity: Common

The creature spends most of its time hiding inside an egg, but it is still quite a Warrior. It usually doesn't attack and keeps defending.

LOB-018 Firegrass

Card Type: Normal Monster
Monster Type: Plant
Attribute: Earth
Level: 2
ATK: 700
DEF: 600
Rarity: Common

Use this Fusion-Material Monster to Summon the Fusion Monster "Darkfire Dragon!" Alone, it will struggle in battle.

LOB-019 Darkfire Dragon

Card Type: Fusion Monster
Monster Type: Dragon
Attribute: Dark
Level: 4
ATK: 1500
DEF: 1250
Rarity: Rare

"Petit Dragon" has wrapped itself in flames and evolved to "Darkfire Dragon." This Fusion Monster has higher ATK than before.

LOB-020 Dark King of the Abyss

Card Type: Normal Monster
Monster Type: Fiend
Attribute: Dark
Level: 3
ATK: 1200
DEF: 800
Rarity: Common

"Dark King of the Abyss" is a Zombie-Type monster with DARK.

LOB-021 Fiend Reflection #2

Card Type: Normal Monster
Monster Type: Winged Beast
Attribute: Light
Level: 4
ATK: 1100
DEF: 1400
Rarity: Common

This Winged Beast flies around at high speed, so it takes steady aim to nail it. Destroy it before it starts calling out for its friends!

LOB-022 Fusionist

Card Type: Fusion Monster
Monster Type: Beast
Attribute: Earth
Level: 3
ATK: 900
DEF: 700
Rarity: Rare

This is a Fusion Monster, but it is not very useful. However, cat lovers will find it irresistible.

Legend of Blue-Eyes White Dragon

LOB-023 Turtle Tiger

Card Type: Normal Monster
Monster Type: Aqua
Attribute: Water
Level: 4
ATK: 1000
DEF: 1500
Rarity: Common

"Turtle Tiger's" high DEF allows it to take attacks head-on!

LOB-024 Petit Dragon

Card Type: Normal Monster
Monster Type: Dragon
Attribute: Wind
Level: 2
ATK: 600
DEF: 700
Rarity: Common

During battles, "Petit Dragon" attacks using its entire body in a crazy manner. Is this a special unique Dragon-fighting style?

LOB-025 Petit Angel

Card Type: Normal Monster
Monster Type: Fairy
Attribute: Light
Level: 3
ATK: 600
DEF: 900
Rarity: Common

This tiny young angel is very speedy! Because ATK is very low, Set in Defense Position.

LOB-026 Hinotama Soul

Card Type: Normal Monster
Monster Type: Pyro
Attribute: Fire
Level: 2
ATK: 600
DEF: 500
Rarity: Common

You'll be toast if this blazing sentient flame crashes into you!

LOB-027 Aqua Madoor

Card Type: Normal Monster
Monster Type: Spellcaster
Attribute: Water
Level: 4
ATK: 1200
DEF: 2000
Rarity: Rare

"Aqua Madoor" has high DEF, and its ATK is not bad either!

LOB-028 Kagemusha of the Blue Flame

Card Type: Normal Monster
Monster Type: Warrior
Attribute: Earth
Level: 2
ATK: 800
DEF: 400
Rarity: Common

This Warrior's ATK is twice as high as his DEF. Therefore, you may want to use it in Attack Position instead of Defense Position.

LOB-029 Flame Ghost

Card Type: Fusion Monster
Monster Type: Zombie
Attribute: Dark
Level: 3
ATK: 1000
DEF: 800
Rarity: Rare

Created when "Dissolverock" walks above a sleeping "Skull Servant," "Flame Ghost" is hot to the touch!

LOB-030 Two-Mouth Darkruler

Card Type: Normal Monster
Monster Type: Dinosaur
Attribute: Earth
Level: 3
ATK: 900
DEF: 700
Rarity: Common

A rare Dinosaur with two mouths, "Two-Mouth Darkruler's" electric attack is powerful but not unbearable!

LOB-031 Dissolverock

Card Type: Normal Monster
Monster Type: Rock
Attribute: Earth
Level: 3
ATK: 900
DEF: 1000
Rarity: Common

This magma monster moves around everywhere! If it suddenly starts getting hot around you, you know "Dissolverrock" has come to pay you a visit.

LOB-032 Root Water

Card Type: Normal Monster
Monster Type: Fish
Attribute: Water
Level: 3
ATK: 900
DEF: 800
Rarity: Common

"Root Water" attacks from the depths of the sea by creating large tsunamis. You should fight on land to avoid drowning!

LOB-033 The Furious Sea King

Card Type: Normal Monster
Monster Type: Aqua
Attribute: Water
Level: 3
ATK: 800
DEF: 700
Rarity: Common

Offer this mid-ranking Aqua-Type monster as a Tribute to summon high-level Monster Cards.

LOB-034 Green Phantom King

Card Type: Normal Monster
Monster Type: Plant
Attribute: Earth
Level: 3
ATK: 500
DEF: 1600
Rarity: Common

This king of plants values all life, so it prefers combat when it's protecting its friends instead of attacking to hurt its enemy.

LOB-035 Ray & Temperature

Card Type:	Normal Monster
Monster Type:	Fairy
Attribute:	Light
Level:	3
ATK:	1000
DEF:	1000
Rarity:	Common

This Fairy specializes in combo attacks! The sun emits thermal rays while the north wind slices through the enemy with its mighty gale!

LOB-036 King Fog

Card Type:	Normal Monster
Monster Type:	Fiend
Attribute:	Dark
Level:	3
ATK:	1000
DEF:	900
Rarity:	Common

This Fiend ambushes the enemy by hiding in smoke. Before you know it, a thick smoke surrounds and blinds you.

LOB-037 Mystical Sheep #2

Card Type:	Normal Monster
Monster Type:	Beast
Attribute:	Earth
Level:	3
ATK:	800
DEF:	1000
Rarity:	Common

This scary Beast will hypnotize you with its long tail. It boasts large horns and a warm-looking coat.

LOB-038 Masaki the Legendary Swordsman

Card Type:	Normal Monster
Monster Type:	Warrior
Attribute:	Earth
Level:	4
ATK:	1100
DEF:	1100
Rarity:	Common

The legendary Warrior has revived in present times. Dressed in the same armor during battle, he strikes his enemy with his favorite sword.

LOB-039 Kurama

Card Type:	Normal Monster
Monster Type:	Winged Beast
Attribute:	Wind
Level:	3
ATK:	800
DEF:	800
Rarity:	Common

Kurama's ATK and DEF are exactly the same. Set this monster in Defense Position until you can summon a stronger monster.

LOB-040 Legendary Sword

Card Type:	Spell
Monster Type:	—
Attribute:	Spell
Level:	—
ATK:	—
DEF:	—
Rarity:	Common

"Legendary Sword" powers up Warrior-Type monsters, regardless of their attribute. It's reassuring to have at least one in your Deck.

LOB-041 Beast Fangs

Card Type:	Spell
Monster Type:	—
Attribute:	Spell
Level:	—
ATK:	—
DEF:	—
Rarity:	Common

Overall, Beast-Type monsters have high DEF, and "Beast Fangs" will strengthen your defense even greater.

LOB-042 Violet Crystal

Card Type:	Spell
Monster Type:	—
Attribute:	Spell
Level:	—
ATK:	—
DEF:	—
Rarity:	Common

Use "Violet Crystal" to power up your Zombie-Type monster and destroy your opponent's monsters.

LOB-043 Book of Secret Arts

Card Type:	Spell
Monster Type:	—
Attribute:	Spell
Level:	—
ATK:	—
DEF:	—
Rarity:	Common

Use this book on "Dark Magician" to easily destroy every Monster Card, except "Blue-Eyes White Dragon!"

LOB-044 Power of Kaishin

Card Type:	Spell
Monster Type:	—
Attribute:	Spell
Level:	—
ATK:	—
DEF:	—
Rarity:	Common

Use "Power of Kaishin" to power up Aqua-Type monsters.

Legend of Blue-Eyes White Dragon

LOB-045 Dragon Capture Jar

Card Type: Trap
Monster Type: —
Attribute: Trap
Level: —
ATK: —
DEF: —
Rarity: Rare

Dragon-Types should be wary of this Trap Card. Even the "Stop Defense" Spell Card can't affect "Dragon Capture Jar!"

LOB-046 Forest

Card Type: Spell
Monster Type: —
Attribute: Spell
Level: —
ATK: —
DEF: —
Rarity: Common

This valuable Spell Card creates a deep forest that aids Insect, Plant, Beast, and Beast-Warrior-Types in battles.

LOB-047 Wasteland

Card Type: Spell
Monster Type: —
Attribute: Spell
Level: —
ATK: —
DEF: —
Rarity: Common

"Wasteland" transforms the field into a desolate withered wasteland. This card powers up Dinosaur, Zombie, and Rock-Types!

LOB-048 Mountain

Card Type: Spell
Monster Type: —
Attribute: Spell
Level: —
ATK: —
DEF: —
Rarity: Common

This Spell Card creates terrain that helps Dragon, Winged Beast, and Thunder-Types. If you power up "Blue-Eyes White Dragon," it will be invincible!

LOB-049 Sogen

Card Type: Spell
Monster Type: —
Attribute: Spell
Level: —
ATK: —
DEF: —
Rarity: Common

This Spell Card transforms the field into a scenic vast grassland. "Sogen" gives Warrior and Beast-Warrior-Types an advantage in battle!

LOB-050 Umi

Card Type: Spell
Monster Type: —
Attribute: Spell
Level: —
ATK: —
DEF: —
Rarity: Common

This terrain allows Sea Serpent, Fish, Thunder, and Aqua-Types to swim freely! On the other hand, Machine and Pyro-Types are weakened.

LOB-051 Yami

Card Type: Spell
Monster Type: —
Attribute: Spell
Level: —
ATK: —
DEF: —
Rarity: Common

Since Fairy-Type monsters crave the light, they're weak in Yami terrain. However, this terrain strengthens Fiend and Spellcaster-Types who thrive on magical powers!

LOB-052 Dark Hole

Card Type: Spell
Monster Type: —
Attribute: Spell
Level: —
ATK: —
DEF: —
Rarity: Super Rare

"Dark Hole" is very effective when the Duel is deadlocked against an opponent who is using monsters with high DEF!

LOB-053 Raigeki

Card Type: Spell
Monster Type: —
Attribute: Spell
Level: —
ATK: —
DEF: —
Rarity: Super Rare

This must-have card destroys all your opponent's monsters. No Monster Card can withstand its powerful destructive force!

LOB-054 Red Medicine

Card Type: Spell
Monster Type: —
Attribute: Spell
Level: —
ATK: —
DEF: —
Rarity: Common

This bubbling red liquid will refill 500 Life Points, but I wonder how it tastes....

LOB-055 Sparks

Card Type: Spell
Monster Type: —
Attribute: Spell
Level: —
ATK: —
DEF: —
Rarity: Common

This hot little magical flame is not that useful, but it can still be annoying when used against you.

LOB-056 Hinotama

Card Type: Spell
Monster Type: —
Attribute: Spell
Level: —
ATK: —
DEF: —
Rarity: Common

"Hinotama" deals 500 points of damage to your opponent's Life Points by hurling fireballs at your opponent. These fireballs aren't very powerful, but they can sometimes cause fires.

LOB-057 Fissure

Card Type: Spell
Monster Type: —
Attribute: Spell
Level: —
ATK: —
DEF: —
Rarity: Rare

This card affects face-up Monster Cards. Even the mightiest Monster Cards cannot escape this effect!

LOB-058 Trap Hole

Card Type: Trap
Monster Type: —
Attribute: Trap
Level: —
ATK: —
DEF: —
Rarity: Super Rare

Activate "Trap Hole" when your opponent Flip Summons a Monster Card face-up or summons a monster face-up directly!

LOB-059 Polymerization

Card Type: Spell
Monster Type: —
Attribute: Spell
Level: —
ATK: —
DEF: —
Rarity: Super Rare

This Spell Card combines various monsters to transform them into a new and powerful Monster Card. This increases your chances for victory!

LOB-060 Remove Trap

Card Type: Spell
Monster Type: —
Attribute: Spell
Level: —
ATK: —
DEF: —
Rarity: Common

This Spell Card destroys one face-up Trap Card on the field. It cannot destroy face-down Trap Cards.

LOB-061 Two-Pronged Attack

Card Type: Trap
Monster Type: —
Attribute: Trap
Level: —
ATK: —
DEF: —
Rarity: Rare

"Two-Pronged Attack" is very useful when you have many monsters on your field. Use it as soon as your opponent Normal Summons or Flip Summons a powerful monster!

LOB-062 Mystical Elf

Card Type: Normal Monster
Monster Type: Spellcaster
Attribute: Light
Level: 4
ATK: 800
DEF: 2000
Rarity: Super Rare

Rely on "Mystical Elf" for defense. However, since she has low ATK, she's easy prey for "Fissure...."

LOB-063 Tyhone

Card Type: Normal Monster
Monster Type: Winged Beast
Attribute: Wind
Level: 4
ATK: 1200
DEF: 1400
Rarity: Common

"Tyhone" launches long-range attacks from the mountains, so look out above when you enter the mountains!

LOB-064 Beaver Warrior

Card Type: Normal Monster
Monster Type: Beast-Warrior
Attribute: Earth
Level: 4
ATK: 1200
DEF: 1500
Rarity: Common

"Beaver Warrior" is one of Yugi's favorite Beast-Warriors. Set this monster first in Defense Position, then switch it to Attack Position when you see an opening!

LOB-065 Gravedigger Ghoul

Card Type: Spell
Monster Type: —
Attribute: Spell
Level: —
ATK: —
DEF: —
Rarity: Rare

Use this card as a countermeasure against "Monster Reborn." However, you won't be able to resurrect the monsters with your "Monster Reborn" either, so use "Gravedigger Ghoul" wisely.

LOB-066 Curse of Dragon

Card Type: Normal Monster
Monster Type: Dragon
Attribute: Dark
Level: 5
ATK: 2000
DEF: 1500
Rarity: Super Rare

This cursed Dragon chars everything with its breath of flame. Instead of Setting it in Defense Position, attack!

LOB-067 Karbonala Warrior

Card Type: Fusion Monster
Monster Type: Warrior
Attribute: Earth
Level: 4
ATK: 1500
DEF: 1200
Rarity: Rare

"Karbonala Warrior" is created when the close-knit "M-Warrior" brothers fuse. However, "Karbonala Warrior's" personality is quite different than before.

LOB-068 Giant Soldier of Stone

Card Type: Normal Monster
Monster Type: Rock
Attribute: Earth
Level: 3
ATK: 1300
DEF: 2000
Rarity: Rare

This card will be the main monster in a Rock-Type Deck. For a Level 3 monster, the ATK and DEF are amazing!

LOB-069 Uraby

Card Type: Normal Monster
Monster Type: Dinosaur
Attribute: Earth
Level: 4
ATK: 1500
DEF: 800
Rarity: Common

This powerful Dinosaur has overwhelming strength and will eat and swallow anyone it sets its sights on.

LOB-070 Red-Eyes B. Dragon

Card Type: Normal Monster
Monster Type: Dragon
Attribute: Dark
Level: 7
ATK: 2400
DEF: 2000
Rarity: Ultra Rare

Joey received this rare card by defeating Rex Raptor. This monster can become even stronger if it fused with another monster by "Polymerization!"

LOB-071 Reaper of the Cards

Card Type: Effect Monster
Monster Type: Fiend
Attribute: Dark
Level: 5
ATK: 1380
DEF: 1930
Rarity: Rare

After destroying a Trap Card on the field, "Reaper of the Cards" can provide strong defense. However, you must offer another monster as a Tribute to Set "Reaper of the Cards."

LOB-072 Witty Phantom

Card Type: Normal Monster
Monster Type: Fiend
Attribute: Dark
Level: 4
ATK: 1400
DEF: 1300
Rarity: Common

This Fiend is a hard-working nice guy and is quite popular with the ladies of the underworld.

LOB-073 Larvas

Card Type: Normal Monster
Monster Type: Beast
Attribute: Earth
Level: 3
ATK: 800
DEF: 1000
Rarity: Common

Although this peculiar creature is a bird, it sides with other Beasts. However, it's so weak.

LOB-074 Hard Armor

Card Type: Normal Monster
Monster Type: Warrior
Attribute: Earth
Level: 3
ATK: 300
DEF: 1200
Rarity: Common

Similar to "Armaill," this Warrior's specialty is defense. Does it have low ATK because it's only armor?

LOB-075 Man Eater

Card Type: Normal Monster
Monster Type: Plant
Attribute: Earth
Level: 2
ATK: 800
DEF: 600
Rarity: Common

This Plant-Type monster has a scary face in the middle of its petals. However, it's not very strong....

LOB-076 M-Warrior #1

Card Type: Normal Monster
Monster Type: Warrior
Attribute: Earth
Level: 3
ATK: 1000
DEF: 500
Rarity: Common

"M-Warrior #1" launches combo attacks with "M-Warrior #2." Its specialty is offense.

LOB-077 M-Warrior #2

Card Type: Normal Monster
Monster Type: Warrior
Attribute: Earth
Level: 3
ATK: 500
DEF: 1000
Rarity: Common

When fused with "M-Warrior #1," this Warrior transforms to "Karbonala Warrior." "M-Warrior #2's" specialty is defense.

LOB-078 Spirit of the Harp

Card Type: Normal Monster
Monster Type: Fairy
Attribute: Light
Level: 4
ATK: 800
DEF: 2000
Rarity: Rare

This female monster has very high DEF. If you use Yami Field Spell Card, "Spirit of the Harp" will power down.

LOB-079 Armaill

Card Type: Normal Monster
Monster Type: Warrior
Attribute: Earth
Level: 3
ATK: 700
DEF: 1300
Rarity: Common

This Warrior has higher DEF than ATK because it wields its three swords expertly when defending.

LOB-080 Terra the Terrible

Card Type: Normal Monster
Monster Type: Fiend
Attribute: Dark
Level: 4
ATK: 1200
DEF: 1300
Rarity: Common

"Terra the Terrible" has average abilities, so you can entrust it with both attack and defense.

LOB-081 Frenzied Panda

Card Type: Normal Monster
Monster Type: Beast
Attribute: Earth
Level: 4
ATK: 1200
DEF: 1000
Rarity: Common

"Frenzied Panda" prefers to eat meat than bamboo leaves. It hunts its prey with a bamboo spear.

LOB-082 Kumootoko

Card Type: Normal Monster
Monster Type: Insect
Attribute: Earth
Level: 3
ATK: 700
DEF: 1400
Rarity: Common

This Insect can move quickly in its web, so it's difficult to strike it!

LOB-083 Meda Bat

Card Type: Normal Monster
Monster Type: Fiend
Attribute: Dark
Level: 2
ATK: 800
DEF: 400
Rarity: Common

"Meda Bat" is an expert at attacking enemies, but it is horrible at defense. If it stares at you with its huge eye, you will definitely be startled.

LOB-084 Enchanting Mermaid

Card Type: Normal Monster
Monster Type: Fish
Attribute: Water
Level: 3
ATK: 1200
DEF: 900
Rarity: Common

This mermaid is as brutal as she is beautiful. She possesses high ATK, so don't be led astray!

LOB-085 Fireyarou

Card Type: Normal Monster
Monster Type: Pyro
Attribute: Fire
Level: 4
ATK: 1300
DEF: 1000
Rarity: Common

"Fireyarou" is one of the few Pyro-Type monsters. He trains throughout the day to increase his own abilities. He's a hard worker!

LOB-086 Dragoness the Wicked Knight

Card Type: Fusion Monster
Monster Type: Warrior
Attribute: Wind
Level: 3
ATK: 1200
DEF: 900
Rarity: Rare

"Dragoness the Wicked Knight" looks really cool, but this Warrior's ATK and DEF are mediocre. Its favorite hobby is flying.

LOB-087 One-Eyed Shield Dragon

Card Type: Normal Monster
Monster Type: Dragon
Attribute: Wind
Level: 3
ATK: 700
DEF: 1300
Rarity: Common

This Dragon has high defense because it carries a shield. It flies to and fro and strikes when you're not ready.

LOB-088 Dark Energy

Card Type: Spell
Monster Type: —
Attribute: Spell
Level: —
ATK: —
DEF: —
Rarity: Common

This energy source for Fiend-Type monsters was created by compressing air from the underworld. Fiends use this energy to power up!

LOB-089 Laser Cannon Armor

Card Type: Spell
Monster Type: —
Attribute: Spell
Level: —
ATK: —
DEF: —
Rarity: Common

This armor has been specially sized for Insects. Equip this card on your Insects to increase their ATK and DEF!

LOB-090 Vile Germs

Card Type: Spell
Monster Type: —
Attribute: Spell
Level: —
ATK: —
DEF: —
Rarity: Common

Use "Vile Germs" to increase the power of your Plant-Type monsters.

LOB-091 Silver Bow and Arrow

Card Type: Spell
Monster Type: —
Attribute: Spell
Level: —
ATK: —
DEF: —
Rarity: Common

Only Fairies can equip this blessed bow and arrow to destroy evil creatures.

LOB-092 Dragon Treasure

Card Type: Spell
Monster Type: —
Attribute: Spell
Level: —
ATK: —
DEF: —
Rarity: Common

Dragons are already powerful to begin with, but this card powers them up even more. This card seems to have no weaknesses!

Legend of Blue-Eyes White Dragon

LOB-093 Electro-Whip

Card Type: Spell
Monster Type: —
Attribute: Spell
Level: —
ATK: —
DEF: —
Rarity: Common

This whip enhances the electricity generated from Thunder-Type monsters. Use this card when the situation calls for it.

LOB-094 Mystical Moon

Card Type: Spell
Monster Type: —
Attribute: Spell
Level: —
ATK: —
DEF: —
Rarity: Common

You can strengthen Beast-Warrior-Type monsters with "Mystical Moon." Include only as many "Mystical Moons" as you need in your Deck.

LOB-095 Stop Defense

Card Type: Spell
Monster Type: —
Attribute: Spell
Level: —
ATK: —
DEF: —
Rarity: Rare

Use "Stop Defense" on monsters that have high DEF that are in Defense Position. Force it to switch to Attack Position.

LOB-096 Machine Conversion Factory

Card Type: Spell
Monster Type: —
Attribute: Spell
Level: —
ATK: —
DEF: —
Rarity: Common

This Spell Card drastically increases a Machine's powers. Rusted joints can now flex smoothly!

LOB-097 Raise Body Heat

Card Type: Spell
Monster Type: —
Attribute: Spell
Level: —
ATK: —
DEF: —
Rarity: Common

This gift will warm up your cold-blooded Dinosaur, allowing it focus on the Duel at hand.

LOB-098 Follow Wind

Card Type: Spell
Monster Type: —
Attribute: Spell
Level: —
ATK: —
DEF: —
Rarity: Common

These divine wings allow Winged Beasts to fly at top speed. Use it to increase their power.

LOB-099 Goblin's Secret Remedy

Card Type: Spell
Monster Type: —
Attribute: Spell
Level: —
ATK: —
DEF: —
Rarity: Rare

After you bite into this secret remedy cherished by goblin fairies, the bitterness will spread throughout your mouth.

LOB-100 Final Flame

Card Type: Spell
Monster Type: —
Attribute: Spell
Level: —
ATK: —
DEF: —
Rarity: Rare

This glowing card does a whopping 600 points of damage to your opponent's Life Points! Save it for the final stroke.

LOB-101 Swords of Revealing Light

Card Type: Spell
Monster Type: —
Attribute: Spell
Level: —
ATK: —
DEF: —
Rarity: Super Rare

This is an extremely powerful Spell Card. However, since this card stays on the field for three turns, it can be destroyed by "De-Spell" or "Heavy Storm."

LOB-102 Metal Dragon

Card Type: Fusion Monster
Monster Type: Machine
Attribute: Wind
Level: 6
ATK: 1850
DEF: 1700
Rarity: Rare

This fusion requires "Steel Ogre Grotto #1," which is not an easy monster to summon. Therefore, use "Polymerization" while the card is in your hand.

LOB-103 Spike Seadra

Card Type: Normal Monster
Monster Type: Sea Serpent
Attribute: Water
Level: 5
ATK: 1600
DEF: 1300
Rarity: Common

"Spike Seadra" lives underwater, but it specializes in electric attacks because its skin is insulated.

LOB-104 Tripwire Beast

Card Type: Normal Monster
Monster Type: Thunder
Attribute: Earth
Level: 4
ATK: 1200
DEF: 1300
Rarity: Common

Stepping on "Tripwire Beast" won't cause it to explode, but it will unleash blasts of lightning!

LOB-105 Skull Red Bird

Card Type: Normal Monster
Monster Type: Winged Beast
Attribute: Wind
Level: 4
ATK: 1550
DEF: 1200
Rarity: Common

"Skull Red Bird" is not as strong as "Rogue Doll," it's a decently powerful Winged Beast. Power it up with the Mountain Field Spell Card!

LOB-106 Armed Ninja

Card Type: Effect Monster
Monster Type: Warrior
Attribute: Earth
Level: 1
ATK: 300
DEF: 300
Rarity: Rare

Use "Armed Ninja" when you do not have enough "De-Spell" cards in your Deck. It's surprisingly useful for a low-level card.

LOB-107 Flower Wolf

Card Type: Fusion Monster
Monster Type: Beast
Attribute: Earth
Level: 5
ATK: 1800
DEF: 1400
Rarity: Rare

This Fusion-Type monster is relatively easy to Summon and has good ATK, so make it part of your normal summoning strategy.

LOB-108 Man-Eater Bug

Card Type: Effect Monster
Monster Type: Insect
Attribute: Earth
Level: 2
ATK: 450
DEF: 600
Rarity: Super Rare

If "Man-Eater Bug" is the only monster on the field, its effect will destroy the "Man-Eater Bug" itself....

LOB-109 Sand Stone

Card Type: Normal Monster
Monster Type: Rock
Attribute: Earth
Level: 5
ATK: 1300
DEF: 1600
Rarity: Common

Though "Sand Stone" is a high-level Rock-Type monster, since its defenses are lower than "Giant Soldier of Stone," this card is difficult to use.

LOB-110 Hane-Hane

Card Type: Effect Monster
Monster Type: Beast
Attribute: Earth
Level: 2
ATK: 450
DEF: 500
Rarity: Rare

Even if face-down "Hane-Hane" is destroyed in battle, you return one monster on the field, but please remember that you can not return "Hane-Hane" itself if it is destroyed.

LOB-111 Misairuzame

Card Type: Normal Monster
Monster Type: Fish
Attribute: Water
Level: 5
ATK: 1400
DEF: 1600
Rarity: Common

If you befriend this extremely intelligent Fish, it will bring you many delicacies from the ocean.

LOB-112 Steel Ogre Grotto #1

Card Type: Normal Monster
Monster Type: Machine
Attribute: Earth
Level: 5
ATK: 1400
DEF: 1800
Rarity: Common

"Steel Ogre Grotto #1" is a high-level Machine-Type monster, but even if you summon it, it seems only to be good for defense....

LOB-113 Lesser Dragon

Card Type: Normal Monster
Monster Type: Dragon
Attribute: Wind
Level: 4
ATK: 1200
DEF: 1000
Rarity: Common

Use this low-level monster as a Tribute to summon other, more powerful Dragons.

LOB-114 Darkworld Thorns

Card Type: Normal Monster
Monster Type: Plant
Attribute: Earth
Level: 3
ATK: 1200
DEF: 900
Rarity: Common

This rose won't attack you unless you get too close. When it rains, it sways its body happily.

Legend of Blue-Eyes White Dragon

LOB-115 Drooling Lizard

Card Type: Normal Monster
Monster Type: Reptile
Attribute: Earth
Level: 3
ATK: 900
DEF: 800
Rarity: Common

There are very few Reptile-Type monsters, and "Drooling Lizard" is one of them. This card may not be very useful.

LOB-116 Armored Starfish

Card Type: Normal Monster
Monster Type: Aqua
Attribute: Water
Level: 4
ATK: 850
DEF: 1400
Rarity: Common

A large starfish with a strong hide, "Armored Starfish's" high DEF makes it useful for strengthening your defense.

LOB-117 Succubus Knight

Card Type: Normal Monster
Monster Type: Warrior
Attribute: Dark
Level: 5
ATK: 1650
DEF: 1300
Rarity: Common

This extremely beautiful female Warrior can be further powered up by "Sword of Dark Destruction" because it has DARK.

LOB-118 Monster Reborn

Card Type: Spell
Monster Type: –
Attribute: Spell
Level: –
ATK: –
DEF: –
Rarity: Ultra Rare

If there's a Monster Card in the Graveyard, use this Spell Card to resurrect it and make it part of your team! This is an extremely important card!

LOB-119 Pot of Greed

Card Type: Spell
Monster Type: –
Attribute: Spell
Level: –
ATK: –
DEF: –
Rarity: Rare

This card is essential when you want to increase the cards in your hand or thin out your Deck.

LOB-120 Right Leg of the Forbidden One

Card Type: Normal Monster
Monster Type: Spellcaster
Attribute: Dark
Level: 1
ATK: 200
DEF: 300
Rarity: Ultra Rare

If at anytime you have five parts of Exodia, you win automatically!

LOB-121 Left Leg of the Forbidden One

Card Type: Normal Monster
Monster Type: Spellcaster
Attribute: Dark
Level: 1
ATK: 200
DEF: 300
Rarity: Ultra Rare

If at anytime you have five parts of Exodia, you win automatically!

LOB-122 Right Arm of the Forbidden One

Card Type: Normal Monster
Monster Type: Spellcaster
Attribute: Dark
Level: 1
ATK: 200
DEF: 300
Rarity: Ultra Rare

If at anytime you have five parts of Exodia, you win automatically!

LOB-123 Left Arm of the Forbidden One

Card Type: Normal Monster
Monster Type: Spellcaster
Attribute: Dark
Level: 1
ATK: 200
DEF: 300
Rarity: Ultra Rare

If at anytime you have five parts of Exodia, you win automatically!

LOB-124 Exodia the Forbidden One

Card Type: Effect Monster
Monster Type: Spellcaster
Attribute: Dark
Level: 3
ATK: 1000
DEF: 1000
Rarity: Ultra Rare

This is one of the five parts necessary to resurrect "Exodia the Forbidden One."

LOB-125 Gaia the Dragon Champion

Card Type: Fusion Monster
Monster Type: Dragon
Attribute: Wind
Level: 7
ATK: 2600
DEF: 2100
Rarity: Secret Rare

It is very difficult to acquire this Secret Rare Card. However, its strength is worth the struggle!

LOB-000 Tri-Horned Dragon

Card Type: Normal Monster
Monster Type: Dragon
Attribute: Dark
Level: 8
ATK: 2850
DEF: 2350
Rarity: Secret Rare

This Dragon is one of the most powerful monsters in existence!

Metal Raiders

MRD-001 Feral Imp

Card Type: Normal Monster
Monster Type: Fiend
Attribute: Dark
Level: 4
ATK: 1300
DEF: 1400
Rarity: Common

This small Fiend's entire body is colored green. Its love of practical jokes makes it troublesome to deal with.

MRD-002 Winged Dragon, Guardian of the Fortress #1

Card Type: Normal Monster
Monster Type: Dragon
Attribute: Wind
Level: 4
ATK: 1400
DEF: 1200
Rarity: Common

Mountain battles are this Dragon's specialty. It frustrates enemies with sneak attacks!

MRD-003 Summoned Skull

Card Type: Normal Monster
Monster Type: Fiend
Attribute: Dark
Level: 6
ATK: 2500
DEF: 1200
Rarity: Ultra Rare

Though "Summoned Skull" is a high-level Fiend, it's easy to summon and extremely useful.

MRD-004 Rock Ogre Grotto #1

Card Type: Normal Monster
Monster Type: Rock
Attribute: Earth
Level: 3
ATK: 800
DEF: 1200
Rarity: Common

Notice that "Rock Ogre Grotto #1's" ATK is lower than its DEF. Other Rock-Type monsters may be better suited to your needs.

MRD-005 Armored Lizard

Card Type: Normal Monster
Monster Type: Reptile
Attribute: Earth
Level: 4
ATK: 1500
DEF: 1200
Rarity: Common

The main offensive card of the Reptile-Type monsters, "Armored Lizard's" strength is that it is good to go in any terrain!

MRD-006 Killer Needle

Card Type: Normal Monster
Monster Type: Insect
Attribute: Wind
Level: 4
ATK: 1200
DEF: 1000
Rarity: Common

No matter the opponent, one poisonous sting from this giant bee and it's history. If they ever swarm you, then duck underwater!

MRD-007 Larvae Moth

Card Type: Effect Monster
Monster Type: Insect
Attribute: Earth
Level: 2
ATK: 500
DEF: 400
Rarity: Common

"Larvae Moth" is the first stage of evolution of "Petit Moth." In order to evolve, it rests in a tree's shadows and gathers its strength. When offering "Cocoon of Evolution," you must have "Larvae Moth" in your hand.

MRD-008 Harpie Lady

Card Type: Normal Monster
Monster Type: Winged Beast
Attribute: Wind
Level: 4
ATK: 1300
DEF: 1400
Rarity: Common

This Winged Beast has average ATK and DEF, but it is indispensable in summoning "Harpie Lady Sisters!"

MRD-009 Harpie Lady Sisters

Card Type: Effect Monster
Monster Type: Winged Beast
Attribute: Wind
Level: 6
ATK: 1950
DEF: 2100
Rarity: Super Rare

Special Summon "Harpie Lady Sisters" using "Elegant Egotist." It has both high ATK and DEF, so it is a force to be reckoned with!

MRD-010 Kojikocy

Card Type: Normal Monster
Monster Type: Warrior
Attribute: Earth
Level: 4
ATK: 1500
DEF: 1200
Rarity: Common

This Warrior has extremely powerful destructive powers! It will definitely be a core force in Warrior-Type Decks.

MRD-011 Cocoon of Evolution

Card Type: Effect Monster
Monster Type: Insect
Attribute: Earth
Level: 3
ATK: 0
DEF: 2000
Rarity: Common

"Cocoon of Evolution" is an Effect Monster Card that you can equip to "Petit Moth." You can Normal Summon this monster although you cannot equip it to "Petit Moth" once it is Normal Summoned and vice versa.

MRD-012 Crawling Dragon

Card Type: Normal Monster
Monster Type: Dragon
Attribute: Earth
Level: 5
ATK: 1600
DEF: 1400
Rarity: Common

This Dragon has been around from the dawn of time, so maybe you should leave this living artifact alone instead of destroying it.

MRD-013 Armored Zombie

Card Type: Normal Monster
Monster Type: Zombie
Attribute: Dark
Level: 3
ATK: 1500
DEF: 0
Rarity: Common

Strong grudges prevented this armored warrior from moving on to the next world. With no reasoning left, all it can do is swing its sword.

MRD-014 Mask of Darkness

Card Type: Effect Monster
Monster Type: Fiend
Attribute: Dark
Level: 2
ATK: 900
DEF: 400
Rarity: Rare

While "Mask of Darkness" can resurrect Trap Cards from the Graveyard, if there are no Trap Cards in the Graveyard, then you cannot recover anything.

MRD-015 Doma The Angel of Silence

Card Type: Normal Monster
Monster Type: Fairy
Attribute: Dark
Level: 5
ATK: 1600
DEF: 1400
Rarity: Common

A Fairy with DARK, this creature is full of mystery. You must offer one monster as a Tribute to summon this monster.

MRD-016 White Magical Hat

Card Type: Effect Monster
Monster Type: Spellcaster
Attribute: Light
Level: 3
ATK: 1000
DEF: 700
Rarity: Rare

This strange Spellcaster appears when the moon is in the sky and only steals from crooks. While its ATK is mediocre, its ability to force your opponent to discard cards from his or her hand is immeasurable. This is especially useful when your opponent is trying to set up a combo.

MRD-017 Big Eye

Card Type: Effect Monster
Monster Type: Fiend
Attribute: Dark
Level: 4
ATK: 1200
DEF: 1000
Rarity: Common

Using all its eyes on its body, this Fiend can see into the future. It can anticipate its opponent's next move to dodge attacks. If your Deck is a Combo Deck, this card makes things interesting. You can draw the exact cards you need earlier, allowing you to form strategies easier. However, "Big Eye" does not go well with cards that require you to shuffle the Deck.

MRD-018 B. Skull Dragon

Card Type: Fusion Monster
Monster Type: Dragon
Attribute: Dark
Level: 9
ATK: 3200
DEF: 2500
Rarity: Ultra Rare

Create one of the fiercest monsters in action by fusing "Summoned Skull" and "Red-Eyes B. Dragon" with "Polymerization." This must-have card has capabilities for powerful combos.

MRD-019 Masked Sorcerer

Card Type: Effect Monster
Monster Type: Spellcaster
Attribute: Dark
Level: 4
ATK: 900
DEF: 1400
Rarity: Rare

A sorcerer adorned with relics from an ancient civilization, he gained the ability to see the future through a steel mask. No one has ever seen his face. With this card, you can prevent losing cards from your hand. "Masked Sorcerer" works well with "Muka Muka," so they should be put into the same Deck. However, it may be hard to get an attack through.

MRD-020 Roaring Ocean Snake

Card Type: Fusion Monster
Monster Type: Aqua
Attribute: Water
Level: 6
ATK: 2100
DEF: 1800
Rarity: Common

Create "Roaring Ocean Snake" by fusing "Mystic Lamp" and "Hyosube" using "Polymerization." Since its Fusion-Material Monsters are weak, "Roaring Ocean Snake" is not the easiest monster to summon, but its ATK is certainly attractive.

MRD-021 Water Omotics

Card Type: Normal Monster
Monster Type: Aqua
Attribute: Water
Level: 4
ATK: 1400
DEF: 1200
Rarity: Common

This water fairy loves dragons. Don't try to sneak up on her unless you're ready to receive punishment.

MRD-022 Ground Attacker Bugroth

Card Type: Normal Monster
Monster Type: Machine
Attribute: Earth
Level: 4
ATK: 1500
DEF: 1000
Rarity: Common

Although "Ground Attacker Bugroth" is a high-performance Machine, it's easy to summon because it's a Level 4 monster! Hit-and-run tactics are its strength!

MRD-023 Petit Moth

Card Type: Normal Monster
Monster Type: Insect
Attribute: Earth
Level: 1
ATK: 300
DEF: 200
Rarity: Common

No one knows what this Insect will evolve into. "Petit Moth" is a challenging card to use.

MRD-024 Elegant Egotist

Card Type: Spell
Monster Type: –
Attribute: Spell
Level: –
ATK: –
DEF: –
Rarity: Rare

After Special Summoning "Harpie Lady Sisters," don't forget to shuffle your Deck.

MRD-025 Sanga of the Thunder

Card Type: Effect Monster
Monster Type: Thunder
Attribute: Light
Level: 7
ATK: 2600
DEF: 2200
Rarity: Super Rare

"Sanga of the Thunder" is the strongest of the three deities. Since it has an electrical current constantly running on the surface of its body, its special powers block damage from opponents that touch it. If your opponent summons a powerful monster that you are not prepared for, "Sanga of the Thunder's" effect can buy you time to draw a useful card from your Deck.

MRD-026 Kazejin

Card Type: Effect Monster
Monster Type: Spellcaster
Attribute: Wind
Level: 7
ATK: 2400
DEF: 2200
Rarity: Super Rare

A rare Spellcaster with WIND, "Kazejin" uses its own breath to create a wall of air to stop its opponent's attacks. Though it is not as powerful as "Sanga of the Thunder" and "Suijin," "Kazejin" has the ability to make the ATK of an opponent's monster 0. However, you have to ask yourself if it's worth it to offer two monsters as a Tribute to summon "Kazejin." If you do summon this monster, then definitely attack!

MRD-027 Suijin

Card Type: Effect Monster
Monster Type: Aqua
Attribute: Water
Level: 7
ATK: 2500
DEF: 2400
Rarity: Super Rare

This magical deity gathers water spirits. WATER monsters usually lack ATK, but "Suijin" boasts incredible ATK. It negates your opponent's attacks with a wall of water. Even if your opponent attacks with "Summoned Skull," "Suijin" will survive while "Summoned Skull" will not if you use "Suijin's" effect. The only drawback is that you need to offer two monsters as a Tribute to summon "Suijin."

MRD-028 Mystic Lamp

Card Type: Effect Monster
Monster Type: Spellcaster
Attribute: Dark
Level: 1
ATK: 400
DEF: 300
Rarity: Common

When you rub this legendary lamp, a genie appears and makes your wishes come true. "Mystic Lamp" also serves as Fusion-Material for "Roaring Ocean Snake." You can fuse this card with "Hyosube," attack your opponent directly, or use it for defense. "Mystic Lamp" is versatile, so it can be quite useful.

MRD-029 Steel Scorpion

Card Type: Effect Monster
Monster Type: Machine
Attribute: Earth
Level: 1
ATK: 250
DEF: 300
Rarity: Common

This monster is very weak, but even "Summoned Skull" cannot avoid this effect when it attacks this monster.

MRD-030 Ocubeam

Card Type: Normal Monster
Monster Type: Fairy
Attribute: Light
Level: 5
ATK: 1550
DEF: 1650
Rarity: Common

Even though "Ocubeam" has high ATK and DEF, you must offer a monster as a Tribute to summon this high-level monster. However, you'll be glad to have "Ocubeam" on your field if you can summon it!

MRD-031 Leghul

Card Type: Effect Monster
Monster Type: Insect
Attribute: Earth
Level: 1
ATK: 300
DEF: 350
Rarity: Common

This pesky Insect pokes enemies with its sharp spikes. Sometimes, it goes unnoticed by large enemies and simply ends up being stamped on. You probably won't use this card unless you power it up with plenty of Spell and Trap Cards. This card is usually used in Decks that destroy your opponent's hand or Decks that contain "Cannon Soldier."

MRD-032 Ooguchi

Card Type: Effect Monster
Monster Type: Aqua
Attribute: Water
Level: 1
ATK: 300
DEF: 250
Rarity: Common

This monster suddenly bites you with its huge mouth from underwater. However, since it's usually an herbivore, its fangs have deteriorated. After using "Swords of Revealing Light," "Ooguchi" can be quite a force with "Cannon Soldier." If you attack and then offer it as a Tribute to "Cannon Soldier," you can cause significant damage to your opponent's Life Points.

MRD-033 Leogun

Card Type: Normal Monster
Monster Type: Beast
Attribute: Earth
Level: 5
ATK: 1750
DEF: 1550
Rarity: Common

A giant lion with a trademark golden mane, "Leogun" is extremely ferocious and will mercilessly fight even a weakened opponent.

MRD-034 Blast Juggler

Card Type: Effect Monster
Monster Type: Machine
Attribute: Fire
Level: 3
ATK: 800
DEF: 900
Rarity: Common

This walking explosive destroys all enemies within its range. You can destroy annoying Effect Monsters in one full sweep, but if left in Attack Position, you can expect your opponent to retaliate. Include this card in your Deck if you have very little removal cards.

MRD-035 Jinzo #7

Card Type: Effect Monster
Monster Type: Machine
Attribute: Dark
Level: 2
ATK: 500
DEF: 400
Rarity: Common

Since this android, created by science, lacks a heart, it feels no pain. It's a horrific creature that continues its carnage until it's destroyed. "Jinzo #7" has one of the highest ATK for a direct damage monster. After powering it up with "Sword of Deep-Seated," force your opponent to lose cards in his or her hand by using "Robbin' Goblin."

MRD-036 Magician of Faith

Card Type: Effect Monster
Monster Type: Spellcaster
Attribute: Light
Level: 1
ATK: 300
DEF: 400
Rarity: Rare

Similar to "Mask of Darkness," "Magician of Faith" can resurrect Spell Cards. Use "Magician of Faith" after using a powerful Spell Card.

Metal Raiders

MRD-037 Ancient Elf

Card Type: Normal Monster
Monster Type: Spellcaster
Attribute: Light
Level: 4
ATK: 1450
DEF: 1200
Rarity: Common

Rumors say this elf has lived for millenniums.

MRD-038 Deepsea Shark

Card Type: Fusion Monster
Monster Type: Fish
Attribute: Water
Level: 5
ATK: 1900
DEF: 1600
Rarity: Common

Create this gigantic shark that lives at the bottom of the ocean by fusing "Bottom Dweller" and "Tongyo" with "Polymerization."

MRD-039 Bottom Dweller

Card Type: Normal Monster
Monster Type: Fish
Attribute: Water
Level: 5
ATK: 1650
DEF: 1700
Rarity: Common

It's quite a challenge to summon this long-lived Fish, but it is certainly worth it when you see it in battle!

MRD-040 Destroyer Golem

Card Type: Normal Monster
Monster Type: Rock
Attribute: Earth
Level: 4
ATK: 1500
DEF: 1000
Rarity: Common

You can count on "Destroyer Golem's" high ATK in combat, but beware—its DEF is surprisingly low!

MRD-041 Kaminari Attack

Card Type: Fusion Monster
Monster Type: Thunder
Attribute: Wind
Level: 5
ATK: 1900
DEF: 1400
Rarity: Common

The Fusion-Material Monsters for this Thunder-Type Fusion Monster are weak, so have the Monster Cards in your hand when you use "Polymerization" to summon "Kaminari Attack."

MRD-042 Rainbow Flower

Card Type: Effect Monster
Monster Type: Plant
Attribute: Earth
Level: 2
ATK: 400
DEF: 500
Rarity: Common

Looks can be deceiving! This eerie flower launches an attack just when its opponent's fears are put to rest by its cute looks. While it can attack the opponent's Life Points directly, it can be destroyed easily next turn because it has low ATK. If you are going to use this card, attack after using "Swords of Revealing Light" first.

MRD-043 Morinphen

Card Type: Normal Monster
Monster Type: Fiend
Attribute: Dark
Level: 5
ATK: 1550
DEF: 1300
Rarity: Common

This strange Fiend, born in the depths of shadows, has long arms and razor-sharp talons.

MRD-044 Mega Thunderball

Card Type: Normal Monster
Monster Type: Thunder
Attribute: Wind
Level: 2
ATK: 750
DEF: 600
Rarity: Common

Since "Mega Thunderball" accumulates so much electricity when it's not moving, it constantly rolls around to expend the extra electricity.

MRD-045 Tongyo

Card Type: Normal Monster
Monster Type: Fish
Attribute: Water
Level: 4
ATK: 1350
DEF: 800
Rarity: Common

"Tongyo" sneaks up from behind and wraps its long tongue around its enemy! If you get caught, it's hard to break free.

MRD-046 Empress Judge

Card Type: Fusion Monster
Monster Type: Warrior
Attribute: Earth
Level: 6
ATK: 2100
DEF: 1700
Rarity: Common

Created by fusing "Queens' Double" and "Hibikime" by "Polymerization," she possesses high-ranking attack powers among all female Warriors. Rumor says she was once an empress who ruled an ancient Eastern land.

MRD-047 Pale Beast

Card Type: Normal Monster
Monster Type: Beast
Attribute: Earth
Level: 4
ATK: 1500
DEF: 1200
Rarity: Common

Living deep in the shadows of a forest, the pair of eyes on "Pale Beast's" chin help it find prey.

MRD-048 Electric Lizard

Card Type: Effect Monster
Monster Type: Thunder
Attribute: Earth
Level: 3
ATK: 850
DEF: 800
Rarity: Common

"Electric Lizard's" effect is useful, but afterwards, it's only useful for being offered as a Tribute for a stronger monster if it is not destroyed by the attack from an opponent's monster.

MRD-049 Hunter Spider

Card Type: Normal Monster
Monster Type: Insect
Attribute: Earth
Level: 5
ATK: 1600
DEF: 1400
Rarity: Common

This spider is not only strong but also quite intelligent! You'll be finished if you find yourself wrapped up in its web.

MRD-050 Ancient Lizard Warrior

Card Type: Normal Monster
Monster Type: Reptile
Attribute: Earth
Level: 4
ATK: 1400
DEF: 1100
Rarity: Common

These warriors are true to their ancient ways, refining their skills with their one-of-a-kind training method.

MRD-051 Queen's Double

Card Type: Effect Monster
Monster Type: Warrior
Attribute: Earth
Level: 1
ATK: 350
DEF: 300
Rarity: Common

"Queen's Double" is a soldier who protects the queen of a prosperous Eastern land. Expertly wielding a knife, she pretends to be the queen to protect her from would-be kidnappers. "Queen's Double" can not only attack your opponent directly, but it is also a Fusion-Material Monster for "Empress Judge." This card works well with "Robbin' Goblin," so use them in the same Deck.

MRD-052 Trent

Card Type: Normal Monster
Monster Type: Plant
Attribute: Earth
Level: 5
ATK: 1500
DEF: 1800
Rarity: Common

"Trent's" DEF is pretty good, but since it requires a Tribute to summon, using this card is a tough call.

MRD-053 Disk Magician

Card Type: Normal Monster
Monster Type: Machine
Attribute: Dark
Level: 4
ATK: 1350
DEF: 1000
Rarity: Common

If you approach the disk, the magician spontaneously appears and attacks. You can often find it guarding ancient ruins and fighting off invaders.

MRD-054 Hyosube

Card Type: Normal Monster
Monster Type: Aqua
Attribute: Water
Level: 4
ATK: 1500
DEF: 900
Rarity: Common

When viewed alone, neither its ATK or DEF are impressive. However, it is useful as Fusion-Material for summoning "Roaring Ocean Snake."

MRD-055 Hibikime

Card Type: Normal Monster
Monster Type: Warrior
Attribute: Earth
Level: 4
ATK: 1450
DEF: 1000
Rarity: Common

This female Warrior prides herself in her ability to emit unpleasant sounds that confuse her opponents. Though she's not powerful on her own, she is Fusion-Material for "Empress Judge."

MRD-056 Fake Trap

Card Type: Trap
Monster Type: –
Attribute: Trap
Level: –
ATK: –
DEF: –
Rarity: Rare

Use this Trap Card to fool your opponent. It's fun to watch your opponent squirm while he or she thinks this card's a Trap Card. However, this card is useless by itself. Fake Trap can protect all your other Trap Cards, making this card indispensable.

MRD-057 Tribute to The Doomed

Card Type: Spell
Monster Type: –
Attribute: Spell
Level: –
ATK: –
DEF: –
Rarity: Super Rare

In ancient Egypt, it was customary to offer tributes upon the Pharaoh's demise, a custom that exists to the present. "Tribute to the Doomed" forces you to discard one card from your hand, but that's not a high price to pay considering that you can destroy your opponent's most powerful monster. It can also destroy Flip Effect Monster Cards without activating their effects.

MRD-058 Soul Release

Card Type: Spell
Monster Type: –
Attribute: Spell
Level: –
ATK: –
DEF: –
Rarity: Common

Free this wandering soul so that it can move on to the spirit world. "Soul Release" prevents powerful Monster, Spell, and Trap Cards from being reused by removing cards in the Graveyard from play. Use it as countermeasure against "Monster Reborn"—"Magician of Faith" combos.

MRD-059 The Cheerful Coffin

Card Type: Spell
Monster Type: –
Attribute: Spell
Level: –
ATK: –
DEF: –
Rarity: Common

A mortician never goes out of business in any day or age. They appear out of nowhere and bury our dead with a smile. You can discard hard-to-summon monsters in the Graveyard, and then revive them with "Monster Reborn." However, this magic is less effective against "Tribute to the Doomed."

MRD-060 Change of Heart

Card Type: Spell
Monster Type: –
Attribute: Spell
Level: –
ATK: –
DEF: –
Rarity: Ultra Rare

The heart is a transient thing, and this is true for monsters' hearts as well—so much that monsters at times forget who their masters are. The monster you worked so hard to summon suddenly defects to your opponent. This effect lasts only the turn "Change of Heart" is activated, so the monster is often offered as a Tribute.

Metal Raiders

MRD-061 Baby Dragon

Card Type: Normal Monster
Monster Type: Dragon
Attribute: Wind
Level: 3
ATK: 1200
DEF: 700
Rarity: Common

Though "Baby Dragon" is still a baby, it has huge potential for power. Fuse "Baby Dragon" with "Time Wizard" to summon "Thousand Dragon!"

MRD-062 Blackland Fire Dragon

Card Type: Normal Monster
Monster Type: Dragon
Attribute: Dark
Level: 4
ATK: 1500
DEF: 800
Rarity: Common

This Dragon lives in the depths of shadows, so it has poor eyesight. However, it more than makes up for it with its keen sense of smell to locate its prey.

MRD-063 Swamp Battleguard

Card Type: Effect Monster
Monster Type: Warrior
Attribute: Earth
Level: 5
ATK: 1800
DEF: 1500
Rarity: Common

This card shows its true colors when it's on the field with "Lava Battleguard," so placing this monster on the field alone is pointless. "Swamp Battleguard" is the offensive arm of the Battleguard brothers. If it is on the field with "Lava Battleguard," its ATK increases by 500 points to 2300. The only catch is that this monster is a Tribute Summon.

MRD-064 Battle Steer

Card Type: Normal Monster
Monster Type: Beast-Warrior
Attribute: Earth
Level: 5
ATK: 1800
DEF: 1300
Rarity: Common

A monster in the form of a steer, "Battle Steer" charges its enemies with its horns. It is constantly excited by the red cape it has wrapped around itself.

MRD-065 Time Wizard

Card Type: Effect Monster
Monster Type: Spellcaster
Attribute: Light
Level: 2
ATK: 500
DEF: 400
Rarity: Ultra Rare

This Spellcaster has the ability to control time. Fuse "Time Wizard" with "Baby Dragon" to summon "Thousand Dragon."

MRD-066 Saggi the Dark Clown

Card Type: Normal Monster
Monster Type: Spellcaster
Attribute: Dark
Level: 3
ATK: 600
DEF: 1500
Rarity: Common

This elusive clown appears out of nowhere, so if you hear an eerie laugh, watch out because chances are that "Saggi the Dark Clown" is nearby!

MRD-067 Dragon Piper

Card Type: Effect Monster
Monster Type: Pyro
Attribute: Fire
Level: 3
ATK: 200
DEF: 1800
Rarity: Common

If you have a Dragon-Type Deck, place "Dragon Piper" in your Side Deck in case your opponent has "Dragon Capture Jar." However, the Spell Card "Remove Trap" may be more versatile....

MRD-068 Illusionist Faceless Mage

Card Type: Normal Monster
Monster Type: Spellcaster
Attribute: Dark
Level: 5
ATK: 1200
DEF: 2200
Rarity: Common

You won't regret offering a monster as a Tribute to summon this Spellcaster with high DEF. As long as you have its defenses, you're in good health.

MRD-069 Sangan

Card Type: Effect Monster
Monster Type: Fiend
Attribute: Dark
Level: 3
ATK: 1000
DEF: 600
Rarity: Rare

Similar to "Witch of the Black Forest," you cannot draw a monster with high ATK, but there are many Effect Monsters that may be useful.

MRD-070 Great Moth

Card Type: Effect Monster
Monster Type: Insect
Attribute: Earth
Level: 8
ATK: 2600
DEF: 2500
Rarity: Rare

There are many Monster Removal cards, so you will find it difficult to protect "Petit Moth" for four turns. Therefore, construct a Deck designed to protect "Petit Moth" in order to Special Summon "Great Moth."

MRD-071 Kuriboh

Card Type: Effect Monster
Monster Type: Fiend
Attribute: Dark
Level: 1
ATK: 300
DEF: 200
Rarity: Super Rare

This card acts as a shield for your Life Points. When you're in a difficult situation, add this card to your hand using "Witch of the Black Forest" or "Sangan."

MRD-072 Jellyfish

Card Type: Normal Monster
Monster Type: Aqua
Attribute: Water
Level: 4
ATK: 1200
DEF: 1500
Rarity: Common

This monster was used by Mako Tsunami. This semi-transparent creature drifts in the sea.

MRD-073 Castle of Dark Illusions

Card Type: Effect Monster
Monster Type: Fiend
Attribute: Dark
Level: 4
ATK: 920
DEF: 1930
Rarity: Common

If your Deck contains many Zombie-Type monsters, then your monsters will power up. If you buy time with "Swords of Revealing Light," your advantage further increases.

MRD-074 King of Yamimakai

Card Type: Normal Monster
Monster Type: Fiend
Attribute: Dark
Level: 5
ATK: 2000
DEF: 1530
Rarity: Common

One of the Fiend kings of the underworld, he has no eyes because he prefers the pitch-black Yami Field.

MRD-075 Catapult Turtle

Card Type: Effect Monster
Monster Type: Aqua
Attribute: Water
Level: 5
ATK: 1000
DEF: 2000
Rarity: Super Rare

"Catapult Turtle" is a beefed-up version of "Cannon Soldier." It requires a Tribute to summon, but you can Special Summon it with "Last Will." If you can lock down a combo with "Ultimate Offering," the battle will be yours for the taking.

MRD-076 Mystic Horseman

Card Type: Normal Monster
Monster Type: Beast
Attribute: Earth
Level: 4
ATK: 1300
DEF: 1550
Rarity: Common

This legendary creature is half-man, half-horse. It can run very fast, making it ideal for swift attacks.

MRD-077 Rabid Horseman

Card Type: Fusion Monster
Monster Type: Beast-Warrior
Attribute: Earth
Level: 6
ATK: 2000
DEF: 1700
Rarity: Common

Created by fusing "Battle Ox" and "Mystic Horseman" using "Polymerization," this relentless Beast-Warrior possesses horrendous destructive capabilities as well as speed and grace.

MRD-078 Crass Clown

Card Type: Effect Monster
Monster Type: Fiend
Attribute: Dark
Level: 4
ATK: 1350
DEF: 1400
Rarity: Common

When first summoned face-down and then switched to Attack Position, it is similar to "Hane-Hane." It's a question of whether you can use this effect again, but it has much higher ATK than "Hane-Hane," so "Crass Clown" may be better.

MRD-079 Pumpking the King of Ghosts

Card Type: Effect Monster
Monster Type: Zombie
Attribute: Dark
Level: 6
ATK: 1800
DEF: 2000
Rarity: Common

When combined with "Castle of Dark Illusions'" effect, "Pumpking the King of Ghosts'" ATK and DEF increase by 100 every turn! If you can make it last five turns, it will have 2300 ATK and 2500 DEF! But remember that even if you have two "Castle of Dark Illusions," you cannot double this card's effect.

MRD-080 Dream Clown

Card Type: Effect Monster
Monster Type: Warrior
Attribute: Earth
Level: 3
ATK: 1200
DEF: 900
Rarity: Common

Since its ATK is low, "Dream Clown" can be easily destroyed before it can activate its effect. However, the effect is very useful. Try using this in a Deck with "Swords of Revealing Light."

MRD-081 Tainted Wisdom

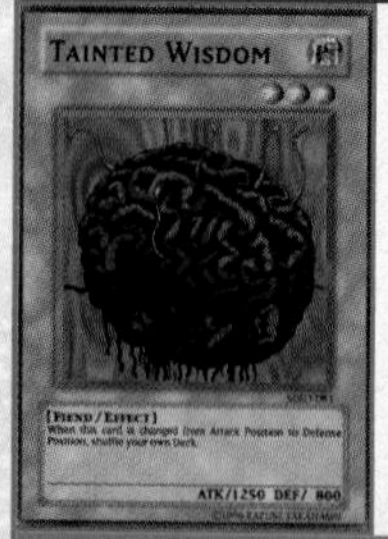

Card Type: Effect Monster
Monster Type: Fiend
Attribute: Dark
Level: 3
ATK: 1250
DEF: 800
Rarity: Common

In order to use this card's effect, it must first be in Attack Position. However, since it has relatively low ATK, it can be easily destroyed...and its effect isn't that great.

MRD-082 Ancient Brain

Card Type: Normal Monster
Monster Type: Fiend
Attribute: Dark
Level: 3
ATK: 1000
DEF: 700
Rarity: Common

This fallen angel was exiled from the heavens due to his research into forbidden evil wisdom. Its brain is large due to the massive amount of information it has acquired.

MRD-083 Guardian of the Labyrinth

Card Type: Normal Monster
Monster Type: Warrior
Attribute: Earth
Level: 4
ATK: 1000
DEF: 1200
Rarity: Common

This monster guards the entrance to the underworld with "Flame Cerebrus." His shield has a mouth that can also attack.

MRD-084 Prevent Rat

Card Type: Normal Monster
Monster Type: Beast
Attribute: Earth
Level: 4
ATK: 500
DEF: 2000
Rarity: Common

This monster has 2000 DEF! Use this card to protect your Life Points.

MRD-085 The Little Swordsman of Aile

Card Type: Effect Monster
Monster Type: Warrior
Attribute: Water
Level: 3
ATK: 800
DEF: 1300
Rarity: Common

If you have Flip Effect Monsters or other monsters that are useless in battle, then use them to power up "The Little Swordsman of Aile" and attack. If you offer two monsters as a Tribute, there will be plenty of damage!

MRD-086 Princess of Tsurugi

Card Type: Effect Monster
Monster Type: Warrior
Attribute: Wind
Level: 3
ATK: 900
DEF: 700
Rarity: Rare

"Princess of Tsurugi" is very effective against opponents who use many Spell and Trap Cards. If used correctly, you can eliminate almost half your opponent's Life Points.

MRD-087 Protector of the Throne

Card Type: Normal Monster
Monster Type: Warrior
Attribute: Earth
Level: 4
ATK: 800
DEF: 1500
Rarity: Common

This queen protects the royal throne while the king is away. The floating crystal possesses various powers that protect the queen from enemies.

MRD-088 Tremendous Fire

Card Type: Spell
Monster Type: —
Attribute: Spell
Level: —
ATK: —
DEF: —
Rarity: Common

Even if you receive 500 damage, dealing 1000 damage is a good deal. If your opponent has less than 1000 Life Points, this can be the finishing blow!

MRD-089 Jirai Gumo

Card Type: Effect Monster
Monster Type: Insect
Attribute: Earth
Level: 4
ATK: 2200
DEF: 100
Rarity: Common

Its ATK are incredible and you don't have to offer another monster as a Tribute! However, the risk is huge! It may be good to attack if you're close to defeat, but until then, it may be best to leave it for protecting your Life Points.

MRD-090 Shadow Ghoul

Card Type: Effect Monster
Monster Type: Zombie
Attribute: Dark
Level: 5
ATK: 1600
DEF: 1300
Rarity: Rare

Summon "Shadow Ghoul" when you have a lot of monsters in your Graveyard. This card works well in Decks that contain "Cannon Soldier" and "Catapult Turtle" because they discard monsters into the Graveyard.

MRD-091 Labyrinth Tank

Card Type: Fusion Monster
Monster Type: Machine
Attribute: Dark
Level: 7
ATK: 2400
DEF: 2400
Rarity: Common

Create "Labyrinth Tank" by fusing "Giga-Tech Wolf" and "Cannon Soldier" using "Polymerization." This tank destroys anyone who enters the labyrinth. However, even the tank itself gets lost in the maze....

MRD-092 Ryu-Kishin Powered

Card Type: Normal Monster
Monster Type: Fiend
Attribute: Dark
Level: 4
ATK: 1600
DEF: 1200
Rarity: Common

Kaiba uses this beefed-up version of "Ryu-Kishin." Its armorlike body and huge sharp claws power up its abilities.

MRD-093 Bickuribox

Card Type: Fusion Monster
Monster Type: Fiend
Attribute: Dark
Level: 7
ATK: 2300
DEF: 2000
Rarity: Common

Create "Bickuribox" by fusing "Crass Clown" and "Dream Clown" with "Polymerization." This Fiend jumps out and attacks anyone that gets near its toy box.

MRD-094 Giltia the D. Knight

Card Type: Fusion Monster
Monster Type: Warrior
Attribute: Light
Level: 5
ATK: 1850
DEF: 1500
Rarity: Common

Fuse "Guardian of the Labyrinth" and "Protector of the Throne" by "Polymerization" to create this Warrior who is also adept at magic. He infuses his magic into his weapon to increase its power.

MRD-095 Launcher Spider

Card Type: Normal Monster
Monster Type: Machine
Attribute: Fire
Level: 7
ATK: 2200
DEF: 2500
Rarity: Common

This Machine-Type monster recklessly launches super-powerful rockets. Though you need to offer two monsters as a Tribute to summon "Launcher Spider," its ATK and DEF are certainly attractive.

MRD-096 Giga-Tech Wolf

Card Type: Normal Monster
Monster Type: Machine
Attribute: Fire
Level: 4
ATK: 1200
DEF: 1400
Rarity: Common

This cyborg wolf is made entirely of steel and can unleash various attacks using its wings and each of its arrowhead tails.

MRD-097 Thunder Dragon

Card Type: Effect Monster
Monster Type: Thunder
Attribute: Light
Level: 5
ATK: 1600
DEF: 1500
Rarity: Common

If you have this card and "Polymerization" in your hand, you can immediately summon the powerful Fusion monster "Twin-Headed Thunder Dragon!" You can only use this effect once, but it is still powerful!

MRD-098 7 Colored Fish

Card Type: Normal Monster
Monster Type: Fish
Attribute: Water
Level: 4
ATK: 1800
DEF: 800
Rarity: Common

"7 Colored Fish" is extremely powerful for a monster that does not have to be a Tribute Summon. Everyone should get this card!

MRD-099 The Immortal of Thunder

Card Type: Effect Monster
Monster Type: Thunder
Attribute: Light
Level: 4
ATK: 1500
DEF: 1300
Rarity: Common

This card acts like a bank for Life Points. When you want to use a Spell, Trap, or Effect Monster Card that requires you to spend Life Points, then "The Immortal of Thunder" gives you a temporary life boost. However, if it is attacked and destroyed, you end up losing 2000 points.

MRD-100 Punished Eagle

Card Type: Fusion Monster
Monster Type: Winged Beast
Attribute: Wind
Level: 6
ATK: 2100
DEF: 1800
Rarity: Common

Summon "Punished Eagle" by fusing "Blue-Winged Crown" and "Niwatori" using "Polymerization." This eagle was sent from above to judge humans. It creates an enormous tornado with a single flap of its wings.

MRD-101 Insect Soldiers of the Sky

Card Type: Effect Monster
Monster Type: Insect
Attribute: Wind
Level: 3
ATK: 1000
DEF: 800
Rarity: Common

Definitely give this card a shot if your opponent is using WIND monsters. However, its original ATK is low, so beware. Once it powers up, then it is a force to be reckoned with.

MRD-102 Hoshiningen

Card Type: Effect Monster
Monster Type: Fairy
Attribute: Light
Level: 2
ATK: 500
DEF: 700
Rarity: Rare

Most LIGHT monsters have low ATK, so this card's effect may not be very effective.

MRD-103 Musician King

Card Type: Fusion Monster
Monster Type: Spellcaster
Attribute: Light
Level: 5
ATK: 1750
DEF: 1500
Rarity: Common

Create "Musician King" by fusing "Witch of the Black Forest" and "Lady of Faith" using "Polymerization." It attacks its enemies with loud sound waves. Its trademarks are its bandanna and guitar.

MRD-104 Yado Karu

Card Type: Effect Monster
Monster Type: Aqua
Attribute: Water
Level: 4
ATK: 900
DEF: 1700
Rarity: Common

Put cards that cannot help you currently at the bottom of your Deck. But be careful not to put a card back in your Deck that you may need real soon....

MRD-105 Cyber Saurus

Card Type: Fusion Monster
Monster Type: Machine
Attribute: Earth
Level: 5
ATK: 1800
DEF: 1400
Rarity: Common

Created by fusing "Blast Juggler" and "Two-Headed King Rex" by "Polymerization," this artificially created dinosaur's body is 90 percent machine.

MRD-106 Cannon Soldier

Card Type: Effect Monster
Monster Type: Machine
Attribute: Dark
Level: 4
ATK: 1400
DEF: 1300
Rarity: Rare

"Cannon Soldier" can offer itself as a Tribute. This card works effectively with monsters that are useless in battle, Effect Monsters whose effects have already been triggered, or cards like "Sangan" and "Witch of the Black Forest" that allow you to add more monsters from your Deck when they are sent to the Graveyard.

MRD-107 Muka Muka

Card Type: Effect Monster
Monster Type: Rock
Attribute: Earth
Level: 2
ATK: 600
DEF: 300
Rarity: Rare

If you summon "Muka Muka" on your first turn, you just summoned a monster with 2100 ATK! Afterwards, try to keep as many cards in your hand. If you need to use a card, then attack first.

MRD-108 The Bistro Butcher

Card Type: Effect Monster
Monster Type: Fiend
Attribute: Dark
Level: 4
ATK: 1800
DEF: 1000
Rarity: Common

You may think it's a drawback to allow your opponent to draw two cards, but if you combine "The Bistro Butcher" with other cards that remove cards from your opponent's hand and Deck, you will make your opponent run out of cards faster!

Metal Raiders

MRD-109 Star Boy

Card Type: Effect Monster
Monster Type: Aqua
Attribute: Water
Level: 2
ATK: 550
DEF: 500
Rarity: Rare

If you play with the rarely-used WATER monster, then "Star Boy's" effect won't affect your opponent's cards and will only power your monsters up. Your main force will be "7 Colored Fish" with 1800 ATK.

MRD-110 Milus Radiant

Card Type: Effect Monster
Monster Type: Beast
Attribute: Earth
Level: 1
ATK: 300
DEF: 250
Rarity: Rare

When you use this card, all EARTH monsters gain 500 ATK while all WIND monsters lose 400 ATK. This effect affects "Milus Radiant" itself.

MRD-111 Flame Cerebrus

Card Type: Normal Monster
Monster Type: Pyro
Attribute: Fire
Level: 6
ATK: 2100
DEF: 1800
Rarity: Common

Ranking quite high among Level 6 monsters, it destroys its enemies with its three pairs of jaws and burning flame. No Level 4 monster can stand up against it.

MRD-112 Niwatori

Card Type: Normal Monster
Monster Type: Winged Beast
Attribute: Earth
Level: 3
ATK: 900
DEF: 800
Rarity: Common

This bird swallows enemies whole and coverts them into energy. It's stomach is so big it can swallow anything!

MRD-113 Dark Elf

Card Type: Effect Monster
Monster Type: Spellcaster
Attribute: Dark
Level: 4
ATK: 2000
DEF: 800
Rarity: Rare

Finally, here's a Level 4 monster that has 2000 ATK. However, it functions as a wall in Attack Position. Paying 1000 Life Points to attack is usually only useful when your opponent has no monsters on the field.

MRD-114 Mushroom Man #2

Card Type: Effect Monster
Monster Type: Warrior
Attribute: Earth
Level: 3
ATK: 1250
DEF: 800
Rarity: Common

Having "Mushroom Man #2" on the field and tossing it back between you and your opponent can be fun. This card may be just for fun, but it can be cool to find a good use for this card.

MRD-115 Lava Battleguard

Card Type: Effect Monster
Monster Type: Warrior
Attribute: Earth
Level: 5
ATK: 1550
DEF: 1800
Rarity: Common

"Lava Battleguard" exerts its true powers when it's on the field with "Swamp Battleguard." "Lava Battleguard's" DEF is higher than its ATK, so it is better suited for defense. However, if "Swamp Battleguard" is also on the field, then its ATK increases by 500, making "Lava Battleguard" suited to attack.

MRD-116 Witch of the Black Forest

Card Type: Effect Monster
Monster Type: Spellcaster
Attribute: Dark
Level: 4
ATK: 1100
DEF: 1200
Rarity: Rare

You can draw most Effect Monster Cards from your Deck while thinning out your Deck at the same time. Also, less than 1500 DEF means that you can add "Summoned Skull" from your Deck!

MRD-117 Little Chimera

Card Type: Effect Monster
Monster Type: Beast
Attribute: Fire
Level: 2
ATK: 600
DEF: 550
Rarity: Rare

Use "Little Chimera" in your Deck if you can easily summon FIRE monsters or if your opponent is using WATER monsters.

MRD-118 Bladefly

Card Type: Effect Monster
Monster Type: Insect
Attribute: Wind
Level: 2
ATK: 600
DEF: 700
Rarity: Rare

Use "Bladefly" when your Deck is centered on WIND monsters. "Bladefly's" effect also affects itself, so this card's ATK is already 500 points higher.

MRD-119 Lady of Faith

Card Type: Normal Monster
Monster Type: Spellcaster
Attribute: Light
Level: 3
ATK: 100
DEF: 800
Rarity: Common

This virtuous monk endured rigorous training, dislikes feuds, and calms our restless souls with her mystical incantations.

MRD-120 Twin-Headed Thunder Dragon

Card Type: Fusion Monster
Monster Type: Thunder
Attribute: Light
Level: 7
ATK: 2800
DEF: 2100
Rarity: Super Rare

Not only is it very easy to create this card by fusing two "Thunder Dragons," but it is quite a force in battle.

MRD-121 Witch's Apprentice

Card Type: Effect Monster
Monster Type: Spellcaster
Attribute: Dark
Level: 2
ATK: 550
DEF: 500
Rarity: Rare

Notice that this card can decrease the ATK of all LIGHT monsters. It's now possible to destroy your opponent's "Blue-Eyes White Dragon" with your "Summoned Skull!"

MRD-122 Blue-Winged Crown

Card Type: Normal Monster
Monster Type: Winged Beast
Attribute: Wind
Level: 4
ATK: 1600
DEF: 1200
Rarity: Common

"Blue-Winged Crown's" body burns in bluish white flames while its head is crowned with red hot fire. Spend any time admiring its beauty and it'll instantly transform you into ash!

MRD-123 Skull Knight

Card Type: Fusion Monster
Monster Type: Spellcaster
Attribute: Dark
Level: 7
ATK: 2650
DEF: 2250
Rarity: Common

Create "Skull Knight" by fusing "Tainted Wisdom" with "Ancient Brain." Clad in bone armor, this guardian of the underworld's weapon attacks are as impressive as its magical powers.

MRD-124 Gazelle the King of Mythical Beasts

Card Type: Normal Monster
Monster Type: Beast
Attribute: Earth
Level: 4
ATK: 1500
DEF: 1200
Rarity: Common

On its own, this monster has no extra abilities.

MRD-125 Garnecia Elefantis

Card Type: Normal Monster
Monster Type: Beast-Warrior
Attribute: Earth
Level: 7
ATK: 2400
DEF: 2000
Rarity: Super Rare

This divine servant from the Southern land, "Garnecia Elefantis" is usually calm, but when it gets rowdy, it is impossible to control.

MRD-126 Barrel Dragon

Card Type: Effect Monster
Monster Type: Machine
Attribute: Dark
Level: 7
ATK: 2600
DEF: 2200
Rarity: Ultra Rare

Bandit Keith punished Joey with this card. It's not risky to play heads or tails because there is no negative effect if you lose. On top of that, "Barrel Dragon" can attack. When "Barrel Dragon" is on the field, use its effect and give your opponent a lot of pressure!

MRD-127 Solemn Judgment

Card Type: Trap
Monster Type: —
Attribute: Trap
Level: —
ATK: —
DEF: —
Rarity: Ultra Rare

You'll get yourself into a bind if you don't use "Solemn Judgment" wisely. This card is more beneficial when your Life Points are low because you'll have less Life Points to lose. Definitely use "Solemn Judgment" when you know negating your opponent's card will guarantee victory.

MRD-128 Magic Jammer

Card Type: Trap
Monster Type: —
Attribute: Trap
Level: —
ATK: —
DEF: —
Rarity: Ultra Rare

Once you Set "Magic Jammer," make sure to have one card that you are willing to discard in your hand. Try not to use "Magic Jammer" until your opponent activates a Spell Card that can seriously cripple you.

MRD-129 Seven Tools of the Bandit

Card Type: Trap
Monster Type: —
Attribute: Trap
Level: —
ATK: —
DEF: —
Rarity: Ultra Rare

Trap Cards can be important cards in your opponent's combo or can seriously damage your strategy. Therefore, paying 1000 Life Points isn't a big deal in comparison!

MRD-130 Horn of Heaven

Card Type: Trap
Monster Type: —
Attribute: Trap
Level: —
ATK: —
DEF: —
Rarity: Ultra Rare

You can negate the summon and destroy your opponent's monster no matter how powerful it is. Also notice that you can destroy an Effect Monster without triggering its effect. However, you cannot use "Horn of Heaven" against Fusion and Ritual Monsters.

MRD-131 Shield & Sword

Card Type: Spell
Monster Type: —
Attribute: Spell
Level: —
ATK: —
DEF: —
Rarity: Rare

Line up Level 4 monsters with 2000 DEF and use "Shield & Sword" to flip ATK and DEF. This simple combo inflicts significant damage to your opponent!

MRD-132 Sword of Deep-Seated

Card Type: Spell
Monster Type: —
Attribute: Spell
Level: —
ATK: —
DEF: —
Rarity: Common

It's great that "Sword of Deep-Seated" raises both ATK and DEF, but if you use it too much, you will only be able to draw this card. Think carefully when using this card.

MRD-133 Block Attack

Card Type: Spell
Monster Type: —
Attribute: Spell
Level: —
ATK: —
DEF: —
Rarity: Common

Use it wisely and you can even destroy the most powerful monsters with your weakest monsters. For example, "Summoned Skull" is usually a difficult monster to destroy. However, with "Block Attack," a weak monster can easily destroy it when "Summoned Skull" is in Defense Position.

MRD-134 The Unhappy Maiden

Card Type: Effect Monster
Monster Type: Spellcaster
Attribute: Light
Level: 1
ATK: 0
DEF: 100
Rarity: Common

With ATK of 0, this card is only useful in face-down Defense Position. However, its effect of ending the Battle Phase is excellent. When your opponent attacks, Setting this monster using "Ultimate Offering" is best.

MRD-135 Robbin' Goblin

Card Type: Trap
Monster Type: —
Attribute: Trap
Level: —
ATK: —
DEF: —
Rarity: Rare

This card is made for combos. You can use this card with monsters that can directly attack your opponent, or you can pair it with "White Magical Hat" to make your opponent discard two cards. This card is a real nuisance.

MRD-136 Germ Infection

Card Type: Spell
Monster Type: —
Attribute: Spell
Level: —
ATK: —
DEF: —
Rarity: Common

First use "Swords of Revealing Light" to prevent your opponent from attacking, then attach "Germ Infection" to one of your opponent's monsters. Three turns later, your opponent's monster's ATK will have decreased by 900!

MRD-137 Paralyzing Potion

Card Type: Spell
Monster Type: —
Attribute: Spell
Level: —
ATK: —
DEF: —
Rarity: Common

After it is equipped on a monster, it is difficult to remove. If your opponent summons a powerful monster, use "Paralyzing Potion." You now have plenty of time to think of how to destroy your opponent's monster.

MRD-138 Mirror Force

Card Type: Trap
Monster Type: —
Attribute: Trap
Level: —
ATK: —
DEF: —
Rarity: Ultra Rare

You are limited to only one "Mirror Force" per Deck, but seeing its power, it's easy to understand. The stronger the monsters your opponent has on his or her field, the more powerful "Mirror Force's" effect is.

MRD-139 Ring of Magnetism

Card Type: Spell
Monster Type: —
Attribute: Spell
Level: —
ATK: —
DEF: —
Rarity: Common

It's best to equip "Ring of Magnetism" on an Effect Monster Card. For example, if you equip it on "Wall of Illusion," your opponent's monsters will return to his or her hand.

MRD-140 Share the Pain

Card Type: Spell
Monster Type: —
Attribute: Spell
Level: —
ATK: —
DEF: —
Rarity: Common

When your opponent summons a powerful monster, you can use "Share the Pain" to offer it as a Tribute. Also, if you offer "Sangan" or "Witch of the Black Forest" as a Tribute, you can move one card from your deck to your hand.

MRD-141 Stim-Pack

Card Type: Spell
Monster Type: —
Attribute: Spell
Level: —
ATK: —
DEF: —
Rarity: Common

This is a prototype chemical, so the ATK decreases over time. However, for three turns, there is an increase in ATK, so use those three turns wisely!

MRD-142 Heavy Storm

Card Type: Spell
Monster Type: —
Attribute: Spell
Level: —
ATK: —
DEF: —
Rarity: Super Rare

You'll also lose your Spell and Trap Cards, but don't stress out. When your opponent lines up Trap Cards, then use "Heavy Storm" and destroy them all!

MRD-143 Thousand Dragon

Card Type: Fusion Monster
Monster Type: Dragon
Attribute: Wind
Level: 7
ATK: 2400
DEF: 2000
Rarity: Secret Rare

"Thousand Dragon" gather much strength and wisdom through the passage of time. You cannot summon this monster until a dragon matures.

MRD-000 Gate Guardian

Card Type: Effect Monster
Monster Type: Warrior
Attribute: Dark
Level: 11
ATK: 3750
DEF: 3400
Rarity: Secret Rare

This monster used by the Paradox Brothers is incredibly powerful but extremely difficult to summon.

Spell Ruler

SPL-001 Penguin Knight

Card Type: Effect Monster
Monster Type: Aqua
Attribute: Water
Level: 3
ATK: 900
DEF: 800
Rarity: Common

When Ritual Monsters or Fusion-Material Monsters are sent to the Graveyard, "Penguin Knight" gives you a second chance. This card is a must-have for Exodia Decks! However, it is a little bit difficult to activate this card's effect because there are rare cases when this card is sent directly from your Deck to the Graveyard.

SPL-002 Axe of Despair

Card Type: Spell
Monster Type: –
Attribute: Spell
Level: –
ATK: –
DEF: –
Rarity: Ultra Rare

It's great that you can equip "Axe of Despair" on any monster. You can also recycle this card. It's fun to equip this card on a monster that can attack your opponent's Life Points directly.

SPL-003 Black Pendant

Card Type: Spell
Monster Type: –
Attribute: Spell
Level: –
ATK: –
DEF: –
Rarity: Super Rare

This is not the strongest Equip Spell Card, but it's useful for defeating monsters that are slightly stronger than yours. Even if your monster is destroyed, there's still a bonus!

SPL-004 Horn of Light

Card Type: Spell
Monster Type: –
Attribute: Spell
Level: –
ATK: –
DEF: –
Rarity: Common

Even if you want to equip "Horn of Light" on a certain monster, it has to be face-up. This card may be hard to use.

SPL-005 Malevolent Nuzzler

Card Type: Spell
Monster Type: –
Attribute: Spell
Level: –
ATK: –
DEF: –
Rarity: Common

This card is better than "Black Pendant" if you want to use this card over and over. If your monster's ATK increases by 700, it can destroy monsters quite a bit stronger than yours.

SPL-006 Spellbinding Circle

Card Type: Trap
Monster Type: –
Attribute: Trap
Level: –
ATK: –
DEF: –
Rarity: Ultra Rare

Not only can you stop your opponent's monster from attacking, but you can also keep Monsters with Flip Effect from a Flip Summon by keeping them in face-down Defense Position!

SPL-007 Metal Fish

Card Type: Normal Monster
Monster Type: Machine
Attribute: Water
Level: 5
ATK: 1600
DEF: 1900
Rarity: Common

"Metal Fish" is unique because it is a Machine-Type monster with WATER. Its ATK and DEF are well-balanced, and its 1900 DEF is very desirable.

SPL-008 Electric Snake

Card Type: Effect Monster
Monster Type: Thunder
Attribute: Light
Level: 3
ATK: 800
DEF: 900
Rarity: Common

"Electric Snake" is a good countermeasure against "White Magical Hat," "Robbin' Goblin," and other cards that make you discard cards from your hand.

SPL-009 Queen Bird

Card Type: Normal Monster
Monster Type: Winged Beast
Attribute: Wind
Level: 5
ATK: 1200
DEF: 2000
Rarity: Common

"Queen Bird" has surprisingly high DEF for a Winged Beast. It can block most monsters' attacks although it needs a Tribute monster to Set.

SPL-010 Ameba

Card Type: Effect Monster
Monster Type: Aqua
Attribute: Water
Level: 1
ATK: 300
DEF: 350
Rarity: Rare

Use this card in the same way as "Griggle." But please remember its effect is NOT activated if it is face-down.

Spell Ruler

SPL-011 Peacock

Card Type: Normal Monster
Monster Type: Winged Beast
Attribute: Wind
Level: 5
ATK: 1700
DEF: 1500
Rarity: Common

This Winged Beast's main characteristic is its brilliantly beautiful rainbow feathers. The fact that you have to offer another monster as a Tribute to summon "Peacock" is a weakness, but it has decent ATK.

SPL-012 Maha Vailo

Card Type: Effect Monster
Monster Type: Spellcaster
Attribute: Light
Level: 4
ATK: 1550
DEF: 1400
Rarity: Super Rare

"Maha Vailo" looks cool, and its effect is just as cool! Construct a Deck that will increase its ATK and DEF quickly.

SPL-013 Guardian of the Throne Room

Card Type: Normal Monster
Monster Type: Machine
Attribute: Light
Level: 4
ATK: 1650
DEF: 1600
Rarity: Common

You can summon "Guardian of the Throne Room" without offering another monster as a Tribute. Its LIGHT can come in handy.

SPL-014 Fire Kraken

Card Type: Normal Monster
Monster Type: Aqua
Attribute: Fire
Level: 4
ATK: 1600
DEF: 1500
Rarity: Common

Though "Fire Kraken" is an Aqua-Type monster, it strangely has FIRE. Its ATK and DEF are both high, so you can count on this card to be useful.

SPL-015 Minar

Card Type: Effect Monster
Monster Type: Insect
Attribute: Earth
Level: 3
ATK: 850
DEF: 750
Rarity: Common

This card is useful against "White Magical Hat" and other cards that make you discard cards from your hand. You can give counter damage in return!

SPL-016 Griggle

Card Type: Effect Monster
Monster Type: Plant
Attribute: Earth
Level: 1
ATK: 350
DEF: 300
Rarity: Common

This card is not just good for "Change of Heart," but it is also effective against "Invader of the Throne." 3000 Life Points will be yours!

SPL-017 Tyhone #2

Card Type: Normal Monster
Monster Type: Dragon
Attribute: Fire
Level: 6
ATK: 1700
DEF: 1900
Rarity: Common

This deep crimson Dragon breathes a burning flame. This is one of the more useful monsters among FIRE monsters.

SPL-018 Ancient One of the Deep Forest

Card Type: Normal Monster
Monster Type: Beast
Attribute: Earth
Level: 6
ATK: 1800
DEF: 1900
Rarity: Common

You must offer one monster as a Tribute to summon "Ancient One of the Deep Forest," but its 1900 DEF can stop most monsters. Its ATK of 1800 is also nothing to sneeze at.

SPL-019 Dark Witch

Card Type: Normal Monster
Monster Type: Fairy
Attribute: Light
Level: 5
ATK: 1800
DEF: 1700
Rarity: Common

This is one of the high-class Fairy-Type monsters with high ATK and DEF.

SPL-020 Weather Report

Card Type: Effect Monster
Monster Type: Aqua
Attribute: Water
Level: 4
ATK: 950
DEF: 1500
Rarity: Common

This is no ordinary snowman! This is a special weapon against "Swords of Revealing Light." Use it and unleash your counterattack!

SPL-021 Mechanical Snail

Card Type: Normal Monster
Monster Type: Machine
Attribute: Dark
Level: 3
ATK: 800
DEF: 1000
Rarity: Common

This looks like a snail with arms and legs, but it is a Machine. Whoever created this robot must be mad.

SPL-022 Giant Turtle Who Feeds on Flames

Card Type: Normal Monster
Monster Type: Aqua
Attribute: Water
Level: 5
ATK: 1400
DEF: 1800
Rarity: Common

This turtle eats flames, but it has WATER. You need to offer another monster as a Tribute to summon "Giant Turtle Who Feeds on Flames," but it has decent DEF to defend your Life Points.

SPL-023 Liquid Beast

Card Type: Normal Monster
Monster Type: Aqua
Attribute: Water
Level: 3
ATK: 950
DEF: 800
Rarity: Common

This gross monster has five eyes and is covered entirely in mud. However, "Liquid Beast" is not as dangerous as it looks.

SPL-024 Hiro's Shadow Scout

Card Type: Effect Monster
Monster Type: Fiend
Attribute: Dark
Level: 2
ATK: 650
DEF: 500
Rarity: Rare

Spell Cards are important in every Deck, especially in setting up combos. By getting rid of your opponent's Spell Cards, you can disrupt his or her strategy.

SPL-025 High Tide Gyojin

Card Type: Normal Monster
Monster Type: Aqua
Attribute: Water
Level: 4
ATK: 1650
DEF: 1300
Rarity: Common

Among Aqua-Type monsters, "High Tide Gyojin" has decently high ATK and DEF. Having 1650 ATK instead of 1600 is actually a huge difference in battle.

SPL-026 Invader of the Throne

Card Type: Effect Monster
Monster Type: Warrior
Attribute: Earth
Level: 4
ATK: 1350
DEF: 1700
Rarity: Super Rare

Since you cannot use "Invader of the Throne's" effect during the Battle Phase, it's important to know when you should summon this monster on to the field. If you use "Swords of Revealing Light" first, then you can safely Flip Summon this card.

SPL-027 Whiptail Crow

Card Type: Normal Monster
Monster Type: Fiend
Attribute: Dark
Level: 4
ATK: 1650
DEF: 1600
Rarity: Common

"Whiptail Crow" has the same ATK and DEF as "Guardian of the Throne Room," but it has DARK. Therefore, use this card if your Deck is geared toward DARK monsters.

SPL-028 Slot Machine

Card Type: Normal Monster
Monster Type: Machine
Attribute: Dark
Level: 7
ATK: 2000
DEF: 2300
Rarity: Common

This card cherished by Bandit Keith has high ATK and DEF.

SPL-029 Relinquished

Card Type: Ritual/Effect Monster
Monster Type: Spellcaster
Attribute: Dark
Level: 1
ATK: 0
DEF: 0
Rarity: Ultra Rare

"Relinquished" is basically a permanent "Change of Heart." Notice that the monsters that "Relinquished" absorbs become Equip Spell Cards. Try to think how to use this fact to your advantage.

SPL-030 Red Archery Girl

Card Type: Normal Monster
Monster Type: Aqua
Attribute: Water
Level: 4
ATK: 1400
DEF: 1500
Rarity: Common

Pegasus punished Yugi with "Red Archery Girl." Its abilities are average, but if you take her lightly, you'd be in bigger trouble than Yugi.

SPL-031 Gravekeeper's Servant

Card Type: Spell
Monster Type: —
Attribute: Spell
Level: —
ATK: —
DEF: —
Rarity: Common

This is a Continuous Spell Card, so it can prove to be a serious nuisance for your opponent. If you are playing an opponent who relies on combos, he or she will be worried about losing the necessary cards to the Graveyard, so your opponent may stop attacking.

SPL-032 Curse of Fiend

Card Type: Spell
Monster Type: —
Attribute: Spell
Level: —
ATK: —
DEF: —
Rarity: Common

This card is best used to switch your opponent's monsters from Attack Position to Defense Position. Even if your opponent's monster has high ATK, it usually has low DEF, which makes it easy to destroy. You can also use this card to switch face-down Defense Position monsters to face-up Attack Position.

SPL-033 Upstart Goblin

Card Type: Spell
Monster Type: —
Attribute: Spell
Level: —
ATK: —
DEF: —
Rarity: Common

You must decide if drawing one card is worth giving your opponent 1000 Life Points. Test this card out first-hand to learn when to use this card.

SPL-034 Toll

Card Type: Spell
Monster Type: —
Attribute: Spell
Level: —
ATK: —
DEF: —
Rarity: Common

Since you will also have to pay Life Points in order to attack, it's best to use this card when you have more Life Points than your opponent. If you use this card incorrectly, it can come back and destroy you.

Spell Ruler

SPL-035 Final Destiny

- **Card Type:** Spell
- **Monster Type:** —
- **Attribute:** Spell
- **Level:** —
- **ATK:** —
- **DEF:** —
- **Rarity:** Common

When using this Spell Card, you have to be careful that your opponent doesn't counter it. If you lose all the cards in your hand and "Final Destiny" is countered, you're in terrible shape. This card is incredibly risky.

SPL-036 Snatch Steal

- **Card Type:** Spell
- **Monster Type:** —
- **Attribute:** Spell
- **Level:** —
- **ATK:** —
- **DEF:** —
- **Rarity:** Ultra Rare

Letting your opponent gain 1000 Life Points every turn may be harsh, but if you immediately offer the monster you took as a Tribute, then you're at an advantage because your opponent will not gain any Life Points. Think of this card as getting another "Change of Heart!"

SPL-037 Chorus of Sanctuary

- **Card Type:** Spell
- **Monster Type:** —
- **Attribute:** Spell
- **Level:** —
- **ATK:** —
- **DEF:** —
- **Rarity:** Common

"Chorus of Sanctuary" makes it difficult for your opponent to damage your Life Points when the defending monsters are stronger. Your opponent will also be more wary to attack your face-down Defense Position monsters.

SPL-038 Confiscation

- **Card Type:** Spell
- **Monster Type:** —
- **Attribute:** Spell
- **Level:** —
- **ATK:** —
- **DEF:** —
- **Rarity:** Super Rare

Paying 1000 Life Points is a pain, but it's great to be able to see your opponent's hand and select one card to discard. If your opponent draws "Witch of the Black Forest" or "Sangan," you can get rid of those annoying cards with "Confiscation."

SPL-039 Delinquent Duo

- **Card Type:** Spell
- **Monster Type:** —
- **Attribute:** Spell
- **Level:** —
- **ATK:** —
- **DEF:** —
- **Rarity:** Ultra Rare

You must pay 1000 Life Points, like "Confiscation," but your opponent has to discard two cards. Though you can't choose which card your opponent has to discard, losing two cards will hurt your opponent.

SPL-040 Darkness Approaches

- **Card Type:** Spell
- **Monster Type:** —
- **Attribute:** Spell
- **Level:** —
- **ATK:** —
- **DEF:** —
- **Rarity:** Common

This Spell Card is made for Effect Monsters. Include "Darkness Approaches" if your Deck contains many Flip Effect Monsters. You'll be able to use "Magician of Faith's" effect twice!

SPL-041 Fairy's Hand Mirror

- **Card Type:** Trap
- **Monster Type:** —
- **Attribute:** Trap
- **Level:** —
- **ATK:** —
- **DEF:** —
- **Rarity:** Common

The greatest joy turns into the greatest pain. Your opponent will now be worried about using other Spell Cards. The only sure bet is to use Spell Cards when there is only one monster on the field.

SPL-042 Tailor of the Fickle

- **Card Type:** Spell
- **Monster Type:** —
- **Attribute:** Spell
- **Level:** —
- **ATK:** —
- **DEF:** —
- **Rarity:** Common

This card is used to counter Equip Spell Cards. Not only does your opponent lose a Spell Card, but you also gain it. Your opponent will be worried about using other Equip Spell Cards.

SPL-043 Rush Recklessly

- **Card Type:** Spell
- **Monster Type:** —
- **Attribute:** Spell
- **Level:** —
- **ATK:** —
- **DEF:** —
- **Rarity:** Rare

Your opponent may think his or her monster's destroying one of your weak monsters, but with this Spell Card, your opponent's in for a surprise! Your opponent will worry about attacking if his or her monster's ATK is only 700 more than yours.

SPL-044 The Reliable Guardian

- **Card Type:** Spell
- **Monster Type:** —
- **Attribute:** Spell
- **Level:** —
- **ATK:** —
- **DEF:** —
- **Rarity:** Common

Similar to "Rush Recklessly," "The Reliable Guardian" is a Quick-Play Spell Card and can be used during your opponent's Battle Phase. You can use this to protect Flip Effect Monsters that you do not want destroyed.

SPL-045 The Forceful Sentry

- **Card Type:** Spell
- **Monster Type:** —
- **Attribute:** Spell
- **Level:** —
- **ATK:** —
- **DEF:** —
- **Rarity:** Ultra Rare

Not only can you see your opponent's hand, you can also get rid of your opponent's most problematic card out of his or her hand without any cost to you. This card has the power to change the tide of battle.

SPL-046 Chain Energy

- **Card Type:** Spell
- **Monster Type:** —
- **Attribute:** Spell
- **Level:** —
- **ATK:** —
- **DEF:** —
- **Rarity:** Common

This card is punishing because doing anything costs Life Points. If you use "Chain Energy" when your opponent is low on Life Points, then you can almost prevent him or her from doing anything.

SPL-047 Mystical Space Typhoon

- **Card Type:** Spell
- **Monster Type:** —
- **Attribute:** Spell
- **Level:** —
- **ATK:** —
- **DEF:** —
- **Rarity:** Ultra Rare

Unlike "Remove Trap," you can now destroy face-down Trap Cards. To counter against "Mystical Space Typhoon," your opponent may now have to place less-useful Spell Cards on the field.

SPL-048 Giant Trunade

- **Card Type:** Spell
- **Monster Type:** —
- **Attribute:** Spell
- **Level:** —
- **ATK:** —
- **DEF:** —
- **Rarity:** Super Rare

This card helps against your opponent's Spell and Trap Cards that are hindering your strategy. Also, it can return Spell and Trap Cards regardless of their position.

SPL-049 Painful Choice

- **Card Type:** Spell
- **Monster Type:** —
- **Attribute:** Spell
- **Level:** —
- **ATK:** —
- **DEF:** —
- **Rarity:** Super Rare

It may be good to choose five cards that you want, but it may also be fun to choose five cards that you do not want at all. This is a unique way to think out your Deck.

SPL-050 Snake Fang

- **Card Type:** Trap
- **Monster Type:** —
- **Attribute:** Trap
- **Level:** —
- **ATK:** —
- **DEF:** —
- **Rarity:** Common

If your monster attacks your opponent's face-down monster in Defense Position, even if your opponent's monster has higher DEF than your monster's ATK, use "Snake Fang" and destroy your opponent's monster.

SPL-051 Black Illusion Ritual

- **Card Type:** Spell
- **Monster Type:** —
- **Attribute:** Spell
- **Level:** —
- **ATK:** —
- **DEF:** —
- **Rarity:** Super Rare

You need this card to Ritual Summon the Ritual Monster "Relinquished." This card is useless by itself, so make sure to get both cards!

SPL-052 Octoberser

- **Card Type:** Normal Monster
- **Monster Type:** Aqua
- **Attribute:** Water
- **Level:** 5
- **ATK:** 1600
- **DEF:** 1400
- **Rarity:** Common

"Octoberser" has the head of a fish and the legs of an octopus.

SPL-053 Psychic Kappa

- **Card Type:** Normal Monster
- **Monster Type:** Aqua
- **Attribute:** Water
- **Level:** 2
- **ATK:** 400
- **DEF:** 1000
- **Rarity:** Common

This creature protects itself against attacks with its various psychic powers.

SPL-054 Horn of the Unicorn

- **Card Type:** Spell
- **Monster Type:** —
- **Attribute:** Spell
- **Level:** —
- **ATK:** —
- **DEF:** —
- **Rarity:** Rare

Not only can you power up any of your monsters, but you can also return this card from your Graveyard to your Deck for additional uses!

SPL-055 Labyrinth Wall

- **Card Type:** Normal Monster
- **Monster Type:** Rock
- **Attribute:** Earth
- **Level:** 5
- **ATK:** 0
- **DEF:** 3000
- **Rarity:** Common

A labyrinth without an exit surrounds the area.

SPL-056 Wall Shadow

- **Card Type:** Effect Monster
- **Monster Type:** Warrior
- **Attribute:** Dark
- **Level:** 7
- **ATK:** 1600
- **DEF:** 3000
- **Rarity:** Common

You cannot Special Summon "Wall Shadow" unless "Labyrinth Wall" is equipped with "Magical Labyrinth" and offer it as a Tribute.

SPL-057 Twin Long Rods #2

- **Card Type:** Normal Monster
- **Monster Type:** Aqua
- **Attribute:** Water
- **Level:** 3
- **ATK:** 850
- **DEF:** 700
- **Rarity:** Common

This aquatic monster swings two tails like whips.

SPL-058 Stone Ogre Grotto

- **Card Type:** Normal Monster
- **Monster Type:** Rock
- **Attribute:** Earth
- **Level:** 5
- **ATK:** 1600
- **DEF:** 1500
- **Rarity:** Common

This giant stone ogre is created by stacks and stacks of boulders.

Spell Ruler

SPL-059 Magical Labyrinth

Card Type: Spell
Monster Type: —
Attribute: Spell
Level: —
ATK: —
DEF: —
Rarity: Common

You need both "Magical Labyrinth" and "Labyrinth Wall" in order to Special Summon "Wall Shadow."

SPL-060 Eternal Rest

Card Type: Spell
Monster Type: —
Attribute: Spell
Level: —
ATK: —
DEF: —
Rarity: Common

You can destroy all monsters with Equip Spell Cards.

SPL-061 Megamorph

Card Type: Spell
Monster Type: —
Attribute: Spell
Level: —
ATK: —
DEF: —
Rarity: Ultra Rare

This is a powerful Equip Spell Card. If you have less Life Points than your opponent, equip this card on one of your monsters. If you have more Life Points than your opponent, equip this card on one of your opponent's monsters.

SPL-062 Commencement Dance

Card Type: Spell
Monster Type: —
Attribute: Spell
Level: —
ATK: —
DEF: —
Rarity: Common

You need this card to Summon the Ritual Monster "Performance of Sword." This card is useless by itself, so make sure to get both cards!

SPL-063 Hamburger Recipe

Card Type: Spell
Monster Type: —
Attribute: Spell
Level: —
ATK: —
DEF: —
Rarity: Common

You need this card to summon the Ritual Monster "Hungry Burger." This card is useless by itself, so make sure to get both cards!

SPL-064 House of Adhesive Tape

Card Type: Trap
Monster Type: —
Attribute: Trap
Level: —
ATK: —
DEF: —
Rarity: Common

This Trap Card helps you destroy monsters with low DEF.

SPL-065 Eatgaboon

Card Type: Trap
Monster Type: —
Attribute: Trap
Level: —
ATK: —
DEF: —
Rarity: Common

Slightly different than "House of Adhesive Tape," this Trap Card lets you destroy monsters with low ATK.

SPL-066 Turtle Oath

Card Type: Spell
Monster Type: —
Attribute: Spell
Level: —
ATK: —
DEF: —
Rarity: Common

You need this card to summon the Ritual Monster "Crab Turtle." This card is useless by itself, so make sure to get both cards!

SPL-067 Performance of Sword

Card Type: Ritual Monster
Monster Type: Warrior
Attribute: Earth
Level: 6
ATK: 1950
DEF: 1850
Rarity: Common

In order to Ritual Summon "Performance of Sword," you must have "Commencement Dance" and offer monsters whose total Level Stars are equal to six or more as a Tribute.

SPL-068 Hungry Burger

Card Type: Ritual Monster
Monster Type: Warrior
Attribute: Dark
Level: 6
ATK: 2000
DEF: 1850
Rarity: Common

In order to Ritual Summon "Hungry Burger," you must have "Hamburger Recipe" and offer monsters whose total Level Stars are equal to six or more as a Tribute.

SPL-069 Crab Turtle

Card Type: Ritual Monster
Monster Type: Aqua
Attribute: Water
Level: 8
ATK: 2550
DEF: 2500
Rarity: Common

In order to Ritual Summon "Crab Turtle," you must have "Turtle Oath" and offer monsters whose total Level Stars are equal to 8 or more as a Tribute.

SPL-070 Ryu-Ran

Card Type: Normal Monster
Monster Type: Dragon
Attribute: Fire
Level: 7
ATK: 2200
DEF: 2600
Rarity: Common

This Dragon may wear an egg shell, but you'll be in big trouble if you treat it with kiddie gloves!

SPL-071 Manga Ryu-Ran

Card Type: Toon Monster
Monster Type: Dragon
Attribute: Fire
Level: 7
ATK: 2200
DEF: 2600
Rarity: Rare

This Toon lets you attack your opponent directly for 2200 damage to his or her Life Points! However, you must have "Toon World" on your side of the field to Special Summon it.

SPL-072 Toon Mermaid

Card Type: Toon Monster
Monster Type: Aqua
Attribute: Water
Level: 4
ATK: 1400
DEF: 1500
Rarity: Ultra Rare

Similar to the other Toons, you can attack your opponent directly. However, you must have "Toon World" on your side of the field to Special Summon it.

SPL-073 Toon Summoned Skull

Card Type: Toon Monster
Monster Type: Fiend
Attribute: Dark
Level: 6
ATK: 2500
DEF: 1200
Rarity: Ultra Rare

Similar to the other Toons, you can attack your opponent directly. However, you must have "Toon World" on your side of the field to Special Summon it.

SPL-074 Jigen Bakudan

Card Type: Effect Monster
Monster Type: Pyro
Attribute: Fire
Level: 2
ATK: 200
DEF: 1000
Rarity: Common

"Jigen Bakudan" allows you to deal direct damage to your opponent's Life Points. If your opponent's Life Points are low, this can be the finishing blow!

SPL-075 Hyozanryu

Card Type: Normal Monster
Monster Type: Dragon
Attribute: Light
Level: 7
ATK: 2100
DEF: 2800
Rarity: Rare

This powerful Dragon is entirely covered in diamonds.

SPL-076 Toon World

Card Type: Spell
Monster Type: —
Attribute: Spell
Level: —
ATK: —
DEF: —
Rarity: Super Rare

Though you must pay 1000 Life Points, you are now able to summon Toon Monsters that can deal Direct Damage to your opponent!

SPL-077 Cyber Jar

Card Type: Effect Monster
Monster Type: Rock
Attribute: Dark
Level: 3
ATK: 900
DEF: 900
Rarity: Rare

Not only does this card act like a "Dark Hole," but it also allows you to draw cards from your Deck and Special Summon monsters onto the field.

SPL-078 Banisher of the Light

Card Type: Effect Monster
Monster Type: Fairy
Attribute: Light
Level: 3
ATK: 100
DEF: 2000
Rarity: Super Rare

This monster has high DEF, but it's main effect is to remove cards from the Duel to prevent your opponent from resurrecting cards from the Graveyard.

SPL-079 Giant Rat

Card Type: Effect Monster
Monster Type: Beast
Attribute: Earth
Level: 4
ATK: 1400
DEF: 1450
Rarity: Rare

When "Giant Rat" is destroyed, you can Special Summon another monster to the field!

SPL-080 Senju of the Thousand Hands

Card Type: Effect Monster
Monster Type: Fairy
Attribute: Light
Level: 4
ATK: 1400
DEF: 1000
Rarity: Rare

This card allows you to search your Deck for the Ritual Monster Card that you need.

Spell Ruler

SPL-081 UFO Turtle

Card Type: Effect Monster
Monster Type: Machine
Attribute: Fire
Level: 4
ATK: 1400
DEF: 1200
Rarity: Rare

When "UFO Turtle" is destroyed, you can Special Summon another monster to the field!

SPL-082 Flash Assailant

Card Type: Effect Monster
Monster Type: Fiend
Attribute: Dark
Level: 4
ATK: 2000
DEF: 2000
Rarity: Common

Though "Flash Assailant" has high ATK and DEF, it is only useful if you have few to no cards in your hand.

SPL-083 Karate Man

Card Type: Effect Monster
Monster Type: Warrior
Attribute: Earth
Level: 3
ATK: 1000
DEF: 1000
Rarity: Rare

You can double the ATK of "Karate Man" for one turn, but it will be destroyed at the end of the turn. Know when to use this effect. Remember this is NOT a Multi-Trigger Effect.

SPL-084 Dark Zebra

Card Type: Effect Monster
Monster Type: Beast
Attribute: Earth
Level: 4
ATK: 1800
DEF: 400
Rarity: Common

"Dark Zebra" has high ATK but very low DEF. Make sure you have additional monsters on the field when you summon "Dark Zebra."

SPL-085 Giant Germ

Card Type: Effect Monster
Monster Type: Fiend
Attribute: Dark
Level: 2
ATK: 1000
DEF: 100
Rarity: Rare

Not only can you damage your opponent's Life Points directly, you can Special Summon another "Giant Germ" and repeat the process again!

SPL-086 Nimble Momonga

Card Type: Effect Monster
Monster Type: Beast
Attribute: Earth
Level: 2
ATK: 1000
DEF: 100
Rarity: Rare

Not only do you regain Life Points, you can Special Summon another "Nimble Momonga" and repeat the process again!

SPL-087 Spear Cretin

Card Type: Effect Monster
Monster Type: Fiend
Attribute: Dark
Level: 2
ATK: 500
DEF: 500
Rarity: Common

"Spear Cretin" can be very effective if your Graveyard contains a powerful monster while your opponent has weak or no monsters in his or her Graveyard.

SPL-088 Shining Angel

Card Type: Effect Monster
Monster Type: Fairy
Attribute: Light
Level: 4
ATK: 1400
DEF: 800
Rarity: Rare

When "Shining Angel" is destroyed, you can Special Summon another monster to the field!

SPL-089 Boar Soldier

Card Type: Effect Monster
Monster Type: Beast-Warrior
Attribute: Earth
Level: 4
ATK: 2000
DEF: 500
Rarity: Common

"Boar Soldier" only has high ATK when your opponent has no monsters on his or her field, so be sure to Flip Summon this monster wisely.

SPL-090 Mother Grizzly

Card Type: Effect Monster
Monster Type: Beast-Warrior
Attribute: Water
Level: 4
ATK: 1400
DEF: 1000
Rarity: Rare

When "Mother Grizzly" is destroyed, you can Special Summon another monster to the field!

SPL-091 Flying Kamakiri #1

Card Type: Effect Monster
Monster Type: Insect
Attribute: Wind
Level: 4
ATK: 1400
DEF: 900
Rarity: Rare

When "Flying Kamakiri #1" is destroyed, you can Special Summon another monster to the field!

SPL-092 Ceremonial Bell

Card Type: Effect Monster
Monster Type: Spellcaster
Attribute: Light
Level: 3
ATK: 0
DEF: 1850
Rarity: Common

You can now see your opponent's hand and learn his or her strategy, but so can your opponent!

SPL-093 Sonic Bird

Card Type: Effect Monster
Monster Type: Winged Beast
Attribute: Wind
Level: 4
ATK: 1400
DEF: 1000
Rarity: Common

This card allows you to search your Deck for the Ritual Spell Card that you need.

SPL-094 Mystic Tomato

Card Type: Effect Monster
Monster Type: Plant
Attribute: Dark
Level: 4
ATK: 1400
DEF: 1100
Rarity: Rare

When "Mystic Tomato" is destroyed, you can Special Summon another monster to the field!

SPL-095 Kotodama

Card Type: Effect Monster
Monster Type: Fairy
Attribute: Earth
Level: 3
ATK: 0
DEF: 1600
Rarity: Common

If your opponent is playing many of the same card, "Kotodama" prevents your opponent from summoning them all to the field.

SPL-096 Gaia Power

Card Type: Spell
Monster Type: —
Attribute: Spell
Level: —
ATK: —
DEF: —
Rarity: Rare

"Gaia Power" increases the ATK of all EARTH monsters, but it also decreases the DEF.

SPL-097 Umiiruka

Card Type: Spell
Monster Type: —
Attribute: Spell
Level: —
ATK: —
DEF: —
Rarity: Common

"Umiiruka" increases the ATK of all WATER monsters, but it also decreases the DEF.

SPL-098 Molten Destruction

Card Type: Spell
Monster Type: —
Attribute: Spell
Level: —
ATK: —
DEF: —
Rarity: Common

"Molten Destruction" increases the ATK of all FIRE monsters, but it also decreases the DEF.

SPL-099 Rising Air Current

Card Type: Spell
Monster Type: —
Attribute: Spell
Level: —
ATK: —
DEF: —
Rarity: Common

"Rising Air Current" increases the ATK of all WIND monsters, but it also decreases the DEF.

SPL-100 Luminous Spark

Card Type: Spell
Monster Type: —
Attribute: Spell
Level: —
ATK: —
DEF: —
Rarity: Common

"Luminous Spark" increases the ATK of all LIGHT monsters, but it also decreases the DEF.

SPL-101 Mystic Plasma Zone

Card Type: Spell
Monster Type: —
Attribute: Spell
Level: —
ATK: —
DEF: —
Rarity: Common

"Mystic Plasma Zone" increases the ATK of all DARK monsters, but it also decreases the DEF.

SPL-102 Messenger of Peace

Card Type: Spell
Monster Type: —
Attribute: Spell
Level: —
ATK: —
DEF: —
Rarity: Super Rare

This card prevents your opponent's strong monsters from attacking. This helps in stalling your opponent until you can summon a strong monster. "Messenger of Peace" is especially useful in Exodia Decks!

SPL-103 Serpent Night Dragon

Card Type: Normal Monster
Monster Type: Dragon
Attribute: Dark
Level: 7
ATK: 2350
DEF: 2400
Rarity: Secret Rare

This Dragon prides itself on its extremely high DEF.

SPL-000 Blue-Eyes Toon Dragon

Card Type: Toon Monster
Monster Type: Dragon
Attribute: Light
Level: 8
ATK: 3000
DEF: 2500
Rarity: Secret Rare

This strongest Toon Monster will deal heavy damage to your opponent's Life Points!

Pharaoh's Servant

PSV-001 Steel Ogre Grotto #2

Card Type: Normal Monster
Monster Type: Machine
Attribute: Earth
Level: 6
ATK: 1900
DEF: 2200
Rarity: Common

This Machine ogre is created out of hard steel and has unbelievable strength.

PSV-002 Three-Headed Geedo

Card Type: Normal Monster
Monster Type: Fiend
Attribute: Dark
Level: 4
ATK: 1200
DEF: 1400
Rarity: Common

This Fiend with three heads has a destructive personality.

PSV-003 Parasite Paracide

Card Type: Effect Monster
Monster Type: Insect
Attribute: Earth
Level: 2
ATK: 500
DEF: 300
Rarity: Super Rare

It's fun to watch your opponent scared to draw his or her next card from the Deck. Also, if "Parasite Paracide" is combined with "Insect Barrier," your opponent's monsters can't damage your Life Points!

PSV-004 7 Completed

Card Type: Spell
Monster Type: —
Attribute: Spell
Level: —
ATK: —
DEF: —
Rarity: Common

If you play with many Machine-Type monsters, "7 Completed" will help increase the ATK of your Machine-Type monsters.

PSV-005 Lightforce Sword

Card Type: Trap
Monster Type: —
Attribute: Trap
Level: —
ATK: —
DEF: —
Rarity: Rare

If you're lucky, "Lightforce Sword" will seal the card your opponent needs for a combo. If your opponent has only one card in his or her hand, then you'll know exactly what you'll hit.

PSV-006 Chain Destruction

Card Type: Trap
Monster Type: —
Attribute: Trap
Level: —
ATK: —
DEF: —
Rarity: Ultra Rare

If you destroy all the monsters necessary in a combo, then the combo can never take place!

PSV-007 Time Seal

Card Type: Trap
Monster Type: —
Attribute: Trap
Level: —
ATK: —
DEF: —
Rarity: Common

Preventing your opponent from drawing a card limits the number of choices he or she can make. You never know when the next card in your opponent's Deck is the card that can destroy you!

PSV-008 Graverobber

Card Type: Trap
Monster Type: —
Attribute: Trap
Level: —
ATK: —
DEF: —
Rarity: Super Rare

2000 Life Points is a lot to pay, so only use "Graverobber" on a very valuable Spell Card that is in your opponent's Graveyard. Make sure it's a Spell Card that can help you achieve victory!

PSV-009 Gift of The Mystical Elf

Card Type: Trap
Monster Type: —
Attribute: Trap
Level: —
ATK: —
DEF: —
Rarity: Common

The more monsters there are on the field, the greater the effect of this card.

PSV-010 The Eye of Truth

Card Type: Trap
Monster Type: —
Attribute: Trap
Level: —
ATK: —
DEF: —
Rarity: Common

Letting your opponent gain 1000 Life Points every turn may be a high price to pay, but being able to see his or her strategy is well worth the cost.

PSV-011 Dust Tornado

Card Type: Trap
Monster Type: —
Attribute: Trap
Level: —
ATK: —
DEF: —
Rarity: Super Rare

Not only does your opponent lose a Spell or Trap Card, but you get to Set one of your own! It's a win-win situation!

PSV-012 Call Of The Haunted

Card Type: Trap
Monster Type: —
Attribute: Trap
Level: —
ATK: —
DEF: —
Rarity: Ultra Rare

Surprise your opponent with this Trap Card to bring back a powerful monster from your Graveyard! If destroying your monster once was difficult, think how hard it will be the second time!

PSV-013 Solomon's Lawbook

Card Type: Trap
Monster Type: —
Attribute: Trap
Level: —
ATK: —
DEF: —
Rarity: Common

Skipping your Standby Phase is useful when you have to pay Life Points during the Standby Phase for cards you are playing.

PSV-014 Earthshaker

Card Type: Trap
Monster Type: —
Attribute: Trap
Level: —
ATK: —
DEF: —
Rarity: Common

If your opponent plays with only a few different attribute monsters, then "Earthshaker" can destroy many monsters in one swoop.

PSV-015 Enchanted Javelin

Card Type: Trap
Monster Type: —
Attribute: Trap
Level: —
ATK: —
DEF: —
Rarity: Common

If used correctly, you can negate the damage from even the strongest monster.

PSV-016 Mirror Wall

Card Type: Trap
Monster Type: —
Attribute: Trap
Level: —
ATK: —
DEF: —
Rarity: Super Rare

Halving your opponent's monsters' ATK can instantly turn the tide of battle! If your opponent's monsters are destroyed, then you don't need to pay 2000 Life Points because you'll no longer need "Mirror Wall."

PSV-017 Gust

Card Type: Trap
Monster Type: —
Attribute: Trap
Level: —
ATK: —
DEF: —
Rarity: Common

Like an eye for an eye, you can destroy one of your opponent's Spell or Trap Cards.

PSV-018 Driving Snow

Card Type: Trap
Monster Type: —
Attribute: Trap
Level: —
ATK: —
DEF: —
Rarity: Common

Similar to "Gust," you can destroy your opponent's Spell or Trap Card when your own Trap Card is destroyed.

PSV-019 Armored Glass

Card Type: Trap
Monster Type: —
Attribute: Trap
Level: —
ATK: —
DEF: —
Rarity: Common

Use this card if your opponent plays with many Equip Spell Cards.

PSV-020 World Suppression

Card Type: Trap
Monster Type: —
Attribute: Trap
Level: —
ATK: —
DEF: —
Rarity: Common

"World Suppression" stops Field Spell Card's effects, which can be useful depending on the status of the Duel.

PSV-021 Mystic Probe

Card Type: Trap
Monster Type: —
Attribute: Trap
Level: —
ATK: —
DEF: —
Rarity: Common

Use this card wisely if your opponent plays a Continuous Spell Card that greatly hinders your strategy.

PSV-022 Metal Detector

Card Type: Trap
Monster Type: —
Attribute: Trap
Level: —
ATK: —
DEF: —
Rarity: Common

"Metal Detector" can be useful when your opponent has you locked down with Continuous Trap Cards.

Pharaoh's Servant

PSV-023 Numinous Healer

Card Type: Trap
Monster Type: —
Attribute: Trap
Level: —
ATK: —
DEF: —
Rarity: Common

The more "Numinous Healer" cards you have in your Deck, the more useful this card is. This card restores a significant portion of your Life Points!

PSV-024 Appropriate

Card Type: Trap
Monster Type: —
Attribute: Trap
Level: —
ATK: —
DEF: —
Rarity: Rare

Since many players know the advantage of drawing extra cards, they include cards that allow them to draw cards during their non-Draw Phases. Therefore, "Appropriate" can be quite useful.

PSV-025 Forced Requisition

Card Type: Trap
Monster Type: —
Attribute: Trap
Level: —
ATK: —
DEF: —
Rarity: Rare

Use "Forced Requisition" if your Deck is geared toward destroying your opponent's hand.

PSV-026 DNA Surgery

Card Type: Trap
Monster Type: —
Attribute: Trap
Level: —
ATK: —
DEF: —
Rarity: Common

"DNA Surgery" allows you to change all different types that have been on the field to one specific type.

PSV-027 The Regulation of Tribe

Card Type: Trap
Monster Type: —
Attribute: Trap
Level: —
ATK: —
DEF: —
Rarity: Common

If your opponent plays with only one or few Monster Types, then "The Regulation of Tribe" severely limits his or her attacking

PSV-028 Backup Soldier

Card Type: Trap
Monster Type: —
Attribute: Trap
Level: —
ATK: —
DEF: —
Rarity: Super Rare

You can only return Normal Monsters, Fusion Monsters, and/or Ritual Monsters without effect from your Graveyard to your hand. Exodia Decks must have this card.

PSV-029 Major Riot

Card Type: Trap
Monster Type: —
Attribute: Trap
Level: —
ATK: —
DEF: —
Rarity: Common

Even if your monsters on the field are weak, you can now Special Summon more powerful monsters on to the field although you cannot Special Summon a high-level monster nor Special Summon a monster like "Gate Guardian."

PSV-030 Ceasefire

Card Type: Trap
Monster Type: —
Attribute: Trap
Level: —
ATK: —
DEF: —
Rarity: Ultra Rare

"Ceasefire" prevents your Effect Monsters' effects from triggering. As a bonus, your opponent will also take damage to his or her Life Points!

PSV-031 Light of Intervention

Card Type: Trap
Monster Type: —
Attribute: Trap
Level: —
ATK: —
DEF: —
Rarity: Common

"Light of Intervention" prevents Flip Effect Monsters' effects from activating. If used correctly, "Light of Intervention" can stop your opponent's combos.

PSV-032 Respect Play

Card Type: Trap
Monster Type: —
Attribute: Trap
Level: —
ATK: —
DEF: —
Rarity: Common

Though this card signifies fair play, how fair is it see each other's strategies....

PSV-033 Magical Hats

Card Type: Trap
Monster Type: —
Attribute: Trap
Level: —
ATK: —
DEF: —
Rarity: Super Rare

If you have a particular monster that you want to protect, play "Magical Hats," and the odds are on your side!

PSV-034 Nobleman of Crossout

Card Type: Spell
Monster Type: —
Attribute: Spell
Level: —
ATK: —
DEF: —
Rarity: Super Rare

"Nobleman of Crossout" may remove a particularly dangerous monster from the Duel. If the monster is part of your opponent's combo, then your opponent's strategy is destroyed!

PSV-035 Nobleman of Extermination

Card Type: Spell
Monster Type: —
Attribute: Spell
Level: —
ATK: —
DEF: —
Rarity: Rare

Not only can you destroy one of your opponent's Spell and Trap Cards, but if you're lucky, you may remove a particularly nasty Trap Card from the Duel!

PSV-036 The Shallow Grave

Card Type: Spell
Monster Type: —
Attribute: Spell
Level: —
ATK: —
DEF: —
Rarity: Rare

"The Shallow Grave" is especially useful if you have a powerful monster in your Graveyard while your opponent has weak monsters in his or her Graveyard.

PSV-037 Premature Burial

Card Type: Spell
Monster Type: —
Attribute: Spell
Level: —
ATK: —
DEF: —
Rarity: Ultra Rare

Though this card is not as powerful as "Monster Reborn," it is another way to retrieve powerful monsters from your Graveyard.

PSV-038 Inspection

Card Type: Spell
Monster Type: —
Attribute: Spell
Level: —
ATK: —
DEF: —
Rarity: Common

You can learn your opponent's strategy if you know what cards he or she is playing, but be careful not to run out of Life Points!

PSV-039 Prohibition

Card Type: Spell
Monster Type: —
Attribute: Spell
Level: —
ATK: —
DEF: —
Rarity: Rare

If your opponent plays with many of the same monsters, "Prohibition" can limit his or her selection.

PSV-040 Morphing Jar #2

Card Type: Effect Monster
Monster Type: Rock
Attribute: Earth
Level: 3
ATK: 800
DEF: 700
Rarity: Rare

"Morphing Jar #2" is useful in various situations. If your opponent has powerful monsters and you have weak monsters on the field, then "Morphing Jar" will act like a "Dark Hole" and return all the monsters to the Decks. It will also allow you to summon new monsters on the field that may be more useful.
Also, if your opponent has few Monster Cards in his or her Deck and many Spell and Trap Cards, then your opponent will probably discard many Spell and Trap Cards into the Graveyard before he or she runs across a Monster Card.

PSV-041 Flame Champion

Card Type: Normal Monster
Monster Type: Pyro
Attribute: Fire
Level: 5
ATK: 1900
DEF: 1300
Rarity: Common

This Warrior blocks all attacks with a flame shield.

PSV-042 Twin-Headed Fire Dragon

Card Type: Normal Monster
Monster Type: Pyro
Attribute: Fire
Level: 6
ATK: 2200
DEF: 1700
Rarity: Common

Born in space, this Dragon is actually twin Dragons sharing the same body.

PSV-043 Darkfire Soldier #1

Card Type: Normal Monster
Monster Type: Pyro
Attribute: Fire
Level: 4
ATK: 1700
DEF: 1150
Rarity: Common

This burning soldier is an expert in explosives.

PSV-044 Mr. Volcano

Card Type: Normal Monster
Monster Type: Pyro
Attribute: Fire
Level: 5
ATK: 2100
DEF: 1300
Rarity: Common

This flame wielder is usually calm, but he is very scary when angry.

PSV-045 Darkfire Soldier #2

Card Type: Normal Monster
Monster Type: Pyro
Attribute: Fire
Level: 4
ATK: 1700
DEF: 1000
Rarity: Common

This swordsman learned to harness flames after he fell into a volcano.

PSV-046 Kiseitai

Card Type: Effect Monster
Monster Type: Fiend
Attribute: Dark
Level: 2
ATK: 300
DEF: 800
Rarity: Common

If this card is played face-down in Defense Position, your opponent will most likely attack "Kiseitai" with his or her most powerful monster. That means you'll gain many Life Points every turn!

PSV-047 Cyber Falcon

Card Type: Normal Monster
Monster Type: Machine
Attribute: Wind
Level: 4
ATK: 1400
DEF: 1200
Rarity: Common

This eagle flies at the speed of sound, thanks to its jet engines.

PSV-048 Flying Kamakiri #2

Card Type: Normal Monster
Monster Type: Insect
Attribute: Wind
Level: 4
ATK: 1500
DEF: 800
Rarity: Common

This flying preying mantis' favorite food is insects.

PSV-049 Harpie's Brother

Card Type: Normal Monster
Monster Type: Winged Beast
Attribute: Wind
Level: 4
ATK: 1800
DEF: 600
Rarity: Common

This birdman flies at incredible speed and can see into great distances with eyes more perceptive than an eagle's.

PSV-050 Buster Blader

Card Type: Effect Monster
Monster Type: Warrior
Attribute: Earth
Level: 7
ATK: 2600
DEF: 2300
Rarity: Ultra Rare

If your opponent plays with many Dragon-Type monsters, then "Buster Blader" is a must-have for your Deck.

PSV-051 Michizure

Card Type: Trap
Monster Type: —
Attribute: Trap
Level: —
ATK: —
DEF: —
Rarity: Rare

"Michizure" is an effective way of getting rid of your opponent's monsters on the field. Your monster may have been destroyed, but so has your opponent's monster!

PSV-052 Minor Goblin Official

Card Type: Trap
Monster Type: —
Attribute: Trap
Level: —
ATK: —
DEF: —
Rarity: Common

"Minor Goblin Official" helps speed up your opponent's demise.

PSV-053 Gamble

Card Type: Trap
Monster Type: —
Attribute: Trap
Level: —
ATK: —
DEF: —
Rarity: Common

Like the card name itself, this card is a gamble. If you win, you will draw much-needed cards that can turn the tide of battle. However, if you lose, you lose an important turn.

PSV-054 Attack and Receive

Card Type: Trap
Monster Type: —
Attribute: Trap
Level: —
ATK: —
DEF: —
Rarity: Common

If you play with "Attack and Receive," try to have three in your Deck. Your opponent will second guess whether to attack you again.

PSV-055 Solemn Wishes

Card Type: Trap
Monster Type: —
Attribute: Trap
Level: —
ATK: —
DEF: —
Rarity: Common

"Solemn Wishes" helps you regain a lot of Life Points because it is a Continuous Trap Card and stays on the field.

PSV-056 Skull Invitation

Card Type: Trap
Monster Type: —
Attribute: Trap
Level: —
ATK: —
DEF: —
Rarity: Rare

This card works great in Decks that force your opponent to discard cards. Also, if your opponent is low on Life Points, he or she will have a hard time playing any card for fear that it will be destroyed.

PSV-057 Bubonic Vermin

Card Type: Effect Monster
Monster Type: Beast
Attribute: Earth
Level: 3
ATK: 900
DEF: 600
Rarity: Common

If you have one "Bubonic Vermin," you can soon fill your field with many "Bubonic Vermin." Find a way to use these creatures to your advantage, such as offering them as a Tribute, because on their own, their low ATK and DEF are not very helpful.

PSV-058 Dark Bat

Card Type: Normal Monster
Monster Type: Winged Beast
Attribute: Wind
Level: 3
ATK: 1000
DEF: 1000
Rarity: Common

These bats search for their prey using sonar.

PSV-059 Oni Tank T-34

Card Type: Normal Monster
Monster Type: Machine
Attribute: Earth
Level: 4
ATK: 1400
DEF: 1700
Rarity: Common

This tank is possessed by the spirit of a fiend and chases after its enemies.

PSV-060 Overdrive

Card Type: Normal Monster
Monster Type: Machine
Attribute: Earth
Level: 4
ATK: 1600
DEF: 1500
Rarity: Common

"Overdrive" is an armored buggy that can drive over any rough terrain.

PSV-061 Burning Land

Card Type: Spell
Monster Type: –
Attribute: Spell
Level: –
ATK: –
DEF: –
Rarity: Common

If your opponent's Life Points are lower than yours, "Burning Land" can help you speed up your opponent's demise.

PSV-062 Cold Wave

Card Type: Spell
Monster Type: –
Attribute: Spell
Level: –
ATK: –
DEF: –
Rarity: Common

Use "Cold Wave" to make sure your opponent cannot interfere with your strategy this turn.

PSV-063 Fairy Meteor Crush

Card Type: Spell
Monster Type: –
Attribute: Spell
Level: –
ATK: –
DEF: –
Rarity: Super Rare

"Fairy Meteor Crush" gives the same effect as "Mad Sword Beast" to any monster. Equip this card on a powerful monster and attack!

PSV-064 Limiter Removal

Card Type: Spell
Monster Type: –
Attribute: Spell
Level: –
ATK: –
DEF: –
Rarity: Super Rare

"Limiter Removal" is very effective in Machine-Type Decks to unleash the final blow to your opponent.

PSV-065 Rain of Mercy

Card Type: Spell
Monster Type: –
Attribute: Spell
Level: –
ATK: –
DEF: –
Rarity: Common

Use this card wisely because it benefits your opponent as much as it benefits you.

PSV-066 Monster Recovery

Card Type: Spell
Monster Type: –
Attribute: Spell
Level: –
ATK: –
DEF: –
Rarity: Rare

If you do not have any useful cards in your hand, use "Monster Recovery" to draw a fresh hand. Also, if you retrieve an Effect Monster Card, you can use its effect again.

PSV-067 Shift

Card Type: Trap
Monster Type: –
Attribute: Trap
Level: –
ATK: –
DEF: –
Rarity: Rare

Make sure you have another monster on the field than the monster you're trying to protect, or this card is useless.

PSV-068 Insect Imitation

Card Type: Spell
Monster Type: –
Attribute: Spell
Level: –
ATK: –
DEF: –
Rarity: Common

Only use this card if you play with many Insect-Type monsters in your Deck.

PSV-069 Dimensionhole

Card Type: Spell
Monster Type: –
Attribute: Spell
Level: –
ATK: –
DEF: –
Rarity: Rare

If you play "Dimensionhole" followed by "Dark Hole," your monster will return next turn while your opponent's monsters are destroyed!

Pharaoh's Servant

PSV-070 Ground Collapse

Card Type: Spell
Monster Type: —
Attribute: Spell
Level: —
ATK: —
DEF: —
Rarity: Common

As long as "Ground Collapse" is on the field, you can limit the number of monsters your opponent can summon to the field. If you have two "Ground Collapses," your opponent can only have one monster on the field!

PSV-071 Magic Drain

Card Type: Trap
Monster Type: —
Attribute: Trap
Level: —
ATK: —
DEF: —
Rarity: Rare

"Magic Drain" can either negate your opponent's Spell Card or force him or her to lose an additional Spell Card. Whichever your opponent chooses, it's a bonus for you!

PSV-072 Infinite Dismissal

Card Type: Trap
Monster Type: —
Attribute: Trap
Level: —
ATK: —
DEF: —
Rarity: Common

Many low-level monsters make up for their lack of ATK and DEF with potent effects. However, "Infinite Dismissal" will destroy these monsters. You can lockdown your opponent if you use "Infinite Dismissal" in combination with "Gravity Bind."

PSV-073 Gravity Bind

Card Type: Trap
Monster Type: —
Attribute: Trap
Level: —
ATK: —
DEF: —
Rarity: Rare

"Gravity Bind" will stop all your opponent's monsters cold! If you play many low-level monsters, "Gravity Bind" will not affect you at all. This card also helps stall your opponent if you're playing an Exodia Deck.

PSV-074 Type Zero Magic Crusher

Card Type: Trap
Monster Type: —
Attribute: Trap
Level: —
ATK: —
DEF: —
Rarity: Common

Play this card if you play with many Spell Cards or if you have useless Spell Cards in your hand when your opponent is low in Life Points.

PSV-075 Shadow of Eyes

Card Type: Trap
Monster Type: —
Attribute: Trap
Level: —
ATK: —
DEF: —
Rarity: Common

"Shadow of Eyes" not only makes your opponent's Flip Effect not activated, but it forces them into Attack Position for your monsters to destroy!

PSV-076 The Legendary Fisherman

Card Type: Effect Monster
Monster Type: Warrior
Attribute: Water
Level: 5
ATK: 1850
DEF: 1600
Rarity: Ultra Rare

Definitely play "The Legendary Fisherman" if you play "Umi" along with your Sea Serpent, Fish, Thunder, and Aqua-Type monsters. "The Legendary Fisherman" is protected against Spell Cards and your opponent's monsters, making it nearly invincible!

PSV-077 Sword Hunter

Card Type: Effect Monster
Monster Type: Warrior
Attribute: Earth
Level: 7
ATK: 2450
DEF: 1700
Rarity: Common

The more monsters "Sword Hunter" destroys, the stronger "Sword Hunter" gets, making it even harder for your opponent to defeat him!

PSV-078 Drill Bug

Card Type: Effect Monster
Monster Type: Insect
Attribute: Earth
Level: 2
ATK: 1000
DEF: 200
Rarity: Common

If you're playing with "Parasite Paracide," make sure to include "Drill Bug" in your Deck to summon "Parasite Paracide" quicker.

PSV-079 Deepsea Warrior

Card Type: Effect Monster
Monster Type: Warrior
Attribute: Water
Level: 5
ATK: 1600
DEF: 1800
Rarity: Common

"Deepsea Warrior" works well with "The Legendary Fisherman" since both are unaffected by your opponent's Spell Card.

PSV-080 Bite Shoes

Card Type: Effect Monster
Monster Type: Fiend
Attribute: Dark
Level: 2
ATK: 500
DEF: 300
Rarity: Common

Many monsters with high ATK have low DEF, so your opponent is in for a surprise when you switch his or her monster to Defense Position and destroy it!

PSV-081 Spikebot

Card Type: Normal Monster
Monster Type: Machine
Attribute: Dark
Level: 5
ATK: 1800
DEF: 1700
Rarity: Common

"Spikebot" swings its spiked balls on its arms wildly, striking both friend and foe.

PSV-082 Invitation to a Dark Sleep

Card Type: Effect Monster
Monster Type: Spellcaster
Attribute: Dark
Level: 5
ATK: 1500
DEF: 1800
Rarity: Common

If your opponent has a powerful monster on the field, "Invitation to a Dark Sleep" prevents it from attacking. This will give you additional time to figure out a way to defeat it.

PSV-083 Thousand-Eyes Idol

Card Type: Normal Monster
Monster Type: Spellcaster
Attribute: Dark
Level: 1
ATK: 0
DEF: 0
Rarity: Common

This Spellcaster's ATK and DEF look absolutely useless, but when fused with "Relinquished," you can summon the mighty "Thousand-Eyes Restrict!"

PSV-084 Thousand-Eyes Restrict

Card Type: Fusion/Effect Monster
Monster Type: Spellcaster
Attribute: Dark
Level: 1
ATK: 0
DEF: 0
Rarity: Ultra Rare

Create "Thousand-Eyes Restrict" by fusing "Thousand-Eyes Idol" and "Relinquished" using "Polymerization." Not only can you absorb your opponent's monsters, your opponent can no longer attack!

PSV-085 Girochin Kuwagata

Card Type: Normal Monster
Monster Type: Insect
Attribute: Wind
Level: 4
ATK: 1700
DEF: 1000
Rarity: Common

This Insect is only about the size of your thumb, but it can cut through steel.

PSV-086 Hayabusa Knight

Card Type: Effect Monster
Monster Type: Warrior
Attribute: Earth
Level: 3
ATK: 1000
DEF: 700
Rarity: Rare

"Hayabusa Knight" can attack twice, but it has low ATK. However, if you power up "Hayabusa Knight," then attacking twice is double the trouble for your opponent!

PSV-087 Bombardment Beetle

Card Type: Effect Monster
Monster Type: Insect
Attribute: Wind
Level: 2
ATK: 400
DEF: 900
Rarity: Common

Not only can "Bombardment Beetle" help you by destroying an Effect Monster, but you can also see what monster your opponent is playing.

PSV-088 4-Starred Ladybug of Doom

Card Type: Effect Monster
Monster Type: Insect
Attribute: Wind
Level: 3
ATK: 800
DEF: 1200
Rarity: Common

Since many useful and powerful monsters are Level 4, "4-Starred Ladybug of Doom" is an effective way to destroy your opponent's monsters.

PSV-089 Gradius

Card Type: Normal Monster
Monster Type: Machine
Attribute: Light
Level: 4
ATK: 1200
DEF: 800
Rarity: Common

Thanks to its power cells, this high-performance fighter has enhanced abilities.

PSV-090 Red-Moon Baby

Card Type: Effect Monster
Monster Type: Zombie
Attribute: Dark
Level: 3
ATK: 700
DEF: 1000
Rarity: Rare

"Red-Moon Baby's" effect is very useful, but since it has low ATK and DEF, make sure to power up "Red-Moon Baby" first.

PSV-091 Mad Sword Beast

Card Type: Effect Monster
Monster Type: Dinosaur
Attribute: Earth
Level: 4
ATK: 1400
DEF: 1200
Rarity: Rare

"Mad Sword Beast" can deal damage to your opponent's Life Points even if your opponent's monster is in Defense Position! Find ways to power up "Mad Sword Beast" to deal even more damage!

PSV-092 Skull Mariner

Card Type: Normal Monster
Monster Type: Warrior
Attribute: Water
Level: 4
ATK: 1600
DEF: 900
Rarity: Normal

This pirate ship has a red skull at its front and plunders tourist and cargo ships.

PSV-093 The All-Seeing White Tiger

Card Type: Normal Monster
Monster Type: Beast
Attribute: Wind
Level: 3
ATK: 1300
DEF: 500
Rarity: Normal

This king of the forest is as feared as it is admired.

PSV-094 Goblin Attack Force

Card Type: Effect Monster
Monster Type: Warrior
Attribute: Earth
Level: 4
ATK: 2300
DEF: 0
Rarity: Ultra Rare

"Goblin Attack Force" has 2300 ATK, and you do not need to offer another monster as a Tribute! You can leave this card in Attack Position and not attack to protect your Life Points, or you can attack and deal a lot of damage. But beware; "Goblin Attack Force" will be destroyed on your opponent's next turn if you attack unless you figure out a way to protect it.

PSV-095 Island Turtle

Card Type: Normal Monster
Monster Type: Aqua
Attribute: Water
Level: 4
ATK: 1000
DEF: 2000
Rarity: Normal

This large turtle is the size of a small island. Trees and animals live on its back because "Island Turtle" never dives underwater.

PSV-096 Wingweaver

Card Type: Normal Monster
Monster Type: Fairy
Attribute: Light
Level: 7
ATK: 2750
DEF: 2400
Rarity: Normal

"Wingweaver" soars with six wings and brings peace and hope to the world.

PSV-097 Science Soldier

Card Type: Normal Monster
Monster Type: Warrior
Attribute: Dark
Level: 3
ATK: 800
DEF: 800
Rarity: Normal

"Science Soldier" is the acme of technology and equipped with high-tech weaponry.

PSV-098 Souls of the Forgotten

Card Type: Normal Monster
Monster Type: Fiend
Attribute: Dark
Level: 2
ATK: 900
DEF: 200
Rarity: Normal

This spirit is an amalgamation of various vengeful souls.

PSV-099 Dokuroyaiba

Card Type: Normal Monster
Monster Type: Fiend
Attribute: Fire
Level: 3
ATK: 1000
DEF: 400
Rarity: Normal

This boomerang won't stop flying until it strikes its enemy.

PSV-100 The Fiend Megacyber

Card Type: Effect Monster
Monster Type: Warrior
Attribute: Dark
Level: 6
ATK: 2200
DEF: 1200
Rarity: Ultra Rare

Summoning a monster with 2200 ATK without having to offer another monster as a Tribute is incredible! You may want to hold off summoning your own monsters until your opponent has two or more than you on the field.

PSV-101 Gearfried the Iron Knight

Card Type: Effect Monster
Monster Type: Warrior
Attribute: Earth
Level: 4
ATK: 1800
DEF: 1600
Rarity: Super Rare

"Gearfried the Iron Knight" has high ATK for a Level 4 monster. Though you can't use Equip Spell Cards on "Gearfried the Iron Knight," neither can your opponent!

PSV-102 Insect Barrier

Card Type: Spell
Monster Type: —
Attribute: Spell
Level: —
ATK: —
DEF: —
Rarity: Normal

If you combo "Insect Barrier" with "Parasite Paracide," you can prevent your opponent's monsters from damaging your Life Points.

PSV-103 Beast of Talwar

Card Type: Normal Monster
Monster Type: Fiend
Attribute: Dark
Level: 6
ATK: 2400
DEF: 2150
Rarity: Ultra Rare

This incredibly powerful monster has both high ATK and DEF, and you only need to offer one monster as a Tribute to summon "Beast of Talwar!"

PSV-104 Imperial Order

Card Type: Trap
Monster Type: —
Attribute: Trap
Level: —
ATK: —
DEF: —
Rarity: Secret Rare

If you prevent your opponent from using Spell Cards, then you can disrupt his or her combos and strategies. Also, without Spell Cards, your opponent will have a hard time destroying "Imperial Order!"

PSV-000 Jinzo

Card Type: Effect Monster
Monster Type: Machine
Attribute: Dark
Level: 6
ATK: 2400
DEF: 1500
Rarity: Secret Rare

"Jinzo" prevents Trap Cards from activating, which can seriously cripple your opponent's strategy if he or she relies on Trap Cards.

Labyrinth of Nightmare

LON-001 The Masked Beast

Card Type: Ritual Monster
Monster Type: Fiend
Attribute: Dark
Level: 8
ATK: 3200
DEF: 1800
Rarity: Ultra Rare

This Ritual Monster has extremely high ATK. Ritual Monsters are tough to Ritual Summon, but this one's well worth the effort!

LON-002 Swordsman of Landstar

Card Type: Normal Monster
Monster Type: Warrior
Attribute: Earth
Level: 3
ATK: 500
DEF: 1200
Rarity: Common

Joey uses this monster, but it has low ATK and DEF.

LON-003 Humanoid Slime

Card Type: Normal Monster
Monster Type: Aqua
Attribute: Water
Level: 4
ATK: 800
DEF: 2000
Rarity: Common

This is a Fusion-Material Monster for "Humanoid Worm Drake." With a high 2000 DEF, this can serve as a great wall in WATER Decks.

LON-004 Worm Drake

Card Type: Normal Monster
Monster Type: Reptile
Attribute: Earth
Level: 4
ATK: 1400
DEF: 1500
Rarity: Common

This is a Fusion-Material Monster for "Humanoid Worm Drake." When compared to other Normal Monsters, this one isn't very good in ATK or DEF.

LON-005 Humanoid Worm Drake

Card Type: Fusion Monster
Monster Type: Aqua
Attribute: Water
Level: 7
ATK: 2200
DEF: 2000
Rarity: Common

This is the Fusion Monster that Strings used against Yugi. Taking into account how difficult it is to Tribute Summon, 2200 ATK feels lacking.

LON-006 Revival Jam

Card Type: Effect Monster
Monster Type: Aqua
Attribute: Water
Level: 4
ATK: 1500
DEF: 500
Rarity: Super Rare

You must pay 1000 Life Points in order to resurrect "Revival Jam." You have to think carefully about your strategy when using this effect.

LON-007 Flying Fish

Card Type: Normal Monster
Monster Type: Fish
Attribute: Wind
Level: 4
ATK: 800
DEF: 500
Rarity: Common

This fish is supposed to bring you luck, but will it in a Duel? Maybe you should put it in your Deck to test the theory.

LON-008 Amphibian Beast

Card Type: Normal Monster
Monster Type: Fish
Attribute: Water
Level: 6
ATK: 2400
DEF: 2000
Rarity: Rare

You can Tribute Summon this powerful monster by offering only one monster as a Tribute. In WATER Decks, this may be more useful than "Summoned Skull."

LON-009 Shining Abyss

Card Type: Normal Monster
Monster Type: Fairy
Attribute: Light
Level: 4
ATK: 1600
DEF: 1800
Rarity: Common

Its ATK and DEF is one step away from being excellent. If you're running low on monsters in a LIGHT Deck, "Shining Abyss" may come in handy.

LON-010 Gadget Soldier

Card Type: Normal Monster
Monster Type: Machine
Attribute: Fire
Level: 6
ATK: 1800
DEF: 2000
Rarity: Common

For a high-Level monster, its ATK and DEF aren't very high.

Labyrinth of Nightmare

LON-011 Grand Tiki Elder

Card Type: Normal Monster
Monster Type: Fiend
Attribute: Dark
Level: 4
ATK: 1500
DEF: 800
Rarity: Common

As a DARK Fiend-Type monster, it doesn't have very high ATK or DEF, but if you're constructing a Mask Deck, it may be worth including.

LON-012 Melchid the Four-Face Beast

Card Type: Normal Monster
Monster Type: Fiend
Attribute: Dark
Level: 4
ATK: 1500
DEF: 1200
Rarity: Common

Its stats are very similar to "Grand Tiki Elder."

LON-013 Nuvia the Wicked

Card Type: Effect Monster
Monster Type: Fiend
Attribute: Dark
Level: 4
ATK: 2000
DEF: 800
Rarity: Rare

Though it has 2000 ATK, not only is it difficult to summon, but this monster's ATK becomes lower depending on the number of monsters your opponent has on his or her field.

LON-014 Chosen One

Card Type: Spell
Monster Type: —
Attribute: Spell
Level: —
ATK: —
DEF: —
Rarity: Common

If you're successful, you can Special Summon a high-Level monster, but the risk may be too high....

LON-015 Mask of Weakness

Card Type: Trap
Monster Type: —
Attribute: Trap
Level: —
ATK: —
DEF: —
Rarity: Common

This card reduces your opponent's monster's ATK greatly. Be confident and use it to surprise your opponent's monster.

LON-016 Curse of the Masked Beast

Card Type: Spell
Monster Type: —
Attribute: Spell
Level: —
ATK: —
DEF: —
Rarity: Common

This Ritual Spell Card is needed to Ritual Summon "The Masked Beast." Offer a second "The Masked Beast" card as a Tribute to satisfy the Level Stars requirement.

LON-017 Mask of Dispel

Card Type: Spell
Monster Type: —
Attribute: Spell
Level: —
ATK: —
DEF: —
Rarity: Super Rare

The controller of the targetted Spell Card takes damage every turn, making this card a unique Direct Damage Spell Card.

LON-018 Mask of Restrict

Card Type: Trap
Monster Type: —
Attribute: Trap
Level: —
ATK: —
DEF: —
Rarity: Ultra Rare

This Continuous Trap Card stops monsters from being offered as a Tribute. Not only does it stop Tribute Summons, but it also stop card effects that require monsters to be offered as a Tribute.

LON-019 Mask of the Accursed

Card Type: Spell
Monster Type: —
Attribute: Spell
Level: —
ATK: —
DEF: —
Rarity: Super Rare

Not only does the monster equipped with this Equip Spell Card lose the ability to attack, but the controller takes damage every turn.

LON-020 Mask of Brutality

Card Type: Spell
Monster Type: —
Attribute: Spell
Level: —
ATK: —
DEF: —
Rarity: Rare

The cost to maintain this card is high, so if you're going to power up your monster, then it's better to use "Axe of Despair." Can you use this to lower your opponent's monster's DEF?

LON-021 Return of the Doomed

Card Type: Spell
Monster Type: —
Attribute: Spell
Level: —
ATK: —
DEF: —
Rarity: Rare

Discard a monster you don't need from your hand to retrieve a destroyed monster back to your hand. Retrieve your key card!

LON-022 Lightning Blade

Card Type: Spell
Monster Type: —
Attribute: Spell
Level: —
ATK: —
DEF: —
Rarity: Common

This Equip Spell Card is geared toward Warrior-Type monsters. It also lowers the ATK of WATER monsters. This card is helpful against WATER Decks.

LON-023 Tornado Wall

Card Type: Trap
Monster Type: —
Attribute: Trap
Level: —
ATK: —
DEF: —
Rarity: Common

As long as "Umi" is active on the field, this protective Trap Card stops you from taking damage from Monster attacks.

LON-024 Fairy Box

Card Type: Trap
Monster Type: —
Attribute: Trap
Level: —
ATK: —
DEF: —
Rarity: Common

You have a fifty percent chance that your opponent's monster's ATK becomes 0. If your opponent attacks your monster in Attack Position, your opponent is going to be hurt instead!

LON-025 Torrential Tribute

Card Type: Trap
Monster Type: —
Attribute: Trap
Level: —
ATK: —
DEF: —
Rarity: Ultra Rare

This Trap Card easily destroys monsters. It works well in Decks that don't rely on monster attacks.

LON-026 Jam Breeding Machine

Card Type: Spell
Monster Type: —
Attribute: Spell
Level: —
ATK: —
DEF: —
Rarity: Rare

For getting a Slime Token every turn, you cannot summon a monster. If you use this card by itself, it's not very helpful, so think of how you can use this Spell Card to your advantage.

LON-027 Infinite Cards

Card Type: Spell
Monster Type: —
Attribute: Spell
Level: —
ATK: —
DEF: —
Rarity: Rare

This Continuous Trap Card gets rid of the limit of the number of cards you can have in your hand. The question is whether you're able to amass a huge number of cards in your hand.

LON-028 Jam Defender

Card Type: Trap
Monster Type: —
Attribute: Trap
Level: —
ATK: —
DEF: —
Rarity: Common

This is a combo card with "Revival Jam," but the cost of resurrecting "Revival Jam" is high, so this card is hard to use.

LON-029 Card of Safe Return

Card Type: Spell
Monster Type: —
Attribute: Spell
Level: —
ATK: —
DEF: —
Rarity: Ultra Rare

Everytime you Special Summon a monster from the Graveyard, you can draw a card. You want to include this card in a combo Deck with "Monster Reborn."

LON-030 Lady Panther

Card Type: Effect Monster
Monster Type: Beast-Warrior
Attribute: Earth
Level: 4
ATK: 1400
DEF: 1300
Rarity: Common

The key point to think about when using this card is whether there's a card in your Graveyard worth returning to your Deck by offering "Lady Panther" on the field as a Tribute.

LON-031 The Unfriendly Amazon

Card Type: Effect Monster
Monster Type: Warrior
Attribute: Earth
Level: 4
ATK: 2000
DEF: 1000
Rarity: Common

This Level 4 monster has a high 2000 ATK, but the cost to maintain "The Unfriendly Amazon" is high. You should think about using this card for only one turn!

LON-032 Amazon Archer

Card Type: Effect Monster
Monster Type: Warrior
Attribute: Earth
Level: 4
ATK: 1400
DEF: 1000
Rarity: Common

Offer two monsters as a Tribute to deal 1200 points of damage. It's slightly better than offering two monsters as a Tribute to "Cannon Soldier."

LON-033 Crimson Sentry

Card Type: Effect Monster
Monster Type: Warrior
Attribute: Fire
Level: 4
ATK: 1500
DEF: 1200
Rarity: Common

This card's effect may not be as good as "Lady Panther's" effect. However, this may come in handy if you need to maintain having cards in your Deck.

LON-034 Fire Princess

Card Type: Effect Monster
Monster Type: Pyro
Attribute: Fire
Level: 4
ATK: 1300
DEF: 1500
Rarity: Super Rare

Everytime you restore Life Points, your opponent takes damage. There are many ways to gain Life Points, so you can construct a Deck with "Fire Princess" as the key card.

Labyrinth of Nightmare

LON-035 Lady Assailant of Flames

Card Type: Effect Monster
Monster Type: Pyro
Attribute: Fire
Level: 4
ATK: 1500
DEF: 1000
Rarity: Common

When this card Flips, you can remove three cards in your Deck from play to deal damage to your opponent. This can be very useful near the end of the Duel.

LON-036 Fire Sorcerer

Card Type: Effect Monster
Monster Type: Spellcaster
Attribute: Fire
Level: 4
ATK: 1000
DEF: 1500
Rarity: Common

When this card Flips, remove two random cards from your hand to deal damage to your opponent. However, it may hinder your strategy to remove two cards from your hand.

LON-037 Spirit of the Breeze

Card Type: Effect Monster
Monster Type: Fairy
Attribute: Wind
Level: 3
ATK: 0
DEF: 1800
Rarity: Rare

As long as this card remains in face-up Attack Position, you gain 1000 Life Points every turn. However, if you leave it in Attack Position without using other cards to help, since it has 0 ATK, it will be destroyed quickly.

LON-038 Dancing Fairy

Card Type: Effect Monster
Monster Type: Fairy
Attribute: Wind
Level: 4
ATK: 1700
DEF: 1000
Rarity: Common

You gain Life Points if this card remains in face-up Defense Position. In order to use its effect to the fullest potential, you will have to find a way to prevent your opponent from attacking.

LON-039 Fairy Guardian

Card Type: Effect Monster
Monster Type: Fairy
Attribute: Wind
Level: 3
ATK: 1000
DEF: 1000
Rarity: Common

You can return a Spell Card in your Graveyard to the bottom of your Deck. However, if you don't find a way to shuffle your Deck, the Spell Card is pratically unusable.

LON-040 Empress Mantis

Card Type: Normal Monster
Monster Type: Insect
Attribute: Wind
Level: 6
ATK: 2200
DEF: 1400
Rarity: Common

This Level 6 monster has 2200 ATK. Unless you're playing an Insect Deck, it's better to use "Summoned Skull."

LON-041 Cure Mermaid

Card Type: Effect Monster
Monster Type: Fish
Attribute: Water
Level: 4
ATK: 1500
DEF: 800
Rarity: Common

You gain Life Points every turn just by having this card face-up on the field. However, since it has low ATK and DEF, you have to find a way to protect her.

LON-042 Hysteric Fairy

Card Type: Effect Monster
Monster Type: Fairy
Attribute: Light
Level: 4
ATK: 1800
DEF: 500
Rarity: Common

If you offer two monsters as a Tribute, you gain 1000 Life Points. You should offer Monster Tokens and Flip Effect Monsters whose effects have already activated.

LON-043 Bio-Mage

Card Type: Normal Monster
Monster Type: Fairy
Attribute: Light
Level: 3
ATK: 1150
DEF: 1000
Rarity: Common

This looks like a mysterious individual, but its powers aren't anything to write home about.

LON-044 The Forgiving Maiden

Card Type: Effect Monster
Monster Type: Fairy
Attribute: Light
Level: 4
ATK: 850
DEF: 2000
Rarity: Common

Other than her effect, the other key features of this card are that she is a LIGHT monster with 2000 DEF. She's excellent as a wall in a LIGHT Deck.

LON-045 St. Joan

Card Type: Fusion Monster
Monster Type: Fairy
Attribute: Light
Level: 7
ATK: 2800
DEF: 2000
Rarity: Common

This Fusion Monster has excellent ATK, making this card a worthwhile addition to your gameplan.

LON-046 Marie the Fallen One

Card Type: Effect Monster
Monster Type: Fiend
Attribute: Dark
Level: 5
ATK: 1700
DEF: 1200
Rarity: Rare

If you send this card to the Graveyard, you can gain Life Points without many ways for your opponent to interfere with your plans. If you have multiple "Marie the Fallen One" cards in your Graveyard, then you will gain even more Life Points!

LON-047 Jar of Greed

Card Type: Trap
Monster Type: —
Attribute: Trap **Level:** —
ATK: —
DEF: —
Rarity: Super Rare

If you use one card to draw one card, then your hand won't increase. However, this card helps you thin out your Deck and can be a ruse against your opponent's "Mystical Space Typhoon."

LON-048 Scroll of Bewitchment

Card Type: Spell
Monster Type: —
Attribute: Spell
Level: —
ATK: —
DEF: —
Rarity: Common

This Equip Spell Card changes a monster's attribute. Now you can use your favorite monster in an Attribute-specific Deck.

LON-049 United We Stand

Card Type: Spell
Monster Type: —
Attribute: Spell
Level: —
ATK: —
DEF: —
Rarity: Ultra Rare

This Equip Spell Card increases ATK and DEF depending on the number of monsters you have on your field. Find a way to get many monsters on your field to strengthen the effect of this card!

LON-050 Mage Power

Card Type: Spell
Monster Type: —
Attribute: Spell
Level: —
ATK: —
DEF: —
Rarity: Ultra Rare

This is similar to "United We Stand," but ATK and DEF increase depending on the number of Spell and Trap Cards on your field. You can play multiple Spell and Trap Cards in one turn, so this card is easy to use!

LON-051 Offerings to the Doomed

Card Type: Spell
Monster Type: —
Attribute: Spell
Level: —
ATK: —
DEF: —
Rarity: Common

A Quick-Play Spell Card that destroys a monster may sound great, but it's painful when you can't draw a card. Only use this on your opponent's strongest monsters.

LON-052 The Portrait's Secret

Card Type: Normal Monster
Monster Type: Fiend
Attribute: Earth
Level: 4
ATK: 1200
DEF: 1500
Rarity: Common

This is one of Bakura's Normal Monsters. Since its ATK and DEF are low, Bakura used this to increase the number of monsters in his Graveyard.

LON-053 The Gross Ghost of Fled Dreams

Card Type: Normal Monster
Monster Type: Fiend
Attribute: Dark
Level: 4
ATK: 1300
DEF: 1800
Rarity: Common

This is one of Bakura's Normal Monsters. Out of the five Normal Monsters that Bakura used, this is one of the stronger ones with 1800 DEF.

LON-054 Headless Knight

Card Type: Normal Monster
Monster Type: Fiend
Attribute: Earth
Level: 4
ATK: 1450
DEF: 1700
Rarity: Common

This is one of Bakura's Normal Monsters. Though it was destroyed in the show, its defense is not too shabby.

LON-055 Earthbound Spirit

Card Type: Normal Monster
Monster Type: Fiend
Attribute: Earth
Level: 4
ATK: 500
DEF: 2000
Rarity: Common

This is one of Bakura's Normal Monsters. A Level 4 monster with 2000 DEF is effective as a wall.

LON-056 The Earl of Demise

Card Type: Normal Monster
Monster Type: Fiend
Attribute: Dark
Level: 5
ATK: 2000
DEF: 700
Rarity: Common

This is one of Bakura's Normal Monsters. 2000 ATK is pretty high, but you need to offer one monster as a Tribute to Tribute Summon "The Earl of Demise."

LON-057 Boneheimer

Card Type: Normal Monster
Monster Type: Aqua
Attribute: Water
Level: 3
ATK: 850
DEF: 400
Rarity: Common

This seahorse-like monster's body is half-transparent. Not only does it look cute, but its ATK is cute as well!

LON-058 Flame Dancer

Card Type: Normal Monster
Monster Type: Pyro
Attribute: Fire
Level: 2
ATK: 550
DEF: 450
Rarity: Common

This strange monster has flames bursting out of its head and hands. For some reason, its feet swing to and fro rapidly.

Labyrinth of Nightmare

LON-059 Spherous Lady

Card Type: Normal Monster
Monster Type: Rock
Attribute: Earth
Level: 3
ATK: 400
DEF: 1400
Rarity: Common

This monster is half-human, half-snake. 1400 DEF is pretty high for a Level 3 monster.

LON-060 Lightning Conger

Card Type: Normal Monster
Monster Type: Thunder
Attribute: Water
Level: 3
ATK: 350
DEF: 750
Rarity: Common

This looks like an advanced form of an electric eel, but with only 350 ATK, it's pretty weak. However, this may come in handy in a Deck that relies on low ATK monsters....

LON-061 Jowgen the Spiritualist

Card Type: Effect Monster
Monster Type: Spellcaster
Attribute: Light
Level: 3
ATK: 200
DEF: 1300
Rarity: Rare

If you discard one card from you hand, then you can destroy all Special Summoned monsters. Use this when your opponent Special Summons a powerful monster!

LON-062 Kycoo the Ghost Destroyer

Card Type: Effect Monster
Monster Type: Spellcaster
Attribute: Dark
Level: 4
ATK: 1800
DEF: 700
Rarity: Super Rare

Remove your opponent's most dangerous monsters in the Graveyard from play so that your opponent can't resurrect them. Also, with 1800 ATK, it's easy to damage your opponent's Life Points.

LON-063 Summoner of Illusions

Card Type: Effect Monster
Monster Type: Spellcaster
Attribute: Light
Level: 3
ATK: 800
DEF: 900
Rarity: Common

The Flip Effect lets you Special Summon any Fusion Monster for one turn. However, since a monster has to be offered as a Tribute, it can be difficult to use.

LON-064 Bazoo the Soul-Eater

Card Type: Effect Monster
Monster Type: Beast
Attribute: Earth
Level: 4
ATK: 1600
DEF: 900
Rarity: Super Rare

If you remove monsters in your Graveyard from play, then "Bazoo the Soul-Eater" powers up instantly to 2500. You can use this as your key card!

LON-065 Dark Necrofear

Card Type: Effect Monster
Monster Type: Fiend
Attribute: Dark
Level: 8
ATK: 2200
DEF: 2800
Rarity: Ultra Rare

Special Summon "Dark Necrofear" by removing three Fiend-Type monsters in your Graveyard from play. If it's destroyed, then it transforms into an Equip Spell Card similar to "Snatch Steal," and you gain control of your opponent's monster.

LON-066 Soul of Purity and Light

Card Type: Effect Monster
Monster Type: Fairy
Attribute: Light
Level: 6
ATK: 2000
DEF: 1800
Rarity: Common

Remove two LIGHT monsters in your Graveyard to Special Summon "Soul of Purity and Light." This excellent monster can't be destroyed by your opponent's monster with 2200 ATK.

LON-067 Spirit of Flames

Card Type: Effect Monster
Monster Type: Pyro
Attribute: Fire
Level: 4
ATK: 1700
DEF: 1000
Rarity: Common

Remove one FIRE monster in your Graveyard from play to Special Summon "Spirit of Flames." During the Battle Phase, this monster's ATK increases.

LON-068 Aqua Spirit

Card Type: Effect Monster
Monster Type: Aqua
Attribute: Water
Level: 4
ATK: 1600
DEF: 1200
Rarity: Common

Remove one WATER monster in your Graveyard from play to Special Summon "Aqua Spirit." Switch the Battle Position of your opponent's monster so that it can't attack.

LON-069 The Rock Spirit

Card Type: Effect Monster
Monster Type: Rock
Attribute: Earth
Level: 4
ATK: 1700
DEF: 1000
Rarity: Common

Remove one EARTH monster in your Graveyard from play to Special Summon "The Rock Spirit." Its ATK increases during your opponent's Battle Phase, so it is difficult to destroy.

LON-070 Garuda the Wind Spirit

Card Type: Effect Monster
Monster Type: Winged Beast
Attribute: Wind
Level: 4
ATK: 1600
DEF: 1200
Rarity: Common

Remove one WIND monster in your Graveyard from play to Special Summon "Garuda the Wind Spirit." Change your opponent's monster's Battle Position so that it is easier to attack.

LON-071 Gilasaurus

Card Type: Effect Monster
Monster Type: Winged Beast
Attribute: Earth
Level: 3
ATK: 1400
DEF: 400
Rarity: Rare

If you Special Summon this monster when your opponent doesn't have any monsters in his or her Graveyard, then there's no risk involved.

LON-072 Tornado Bird

Card Type: Effect Monster
Monster Type: Winged Beast
Attribute: Wind
Level: 4
ATK: 1100
DEF: 1000
Rarity: Rare

Be careful, you must return two cards on the field back to the hand.

LON-073 Dreamsprite

Card Type: Effect Monster
Monster Type: Plant
Attribute: Light
Level: 2
ATK: 300
DEF: 200
Rarity: Common

You can switch your opponent's monster's attack to a different monster. Make your opponent's monster attacks a wall monster or a Flip Effect Monster!

LON-074 Zombyra the Dark

Card Type: Effect Monster
Monster Type: Warrior
Attribute: Dark
Level: 4
ATK: 2100
DEF: 500
Rarity: Common

It loses ATK for every monster it destroys, but even if it destroys one monster, is still has 1900 ATK. It can be very useful in your offensive force.

LON-075 Supply

Card Type: Effect Monster
Monster Type: Warrior
Attribute: Earth
Level: 4
ATK: 1300
DEF: 800
Rarity: Common

You can return two Fusion-Material Monsters back to your hand. This helps rebuild your forces, and you can also use them as Fusion-Material Monsters again.

LON-076 Maryokutai

Card Type: Effect Monster
Monster Type: Aqua
Attribute: Water
Level: 3
ATK: 900
DEF: 900
Rarity: Common

If you offer this card as a Tribute, then you can stop your opponent's Spell Card. The hard part is that this monster can be easily destroyed in battle.

LON-077 The Last Warrior from Another Planet

Card Type: Fusion/Effect Monster
Monster Type: Warrior
Attribute: Earth
Level: 7
ATK: 2350
DEF: 2300
Rarity: Ultra Rare

When this monster is Special Summoned, other monsters can only be Set. If you have "Light of Intervention," then monsters can't even be Set!

LON-078 Collected Power

Card Type: Trap
Monster Type: —
Attribute: Trap
Level: —
ATK: —
DEF: —
Rarity: Common

All Equip Spell Cards on the field are placed on one monster. You want to combo this card with "Maha Vailo."

LON-079 Dark Spirit of the Silent

Card Type: Trap
Monster Type: —
Attribute: Trap
Level: —
ATK: —
DEF: —
Rarity: Super Rare

Not only does it stop your opponent's powerful monster's attack, but you can attack with one of your monsters to gain the advantage.

LON-080 Royal Command

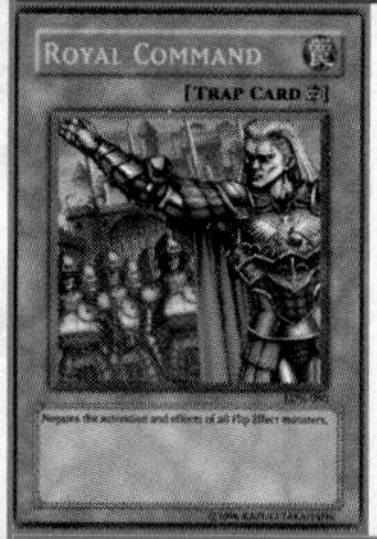

Card Type: Trap
Monster Type: —
Attribute: Trap
Level: —
ATK: —
DEF: —
Rarity: Ultra Rare

This card stops the activation and effects of Flip Effect Monsters. Use this card if your opponent plays with "Morphing Jar" or "Cyber Jar."

LON-081 Riryoku Field

Card Type: Trap
Monster Type: —
Attribute: Trap
Level: —
ATK: —
DEF: —
Rarity: Super Rare

This Counter Trap Card protects one of your monsters from your opponent's Spell Card. This excellent Trap Card can also counter "Monster Reborn."

LON-082 Skull Lair

- Card Type: Trap
- Monster Type: —
- Attribute: Trap
- Level: —
- ATK: —
- DEF: —
- Rarity: Common

Destroy a monster on the field with the same number of Level Stars equal to the number of cards you remove from your Graveyard from play. It's difficult to destroy your opponent's high-Level monsters.

LON-083 Graverobber's Retribution

- Card Type: Trap
- Monster Type: —
- Attribute: Trap
- Level: —
- ATK: —
- DEF: —
- Rarity: Common

You inflict damage to your opponent's Life Points every turn for the number of your opponent's monsters that have been removed from play. This card works well if you play with cards that removes cards from the Graveyard.

LON-084 Deal of Phantom

- Card Type: Trap
- Monster Type: —
- Attribute: Trap
- Level: —
- ATK: —
- DEF: —
- Rarity: Common

This power-up Trap Card is determined by the number of monsters in your Graveyard. For it to have the same effect as "Rush Recklessly," you need seven monsters in your Graveyard.

LON-085 Destruction Punch

- Card Type: Trap
- Monster Type: —
- Attribute: Trap
- Level: —
- ATK: —
- DEF: —
- Rarity: Rare

You can destroy your opponent's monster with your wall monster. When your opponent attacks your face-down wall monster, that's your chance to activate this card!

LON-086 Blind Destruction

- Card Type: Trap
- Monster Type: —
- Attribute: Trap
- Level: —
- ATK: —
- DEF: —
- Rarity: Common

This Trap Card destroys all monsters with the same Level as the dice roll. This card is a gamble that both you and your opponent has to worry about!

LON-087 The Emperor's Holiday

- Card Type: Trap
- Monster Type: —
- Attribute: Trap
- Level: —
- ATK: —
- DEF: —
- Rarity: Common

You can stop the effect of powerful Equip Spell Cards, such as "Megamorph." If you activate this Trap Card right before your opponent attacks, you'll mess up your opponent's calculations.

LON-088 Destiny Board

- Card Type: Trap
- Monster Type: —
- Attribute: Trap
- Level: —
- ATK: —
- DEF: —
- Rarity: Ultra Rare

This is a special victory card, such as "Exodia the Forbidden One." Protect this card until you get all five letters!

LON-089 Spirit Message "I"

- Card Type: Spell
- Monster Type: —
- Attribute: Spell
- Level: —
- ATK: —
- DEF: —
- Rarity: Rare

This is one of the alphabet cards needed for "Destiny Board." If you get all five, then you win.

LON-090 Spirit Message "N"

- Card Type: Spell
- Monster Type: —
- Attribute: Spell
- Level: —
- ATK: —
- DEF: —
- Rarity: Rare

This is one of the alphabet cards needed for "Destiny Board." If you get all five, then you win.

LON-091 Spirit Message "A"

- Card Type: Spell
- Monster Type: —
- Attribute: Spell
- Level: —
- ATK: —
- DEF: —
- Rarity: Rare

This is one of the alphabet cards needed for "Destiny Board." If you get all five, then you win.

LON-092 Spirit Message "L"

- Card Type: Spell
- Monster Type: —
- Attribute: Spell
- Level: —
- ATK: —
- DEF: —
- Rarity: Rare

This is one of the alphabet cards needed for "Destiny Board." If you get all five, then you win.

LON-093 The Dark Door

- Card Type: Spell
- Monster Type: —
- Attribute: Spell
- Level: —
- ATK: —
- DEF: —
- Rarity: Common

Since only one monster can attack, damage from monster attacks decrease greatly. This card is a perfect fit if your Deck doesn't use monsters.

LON-094 Spiritualism

Card Type: Spell
Monster Type: —
Attribute: Spell
Level: —
ATK: —
DEF: —
Rarity: Rare

This Spell Card can't even be stopped by Counter Trap Cards. Use this card when you want to definitely remove one of your opponent's Spell or Trap Cards from the field, even for one turn.

LON-095 Cyclon Laser

Card Type: Equip Spell Card
Monster Type: —
Attribute: Spell
Level: —
ATK: —
DEF: —
Rarity: Common

This Equip Spell Card is designed for "Gradius." Not only does it increase ATK, but it also has the effect of "Fairy Meteor Crush."

LON-096 Bait Doll

Card Type: Spell
Monster Type: —
Attribute: Spell
Level: —
ATK: —
DEF: —
Rarity: Common

Force your opponent's Trap Card to activate and mess up your opponent's strategy. If you destroyed the Trap Card, then you can put this card back in your Deck so that you can use it again.

LON-097 De-Fusion

Card Type: Spell
Monster Type: —
Attribute: Spell
Level: —
ATK: —
DEF: —
Rarity: Super Rare

Separate a Fusion Monster and Special Summon the Fusion-Material Monsters from the Graveyard back to the field. Notice that this card is a Quick-Play Spell Card.

LON-098 Fusion Gate

Card Type: Spell
Monster Type: —
Attribute: Spell
Level: —
ATK: —
DEF: —
Rarity: Common

Instead of using "Polymerization," you can use this Field Spell Card to Special Summon Fusion Monsters. However, the Fusion-Material Monsters are removed from play instead of placed in the Graveyard.

LON-099 Ekibyo Drakmord

Card Type: Equip Spell Card
Monster Type: —
Attribute: Spell
Level: —
ATK: —
DEF: —
Rarity: Common

This Equip Spell Card destroys monsters. Even though it takes time for the effect to be successful, it returns to the hand, so you can use this card many times.

LON-100 Miracle Dig

Card Type: Spell
Monster Type: —
Attribute: Spell
Level: —
ATK: —
DEF: —
Rarity: Common

You can return monsters removed from play back into the Graveyard. You may need this card if you play with cards that have effects that remove monsters in the Graveyard from play.

LON-101 Dragonic Attack

Card Type: Spell
Monster Type: —
Attribute: Spell
Level: —
ATK: —
DEF: —
Rarity: Common

Transform Warrior-Type monsters into Dragon-Type monsters and power them up. They can now receive "Lord of D.'s" effect.

LON-102 Spirit Elimination

Card Type: Spell
Monster Type: —
Attribute: Spell
Level: —
ATK: —
DEF: —
Rarity: Common

Instead of removing monsters in the Graveyard from play, you remove monsters on the field from play. Use this in the beginning of a Duel when there are no cards in the Graveyard.

LON-103 Vengeful Bog Spirit

Card Type: Spell
Monster Type: —
Attribute: Spell
Level: —
ATK: —
DEF: —
Rarity: Common

Monsters cannot attack in the turn they were summoned. This stops instant attack combos using "Monster Reborn."

LON-104 Magic Cylinder

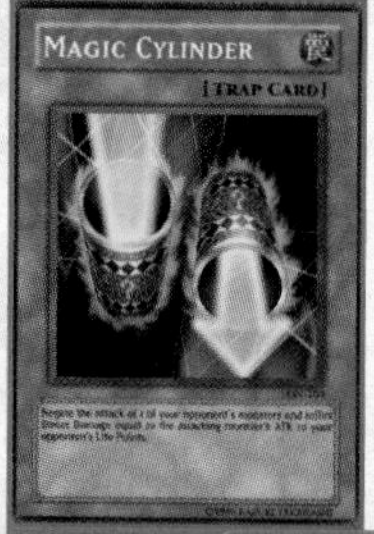

Card Type: Trap
Monster Type: —
Attribute: Trap
Level: —
ATK: —
DEF: —
Rarity: Secret Rare

Send your opponent's monster's attack back at your opponent. Use this on your opponent's strongest monster.

LON-000 Gemini Elf

Card Type: Normal Monster
Monster Type: Spellcaster
Attribute: Earth
Level: 4
ATK: 1900
DEF: 900
Rarity: Secret Rare

This is the strongest Level 4 Normal Monster, making this card extremely useful.

Legacy of Darkness

LOD-001 Dark Ruler Ha Des

Card Type: Effect Monster
Monster Type: Fiend
Attribute: Dark
Level: 6
ATK: 2450
DEF: 1600
Rarity: Ultra Rare

This card is the boss of the Fiend-Type monsters. When this monster is face-up on the field, it can stop the effects of Effect Monsters that your Fiend-Type monsters destroyed in battle.

LOD-002 Dark Balter the Terrible

Card Type: Fusion/Effect Monster
Monster Type: Fiend
Attribute: Dark
Level: 5
ATK: 2000
DEF: 1200
Rarity: Super Rare

This Fusion Monster is created from Fiend-Type and Spellcaster-Type monsters. It's also a powerful Effect monster that can negate the effects of Spell Cards!

LOD-003 Lesser Fiend

Card Type: Effect Monster
Monster Type: Fiend
Attribute: Dark
Level: 5
ATK: 2100
DEF: 1000
Rarity: Rare

Monsters destroyed by this card are removed from play. It's useful against monsters like "Sangan" and "Giant Rat."

LOD-004 Possessed Dark Soul

Card Type: Effect Monster
Monster Type: Fiend
Attribute: Dark
Level: 3
ATK: 1200
DEF: 800
Rarity: Common

When this card is offered as a Tribute, you can take control of your opponent's Level or lower monster. Take an Effect Monster with an excellent effect.

LOD-005 Winged Minion

Card Type: Effect Monster
Monster Type: Fiend
Attribute: Dark
Level: 2
ATK: 700
DEF: 700
Rarity: Common

Offer this monster as a Tribute to strengthen your Fiend-Type monster. Not only is this monster easy to search for, but you don't have to worry about it being destroyed like an Equip Spell Card.

LOD-006 Skull Knight #2

Card Type: Effect Monster
Monster Type: Fiend
Attribute: Dark
Level: 3
ATK: 1000
DEF: 1200
Rarity: Common

When this monster is offered as a Tribute to summon a Fiend-Type Monster, then you can Special Summon another "Skull Knight #2" from your Deck. The number of monsters on your field doesn't decrease, so it's great!

LOD-007 Ryu-Kishin Clown

Card Type: Effect Monster
Monster Type: Fiend
Attribute: Dark
Level: 2
ATK: 800
DEF: 500
Rarity: Common

This card activates when it is summoned. Since it's not a Flip Effect, you can use this effect with pinpoint accuracy.

LOD-008 Twin-Headed Wolf

Card Type: Effect Monster
Monster Type: Fiend
Attribute: Dark
Level: 4
ATK: 1500
DEF: 1000
Rarity: Common

As long as you have another Fiend-Type monster on your field, you can attack without having to worry about the Flip Effects of the Effect Monsters this card destroyed. You don't have to be afraid of "Man-Eater Bug!"

LOD-009 Opticlops

Card Type: Normal Monster
Monster Type: Fiend
Attribute: Dark
Level: 4
ATK: 1800
DEF: 1700
Rarity: Rare

"Opticlops" and "La Jinn the Mystical Genie of the Lamp" form the main force of Level 4 Fiend-Type monsters. 1800 ATK comes in very handy.

LOD-010 Bark of Dark Ruler

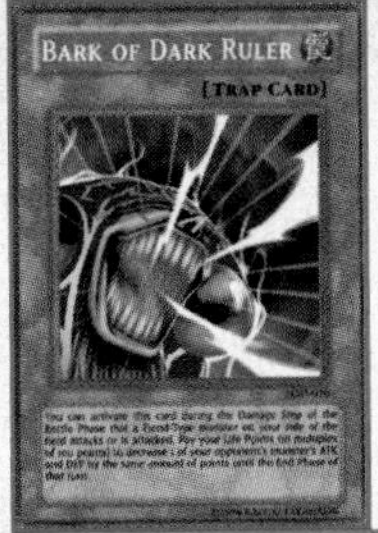

Card Type: Trap
Monster Type: —
Attribute: Trap
Level: —
ATK: —
DEF: —
Rarity: Common

Exchange your Life Points to weaken your opponent's monster. This effect is used during battle, so your opponent will definitely be surprised.

LOD-011 Fatal Abacus

Card Type: Trap
Monster Type: —
Attribute: Trap
Level: —
ATK: —
DEF: —
Rarity: Rare

This card deals damage for every monster on the field that goes to the Graveyard. Damage is dealt even when a monster is offered as a Tribute, so be careful.

LOD-012 Life Absorbing Machine

Card Type: Trap
Monster Type: —
Attribute: Trap
Level: —
ATK: —
DEF: —
Rarity: Common

Life Points that you paid as a cost will be partially restored. This card is perfect for Fiend-Type Decks because many cards require Life Points to be paid as a cost.

LOD-013 The Puppet Magic of Dark Ruler

Card Type: Spell
Monster Type: —
Attribute: Spell
Level: —
ATK: —
DEF: —
Rarity: Common

This Spell Card requires you to remove monsters on the field from play to Special Summon a monster from the Graveyard.

LOD-014 Soul Demolition

Card Type: Trap
Monster Type: —
Attribute: Trap
Level: —
ATK: —
DEF: —
Rarity: Common

This card removes a Monster Card in the Graveyard from play. If you chain this card to your opponent's card that resurrects monsters, such as "Monster Reborn," your opponent will waste his card.

LOD-015 Double Snare

Card Type: Spell
Monster Type: —
Attribute: Spell
Level: —
ATK: —
DEF: —
Rarity: Common

This card can destroy any card that negates the effects of Trap Cards. This includes "Jinzo!"

LOD-016 Freed the Matchless General

Card Type: Effect Monster
Monster Type: Warrior
Attribute: Earth
Level: 5
ATK: 2300
DEF: 1700
Rarity: Ultra Rare

Spell Cards do not work on this boss Warrior-Type monster. Also, you can draw a Level 4 or lower Warrior-Type monster during your Draw Phase!

LOD-017 Throwstone Unit

Card Type: Effect Monster
Monster Type: Warrior
Attribute: Earth
Level: 4
ATK: 900
DEF: 2000
Rarity: Common

Offer your own Warrior-Type monster as a Tribute to destroy your opponent's monster. Even if your opponent's monster has high ATK, if it has low DEF, then it's an excellent target.

LOD-018 Marauding Captain

Card Type: Effect Monster
Monster Type: Warrior
Attribute: Earth
Level: 3
ATK: 1200
DEF: 400
Rarity: Ultra Rare

Not only can you Special Summon a monster, but your opponent can't attack a different Warrior-Type monster. You can increase your offensive power in one turn!

LOD-019 Ryu Senshi

Card Type: Fusion/Effect Monster
Monster Type: Warrior
Attribute: Earth
Level: 6
ATK: 2000
DEF: 1200
Rarity: Super Rare

This Fusion Monster is created from Warrior-Type and Dragon-Type monsters. It's also strong against Spell Cards and can negate the effects of Trap Cards. If you can bring out this monster, it's very powerful!

LOD-020 Warrior Dai Grepher

Card Type: Normal Monster
Monster Type: Warrior
Attribute: Earth
Level: 4
ATK: 1700
DEF: 1600
Rarity: Common

This Fusion-Material Monster for "Ryu Senshi" is useful on its own with its 1700 ATK.

LOD-021 Mysterious Guard

Card Type: Effect Monster
Monster Type: Spellcaster
Attribute: Earth
Level: 3
ATK: 800
DEF: 1200
Rarity: Common

If you return one of your opponent's monsters on to the top of his or her Deck, then your opponent's next draw is a waste.

Legacy of Darkness

LOD-022 Frontier Wiseman

Card Type: Effect Monster
Monster Type: Spellcaster
Attribute: Earth
Level: 3
ATK: 1600
DEF: 800
Rarity: Common

As long as this card remains face-up on your side of the field, your Warrior-Type monsters are protected from Spell Cards. However, this card can be easily destroyed, so find ways to protect it.

LOD-023 Exiled Force

Card Type: Effect Monster
Monster Type: Warrior
Attribute: Earth
Level: 4
ATK: 1000
DEF: 1000
Rarity: Super Rare

When you offer this card as a Tribute, then you can destroy a powerful monster of a face-down Defense Position monster with no problem. You can almost treat this card like a Spell Card.

LOD-024 The Hunter with 7 Weapons

Card Type: Effect Monster
Monster Type: Warrior
Attribute: Earth
Level: 3
ATK: 1000
DEF: 600
Rarity: Common

During battle, one selected Monster Type will power up. If you build a Deck focused on one Monster Type, then this card's power is truly unleashed!

LOD-025 Shadow Tamer

Card Type: Effect Monster
Monster Type: Warrior
Attribute: Earth
Level: 3
ATK: 800
DEF: 700
Rarity: Rare

The Flip Effect works like "Change of Heart" on a Fiend-Type monster. Use this card to counteract Fiend-Type Decks!

LOD-026 Dragon Manipulator

Card Type: Effect Monster
Monster Type: Warrior
Attribute: Earth
Level: 3
ATK: 700
DEF: 800
Rarity: Common

The Flip Effect works like "Change of Heart" on a Dragon-Type monster. Take your opponent's powerful dragon!

LOD-027 The A. Forces

Card Type: Spell
Monster Type: –
Attribute: Spell
Level: –
ATK: –
DEF: –
Rarity: Rare

You only need a Warrior-Type monster and Spellcaster-Type monster to use this power up. Use "Marauding Captain" to Special Summon a Spellcaster-Type monster.

LOD-028 Reinforcement of the Army

Card Type: Spell
Monster Type: –
Attribute: Spell
Level: –
ATK: –
DEF: –
Rarity: Super Rare

You can draw a Level 4 or below Warrior-Type monster from your Deck. Aim for "Marauding Captain" or "Exiled Force!"

LOD-029 Array of Revealing Light

Card Type: Spell
Monster Type: –
Attribute: Spell
Level: –
ATK: –
DEF: –
Rarity: Rare

This Continuous Spell Card makes it so that a selected Monster Type cannot attack on the turn in which it was summoned. This card can protect against a final blow and is especially useful if your opponent uses a Deck with one Monster Type.

LOD-030 The Warrior Returning Alive

Card Type: Spell
Monster Type: –
Attribute: Spell
Level: –
ATK: –
DEF: –
Rarity: Rare

You can bring back one Warrior-Type monster in your Graveyard back to your hand. You can easily resurrect a destroyed key card. You can use "Exiled Force" again!

LOD-031 Ready for Intercepting

Card Type: Trap
Monster Type: –
Attribute: Trap
Level: –
ATK: –
DEF: –
Rarity: Common

Use this card on a Flip Effect Warrior-Type or Spellcaster-Type monster whose effect has already activated. You can use its effect again.

LOD-032 A Feint Plan

Card Type: Trap
Monster Type: –
Attribute: Trap
Level: –
ATK: –
DEF: –
Rarity: Common

Face-down Defense Position monsters cannot be attacked. Use this to protect your Flip Effect Monsters that you want to use on your turn.

LOD-033 Emergency Provisions

Card Type: Spell
Monster Type: –
Attribute: Spell
Level: –
ATK: –
DEF: –
Rarity: Common

Send Spell and Trap Cards on your field to the Graveyard to regain Life Points. This may help you in dire situations.

LOD-034 Tyrant Dragon

Card Type: Effect Monster
Monster Type: Dragon
Attribute: Fire
Level: 8
ATK: 2900
DEF: 2500
Rarity: Ultra Rare

Trap Cards do not work on this monster, so you don't have to worry about "Ring of Destruction." After attacking, if your opponent has another monster, you can attack again!

LOD-035 Spear Dragon

Card Type: Effect Monster
Monster Type: Dragon
Attribute: Wind
Level: 4
ATK: 1900
DEF: 0
Rarity: Super Rare

This monster has the the effect of "Fairy Meteor Crush." After attacking, it is switched to Defense Position, but you can certainly deal damage.

LOD-036 Spirit Ryu

Card Type: Effect Monster
Monster Type: Dragon
Attribute: Wind
Level: 4
ATK: 1000
DEF: 1000
Rarity: Common

Discarding a Dragon-Type monster from your hand to the Graveyard increases ATK and DEF of "Spirit Ryu" by a whopping 1000 points! If you have plenty of Dragon-Type monsters in your hand, then this is a very powerful effect!

LOD-037 The Dragon Dwelling in the Cave

Card Type: Normal Monster
Monster Type: Dragon
Attribute: Wind
Level: 4
ATK: 1300
DEF: 2000
Rarity: Common

Until now, there hasn't been a Dragon-Type monster that functions like a wall. Use this card in a Dragon-Type Deck to function as a wall and to offer as a Tribute.

LOD-038 Lizard Soldier

Card Type: Normal Monster
Monster Type: Dragon
Attribute: Wind
Level: 3
ATK: 1100
DEF: 800
Rarity: Common

This Normal Monster has low ATK and DEF. Only use this card if you need Dragon-Type monsters in your Deck.

LOD-039 Fiend Skull Dragon

Card Type: Fusion/Effect Monster
Monster Type: Dragon
Attribute: Wind
Level: 5
ATK: 2000
DEF: 1200
Rarity: Super Rare

This Fusion Monster is created from Dragon-Type and Fiend-Type monsters. It's also strong against Trap Cards and can negate the effects of Flip Effect Monsters.

LOD-040 Cave Dragon

Card Type: Effect Monster
Monster Type: Dragon
Attribute: Wind
Level: 4
ATK: 2000
DEF: 100
Rarity: Common

There are limits on how this monster can be summoned, but if you are able to successfully summon it, then it can be a powerful force in your Dragon-Type Deck.

LOD-041 Gray Wing

Card Type: Effect Monster
Monster Type: Dragon
Attribute: Wind
Level: 3
ATK: 1300
DEF: 700
Rarity: Common

If you discard one card from your hand, this monster can attack twice. Its ATK is 1300, so it's better than "Hayabusa Knight." Use it wisely!

LOD-042 Troop Dragon

Card Type: Effect Monster
Monster Type: Dragon
Attribute: Wind
Level: 2
ATK: 700
DEF: 800
Rarity: Common

When this card is destroyed, you can Special Summon another "Troop Dragon" from your Deck. Use this monster to offer as a Tribute.

LOD-043 The Dragon's Bead

Card Type: Trap
Monster Type: —
Attribute: Trap
Level: —
ATK: —
DEF: —
Rarity: Rare

You can protect Dragon-Type monsters from Trap Cards. Use this to stop "Ring of Destruction," "Magic Cylinder," or "Spellbinding Circle!"

LOD-044 A Wingbeat of Giant Dragon

Card Type: Spell
Monster Type: —
Attribute: Spell
Level: —
ATK: —
DEF: —
Rarity: Common

If you return a Level 5 or above Dragon-Type monster to your hand, this card works like "Heavy Storm." This card is useful if your opponent uses many Spell and Trap Cards.

LOD-045 Dragon's Gunfire

Card Type: Spell
Monster Type: —
Attribute: Spell
Level: —
ATK: —
DEF: —
Rarity: Common

This unique Spell Card has two different effects to use, depending on the situation. Even better, both effects are pretty useful!

Legacy of Darkness

LOD-046 Stamping Destruction

Card Type: Spell
Monster Type: —
Attribute: Spell
Level: —
ATK: —
DEF: —
Rarity: Common

Not only do you destroy a Spell or Trap Card, you get the added bonus of dealing damage to your opponent's Life Points. Definitely put this in your Dragon-Type Deck.

LOD-047 Super Rejuvenation

Card Type: Spell
Monster Type: —
Attribute: Spell
Level: —
ATK: —
DEF: —
Rarity: Common

You can draw as many cards as monsters you offered as a Tribute. This card is a must for Dragon-Type Decks that have effects which require offering monsters as a Tribute.

LOD-048 Dragon's Rage

Card Type: Trap
Monster Type: —
Attribute: Trap
Level: —
ATK: —
DEF: —
Rarity: Common

All your Dragon-Type monsters gain the effect of "Fairy Meteor Crush." You can definitely deal damage to your opponent's Lilfe Points.

LOD-049 Burst Breath

Card Type: Trap
Monster Type: —
Attribute: Trap
Level: —
ATK: —
DEF: —
Rarity: Common

If used correctly, you can destroy all your opponent's monsters by offering one Dragon-Type monster as a Tribute. This is a Trap Card, so you can use it even on your opponent's turn.

LOD-050 Luster Dragon

Card Type: Normal Monster
Monster Type: Dragon
Attribute: Wind
Level: 6
ATK: 2400
DEF: 1400
Rarity: Super Rare

By offering one monster as a Tribute, you can summon this excellent monster. Out of Level 5 or 6 Dragon-Type monsters, this one is the strongest!

LOD-051 Robotic Knight

Card Type: Normal Monster
Monster Type: Machine
Attribute: Fire
Level: 4
ATK: 1600
DEF: 1800
Rarity: Common

For a Level 4 FIRE monster, it is average, but you can't count on its 1600 ATK. If you use a Deck that relies on high DEF, then this card may be useful.

LOD-052 Wolf Axwielder

Card Type: Normal Monster
Monster Type: Beast-Warrior
Attribute: Earth
Level: 4
ATK: 1650
DEF: 1000
Rarity: Common

This monster has pretty high ATK for a Beast-Warrior-Type.

LOD-053 The Illusory Gentleman

Card Type: Normal Monster
Monster Type: Spellcaster
Attribute: Dark
Level: 4
ATK: 1500
DEF: 1600
Rarity: Common

This monster has excellent ATK and DEF for a Spellcaster-Type. However, it is only average for a Normal Monster.

LOD-054 Robolady

Card Type: Normal Monster
Monster Type: Machine
Attribute: Earth
Level: 3
ATK: 450
DEF: 900
Rarity: Common

This is the first Machine-Type monster that is a Fusion-Material Monster for a Fusion/Effect Monster. This card is used along with "Roboyarou."

LOD-055 Roboyarou

Card Type: Normal Monster
Monster Type: Machine
Attribute: Earth
Level: 3
ATK: 900
DEF: 450
Rarity: Common

This card fuses with "Robolady." If you look at its abilities alone, then it is pretty weak.

LOD-056 Fiber Jar

Card Type: Effect Monster
Monster Type: Plant
Attribute: Earth
Level: 3
ATK: 500
DEF: 500
Rarity: Ultra Rare

When you Flip this card, other than the Life Points and cards removed from play, the Duel restarts. However, you can summon a monster and attack immediately!

LOD-057 Serpentine Princess

Card Type: Effect Monster
Monster Type: Reptile
Attribute: Water
Level: 4
ATK: 1400
DEF: 2000
Rarity: Common

When this card is face-up and returns to your Deck, you can Special Summon a monster from your Deck. You can combo this card with "Fiber Jar."

LOD-058 Patrician of Darkness

Card Type: Effect Monster
Monster Type: Zombie
Attribute: Dark
Level: 5
ATK: 2000
DEF: 1400
Rarity: Common

As long as this monster remains face-up on the field, you can choose the target of your opponent's attacks. Your opponent now has to think harder before attacking!

LOD-059 Thunder Nyan Nyan

Card Type: Effect Monster
Monster Type: Thunder
Attribute: Light
Level: 4
ATK: 1900
DEF: 800
Rarity: Rare

If you play a LIGHT Deck, then you can Normal Summon this monster with 1900 ATK. If you have "Luminous Spark," this card's ATK is 2400!

LOD-060 Gradius' Option

Card Type: Effect Monster
Monster Type: Machine
Attribute: Light
Level: 3
ATK: ?
DEF: ?
Rarity: Common

This is a unique Monster Card that imiates "Gradius." If you power up the original, then "Gradius' Option" also becomes stronger!

LOD-061 Woodland Sprite

Card Type: Effect Monster
Monster Type: Plant
Attribute: Earth
Level: 3
ATK: 900
DEF: 400
Rarity: Common

If an Equip Spell Card equipped to this monster is sent to the Graveyard, then it deal Direct Damage to your opponent's Life Points. How about gathering Equip Spell Cards using "Collected Power?"

LOD-062 Airknight Parshath

Card Type: Effect Monster
Monster Type: Fairy
Attribute: Light
Level: 5
ATK: 1900
DEF: 1400
Rarity: Ultra Rare

Not only does it have the effect of "Fairy Meteor Crush," but when this monster deals damage to your opponent, then you can draw one card.

LOD-063 Twin-Headed Behemoth

Card Type: Effect Monster
Monster Type: Dragon
Attribute: Wind
Level: 3
ATK: 1500
DEF: 1200
Rarity: Super Rare

Even if this monster is destroyed, it resurrects as a monster with 1000 ATK and DEF. This monster can be useful as a wall or offered as a Tribute.

LOD-064 Maharaghi

Card Type: Spirit Monster
Monster Type: Rock
Attribute: Earth
Level: 4
ATK: 1200
DEF: 1700
Rarity: Common

Look at your card, and if you have no use for it, then place it at the bottom of your Deck. If you do need it, then place it back at the top of your Deck. You can choose which card you will draw on your next turn.

LOD-065 Inaba White Rabbit

Card Type: Spirit Monster
Monster Type: Beast
Attribute: Earth
Level: 2
ATK: 700
DEF: 500
Rarity: Common

You can attack your opponent's Life Points directly every turn. It has only 700 ATK, but it can be an excellent combo with "Robbin' Goblin."

LOD-066 Susa Soldier

Card Type: Spirit Monster
Monster Type: Thunder
Attribute: Earth
Level: 4
ATK: 2000
DEF: 1600
Rarity: Rare

Damage inflicted to your opponent's Life Points is halved, but this is a Level 4 monster with 2000 ATK. This is an excellent monster for wiping out your opponent's monsters!

LOD-067 Yamata Dragon

Card Type: Spirit Monster
Monster Type: Dragon
Attribute: Fire
Level: 7
ATK: 2600
DEF: 3100
Rarity: Ultra Rare

If this card deals damage to your opponent's Life Points, then you can draw cards until there are five cards in your hand. Though you need to offer monsters as a Tribute to summon "Yamata Dragon," you can quickly refill your hand!

Legacy of Darkness

LOD-068 Great Long Nose

Card Type: Spirit Monster
Monster Type: Beast-Warrior
Attribute: Dark
Level: 5
ATK: 1900
DEF: 1700
Rarity: Common

When this card deals damage to your opponent's Life Points, your opponent skips his or her Battle Phase. The fact that you need to offer one monster as a Tribute to summon "Great Long Nose" is a drawback.

LOD-069 Otohime

Card Type: Spirit Monster
Monster Type: Spellcaster
Attribute: Light
Level: 3
ATK: 0
DEF: 100
Rarity: Common

When this monster is summoned, you can change the Battle Position of one of your opponent's monsters. As long as the summon is not negated, this effect can definitely be used.

LOD-070 Hino-Kagu-Tsuchi

Card Type: Spirit Monster
Monster Type: Pyro
Attribute: Fire
Level: 8
ATK: 2800
DEF: 2900
Rarity: Ultra Rare

When this monster deals damage to your opponent's Life Points, your opponent has to discard his or her entire hand. If you next attack with "Yata-Garasu," you've established a perfect lockdown combo!

LOD-071 Asura Priest

Card Type: Spirit Monster
Monster Type: Fairy
Attribute: Light
Level: 4
ATK: 1700
DEF: 1200
Rarity: Super Rare

This monster can attack each of your opponent's monsters once. You can destroy wall monsters, such as "Scapegoat" and "Giant Rat," with this one card!

LOD-072 Fushi No Tori

Card Type: Spirit Monster
Monster Type: Winged Beast
Attribute: Fire
Level: 4
ATK: 1200
DEF: 0
Rarity: Common

You gain Life Points equal to the damage you inflicted to your opponent. Gaining 1200 Life Points at a time is not too shabby.

LOD-073 Super Robolady

Card Type: Fusion/Effect Monster
Monster Type: Machine
Attribute: Earth
Level: 6
ATK: 1200
DEF: 500
Rarity: Common

This Fusion Monster's ATK rises when it deals Direct Damage to your opponent. During your Main Phase, you can exchange this card with "Super Roboyarou."

LOD-074 Super Roboyarou

Card Type: Fusion/Effect Monster
Monster Type: Machine
Attribute: Earth
Level: 6
ATK: 1200
DEF: 500
Rarity: Common

During battle with your opponent's monsters, this Fusion Monster's ATK increases. During your Main Phase, you can exchange this card with "Super Robolady."

LOD-075 Fengsheng Mirror

Card Type: Spell
Monster Type: —
Attribute: Spell
Level: —
ATK: —
DEF: —
Rarity: Common

Discard your opponent's Spirit monster from his or her hand to the Graveyard. Since Spirit monsters cannot be Special Summoned, once it's in the Graveyard, it won't come back!

LOD-076 Spring of Rebirth

Card Type: Spell
Monster Type: —
Attribute: Spell
Level: —
ATK: —
DEF: —
Rarity: Common

When a monster on the field is returned to the hand, you gain Life Points. This card works perfectly with Spirit monsters.

LOD-077 Heart of Clear Water

Card Type: Spell
Monster Type: —
Attribute: Spell
Level: —
ATK: —
DEF: —
Rarity: Common

Monsters equipped with this card are practically invincible. How about equpping it on "Lord of D." or "White Magical Hat?"

LOD-078 A Legendary Ocean

Card Type: Spell
Monster Type: —
Attribute: Spell
Level: —
ATK: —
DEF: —
Rarity: Common

The Level of WATER monsters decrease by one, so you can Normal Summon "The Legendary Fisherman" without offering another monster as a Tribute.

LOD-079 Fusion Sword Murasame Blade

Card Type: Spell
Monster Type: —
Attribute: Spell
Level: —
ATK: —
DEF: —
Rarity: Rare

This Equip Spell Card is geared toward Warrior-Type monsters, and it cannot be destroyed by "Mystical Space Typhoon."

LOD-080 Smoke Grenade of the Thief

Card Type: Spell
Monster Type: —
Attribute: Spell
Level: —
ATK: —
DEF: —
Rarity: Common

This excellent hand destruction card allows you to select one card from your opponent's hand and discard it to the Graveyard. The problem is deciding when to activate this card.

LOD-081 Creature Swap

Card Type: Spell
Monster Type: —
Attribute: Spell
Level: —
ATK: —
DEF: —
Rarity: Ultra Rare

Each player selects one monster and exchanges it with the opponent. Select one monster that you don't need it and exchange it!

LOD-082 Spiritual Energy Settle Machine

Card Type: Spell
Monster Type: —
Attribute: Spell
Level: —
ATK: —
DEF: —
Rarity: Common

Spirit monsters no longer return to the hand. Even if you do not pay this card's cost, Spirit monsters summoned on the same turn do not return to the hand.

LOD-083 Second Coin Toss

Card Type: Spell
Monster Type: —
Attribute: Spell
Level: —
ATK: —
DEF: —
Rarity: Rare

Discard the result of the failed coin toss, and you can toss the coin again. The chances of success for "Time Wizard's" effect increases greatly!

LOD-084 Convulsion of Nature

Card Type: Spell
Monster Type: —
Attribute: Spell
Level: —
ATK: —
DEF: —
Rarity: Common

The Decks flip over, so both players can see what card is going to be drawn next. It's now very important to strategize in advance.

LOD-085 The Secret of the Bandit

Card Type: Spell
Monster Type: —
Attribute: Spell
Level: —
ATK: —
DEF: —
Rarity: Common

Any monster turns into "White Magical Hat" for one turn. This card is very effective if you use monsters that can deal Direct Damage to your opponent's Life Points or can attack multiple times!

LOD-086 After Genocide

Card Type: Spell
Monster Type: —
Attribute: Spell
Level: —
ATK: —
DEF: —
Rarity: Rare

No matter how high ATK or DEF is, all monsters in battle are destroyed. Attack with your weak monsters to destroy your opponent's powerful monsters!

LOD-087 Magic Reflector

Card Type: Spell
Monster Type: —
Attribute: Spell
Level: —
ATK: —
DEF: —
Rarity: Rare

If you remove a counter, you can protect a Continuous Spell Card or Equip Spell Card. This card helps preserve combos.

LOD-088 Blast with Chain

Card Type: Trap
Monster Type: —
Attribute: Trap
Level: —
ATK: —
DEF: —
Rarity: Rare

Instead of the power up effect, focus more on the effect when this card is destroyed. You can destroy any card on the field!

LOD-089 Disappear

Card Type: Trap
Monster Type: —
Attribute: Trap
Level: —
ATK: —
DEF: —
Rarity: Common

This Trap Card removes one card in your opponent's Graveyard from play. If you chain this card to "Monster Reborn," you can stop it!

LOD-090 Bubble Crash

Card Type: Trap
Monster Type: —
Attribute: Trap
Level: —
ATK: —
DEF: —
Rarity: Common

When your opponent has many cards in his or her hand and on the field, use this card. Your opponent will have a hard time choosing which five cards to keep.

LOD-091 Royal Oppression

Card Type: Trap
Monster Type: —
Attribute: Trap
Level: —
ATK: —
DEF: —
Rarity: Rare

Either player can pay the cost to negate a Special Summon. This card can stop cards that resurrect monsters, such as "Monster Reborn" and "Premature Burial."

Legacy of Darkness

LOD-092 Bottomless Trap Hole

Card Type: Trap
Monster Type: —
Attribute: Trap
Level: —
ATK: —
DEF: —
Rarity: Rare

The summoned monster is removed from play. Use this card so that dangerous monsters can't be resurrected.

LOD-093 Bad Reaction to Simochi

Card Type: Trap
Monster Type: —
Attribute: Trap
Level: —
ATK: —
DEF: —
Rarity: Common

Your opponent is trying to restore Life Points, but instead, he or she takes damage instead!

LOD-094 Ominous Fortunetelling

Card Type: Trap
Monster Type: —
Attribute: Trap
Level: —
ATK: —
DEF: —
Rarity: Common

If you use a different card's effect to see the cards in your opponent's hand, then you are guaranteed to deal damage! However, this card is useless if your opponent doesn't have any cards in his or her hand.

LOD-095 Spirit's Invitation

Card Type: Trap
Monster Type: —
Attribute: Trap
Level: —
ATK: —
DEF: —
Rarity: Common

When your Spirit monster returns to your hand, then your opponent's monster also returns to his or her hand. This helps limit the overall combined strength of your opponent's monsters.

LOD-096 Nutrient Z

Card Type: Trap
Monster Type: —
Attribute: Trap
Level: —
ATK: —
DEF: —
Rarity: Common

Turn a negative into a positive! Big damage to your Life Points can become your chance to restore a lot of your Life Points! If your opponent executes a last ditch attack to deal the finishing blow, this card can overcome it.

LOD-097 Drop Off

Card Type: Trap
Monster Type: —
Attribute: Trap
Level: —
ATK: —
DEF: —
Rarity: Super Rare

The card your opponent just drew is sent to the Graveyard immediately. If you know what card your opponent is drawing next, you can aim for your opponent's dangerous cards!

LOD-098 Fiend Comedian

Card Type: Trap
Monster Type: —
Attribute: Trap
Level: —
ATK: —
DEF: —
Rarity: Common

Whether you succeed in the coin toss or not, the effect is quite powerful. The question is: How are you going to use either effect to your advantage?

LOD-099 Last Turn

Card Type: Trap
Monster Type: —
Attribute: Trap
Level: —
ATK: —
DEF: —
Rarity: Ultra Rare

It's a one-on-one battle with the last one standing as the winner! You don't know which monster is in your opponent's Deck, so this card can be a huge gamble.

LOD-100 Injection Fairy Lily

Card Type: Effect Monster
Monster Type: Spellcaster
Attribute: Earth
Level: 3
ATK: 400
DEF: 1500
Rarity: Secret Rare

If you pay 2000 Life Points, "Injection Fairy Lily's" ATK becomes 3400. If you can attack your opponent directly, your opponent won't stand a chance. You may want to use cards that restore your Life Points when using this card!

LOD-000 Yata-Garasu

Card Type: Spirit Monster
Monster Type: Fiend
Attribute: Wind
Level: 2
ATK: 200
DEF: 100
Rarity: Secret Rare

Don't underestimate "Yata-Garasu" because it only has 200 ATK! If your opponent has no cards in his or her hand and no cards on the field, then you've established a perfect lock!

Pharaonic Guardian

PGD-001 Molten Behemoth

Card Type: Normal Monster
Monster Type: Pyro
Type: Fire
Level: 5
ATK: 1000
DEF: 2200
Rarity: Common

You need to offer another monster as a Tribute in order to Tribute Summon "Molten Behemoth." With 2200 DEF, this monster works excellent as a wall monster.

PGD-002 Shapesnatch

Card Type: Normal Monster
Monster Type: Machine
Type: Dark
Level: 5
ATK: 1200
DEF: 1700
Rarity: Common

This is a Level 5 Machine-Type monster. When including this card in your Deck, make sure to include other cards that will power it up, such as "Machine Conversion Factory."

PGD-003 Souleater

Card Type: Normal Monster
Monster Type: Fish
Type: Earth
Level: 4
ATK: 1200
DEF: 0
Rarity: Common

Though this is an EARTH monster, it is also a Fish-Type. This card is useful in both EARTH Decks and "Umi" Decks. Pay attention to the fact that its DEF is 0.

PGD-004 King Tiger Wanghu

Card Type: Effect Monster
Monster Type: Beast
Type: Earth
Level: 4
ATK: 1700
DEF: 1000
Rarity: Rare

Most monsters with 1400 ATK or below will be unable to be summoned. When including this card in your Deck, be careful of the ATK of the other monsters you put in your Deck.

PGD-005 Birdface

Card Type: Effect Monster
Monster Type: Winged Beast
Type: Wind
Level: 4
ATK: 1600
DEF: 1600
Rarity: Common

Definitely include this card in your Deck if you play a "Harpie Lady" Deck.

PGD-006 Kryuel

Card Type: Effect Monster
Monster Type: Fiend
Type: Dark
Level: 4
ATK: 1000
DEF: 1700
Rarity: Common

When playing with this card, include "Second Coin Toss" in your Deck to increase your chances for success.

PGD-007 Arsenal Bug

Card Type: Effect Monster
Monster Type: Insect
Type: Earth
Level: 3
ATK: 2000
DEF: 2000
Rarity: Common

If all other monsters are Insect-Type, then you can use this card as a 2000 ATK monster without a hitch. It will be your main force in an Insect-Type Deck!

PGD-008 Maiden of the Aqua

Card Type: Effect Monster
Monster Type: Aqua
Type: Water
Level: 4
ATK: 700
DEF: 2000
Rarity: Common

This monster transform the field into the "Umi" Field. Level 4 with a high 2000 DEF, think of using this card when creating an "Umi" Deck.

PGD-009 Jowls of Dark Demise

Card Type: Effect Monster
Monster Type: Fiend
Type: Water
Level: 2
ATK: 200
DEF: 100
Rarity: Rare

You can deal Direct Damage to your opponent's Life Points using your opponent's monster that you gained control of. If you combo this card with "Book of Taiyou," it is extremely powerful!

PGD-010 Timeater

Card Type: Effect Monster
Monster Type: Machine
Type: Dark
Level: 6
ATK: 1900
DEF: 1700
Rarity: Common

If you destroy your opponent's monster in battle, your opponent has to skip Main Phase 1. Increase its low ATK using Equip Spell Cards.

PGD-011 Mucus Yolk

Card Type: Effect Monster
Monster Type: Aqua
Type: Dark
Level: 3
ATK: 0
DEF: 100
Rarity: Common

This card can attack your opponent's Life Points directly, but it has 0 ATK. Therefore, if you power it up with cards like "Axe of Despair," then it will power up to untold heights!

PGD-012 Servant of Catabolism

Card Type: Effect Monster
Monster Type: Aqua
Type: Light
Level: 3
ATK: 700
DEF: 500
Rarity: Common

Out of the monsters that can attack your opponent's Life Points directly, this monster has high ATK. This card can replace "Jinzo #7" in a Direct Damage Deck.

Pharaonic Guardian

PGD-013 Moisture Creature

Card Type: Effect Monster
Monster Type: Fairy
Type: Light
Level: 9
ATK: 2800
DEF: 2900
Rarity: Rare

If you offer three monsters as a Tribute to Tribute Summon "Moisture Creature," then this card also works like a "Harpie Feather Duster." You can attack without having to worry about your opponent's Spell and Trap Cards.

PGD-014 Gora Turtle

Card Type: Effect Monster
Monster Type: Aqua
Type: Water
Level: 3
ATK: 1100
DEF: 1100
Rarity: Rare

As long as this card is face-up on the field, monsters with 1900 ATK or above cannot attack. It's a good idea to Special Summon this monster using "Mother Grizzly's" effect.

PGD-015 Sasuke Samurai

Card Type: Effect Monster
Monster Type: Warrior
Type: Wind
Level: 2
ATK: 500
DEF: 800
Rarity: Super Rare

You can destroy face-down Defense Position monsters without worry. You can destroy cards like "Cyber Jar" without having to worry about its effect activating.

PGD-016 Poison Mummy

Card Type: Effect Monster
Monster Type: Zombie
Type: Earth
Level: 4
ATK: 1000
DEF: 1800
Rarity: Common

This Zombie-Type monster's Flip Effect deals 500 points of damage to your opponent's Life Points. Its 1800 DEF is also pretty high.

PGD-017 Dark Dust Spirit

Card Type: Spirit Monster
Monster Type: Zombie
Type: Earth
Level: 6
ATK: 2200
DEF: 1800
Rarity: Common

When this card is summoned, all face-up monsters are destroyed. Remember that since it's a Spirit monster, it returns to your hand at the End Phase.

PGD-018 Royal Keeper

Card Type: Effect Monster
Monster Type: Zombie
Type: Earth
Level: 4
ATK: 1600
DEF: 1700
Rarity: Common

Once per turn, this monster can flip face-down in Defense Position. This card is prefect for Zombie-Type Decks that power up from Flip Effects.

PGD-019 Wandering Mummy

Card Type: Effect Monster
Monster Type: Zombie
Type: Earth
Level: 4
ATK: 1500
DEF: 1500
Rarity: Rare

If you use its effect, you can change the order of your face-down Defense Position monsters and Set them. Use this effect to confuse your opponent.

PGD-020 Great Dezard

Card Type: Effect Monster
Monster Type: Spellcaster
Type: Dark
Level: 6
ATK: 1900
DEF: 2300
Rarity: Ultra Rare

This monster gains abilities when it destroys monsters in battle. This is also a key card to Special Summon "Fushioh Richie."

PGD-021 Swarm of Scarabs

Card Type: Effect Monster
Monster Type: Insect
Type: Dark
Level: 3
ATK: 500
DEF: 1000
Rarity: Common

Once per turn, this monster can flip face-down in Defense Position. Every time this monster is Flip Summoned, you can destroy one of your opponent's monsters.

PGD-022 Swarm of Locusts

Card Type: Effect Monster
Monster Type: Insect
Type: Dark
Level: 3
ATK: 1000
DEF: 500
Rarity: Common

Once per turn, this monster can flip face-down in Defense Position. While "Swarm of Scarabs" destroys Monster Cards, "Swarm of Locusts" destroys Spell and Trap Cards.

PGD-023 Giant Axe Mummy

Card Type: Effect Monster
Monster Type: Zombie
Type: Earth
Level: 5
ATK: 1700
DEF: 2000
Rarity: Common

When this monster is attacked while in face-down Defense Position, as long as your opponent's monster is less than 2000, then the attacking Monster is destroyed.

PGD-024 8-Claws Scorpion

Card Type: Effect Monster
Monster Type: Insect
Type: Dark
Level: 2
ATK: 300
DEF: 200
Rarity: Common

When this monster attacks a face-down Defense Position monster, then its ATK rises to 2400! Equip this card with "Fairy Meteor Crush" to deal painful damage to your opponent's Life Points!

PGD-025 Guardian Sphinx

Card Type: Effect Monster
Monster Type: Rock
Type: Earth
Level: 5
ATK: 1700
DEF: 2400
Rarity: Ultra Rare

When this card is Flip Summoned, all of your opponent's monsters on the field return to his or her hand. This is usually a powerful effect, but be careful of cards like "Sasuke Samurai."

PGD-026 Pyramid Turtle

Card Type: Effect Monster
Monster Type: Zombie
Type: Earth
Level: 4
ATK: 1200
DEF: 1400
Rarity: Rare

When this monster is destroyed in battle, you can Special Summon a Zombie-Type monster with 2000 DEF or below from your Deck.

PGD-027 Dice Jar

Card Type: Effect Monster
Monster Type: Rock
Type: Light
Level: 3
ATK: 200
DEF: 300
Rarity: Common

Even if you lose the dice roll, if you use "Barrel Behind the Door," you can deal damage to your opponent instead.

PGD-028 Dark Scorpion Burglars

Card Type: Effect Monster
Monster Type: Warrior
Type: Dark
Level: 4
ATK: 1000
DEF: 1000
Rarity: Common

When "Dark Scorpion Burglars" deal Battle Damage to your opponent's Life Points, your opponent has to discard one Spell Card in his or her Deck into the Graveyard. Since this card's ATK is low, use Spell Cards to power it up before attacking.

PGD-029 Don Zaloog

Card Type: Effect Monster
Monster Type: Warrior
Type: Dark
Level: 4
ATK: 1400
DEF: 1500
Rarity: Ultra Rare

"Don Zaloog" is the leader of the "Dark Scorpion Burglars." When he deals Battle Damage to your opponent's Life Points, two different effects can activate. Choose the proper effect depending on the situation of the Duel.

PGD-030 Des Lacooda

Card Type: Effect Monster
Monster Type: Zombie
Type: Earth
Level: 3
ATK: 500
DEF: 600
Rarity: Common

You can draw one card when this card is Flip Summoned. When this card flips face-up when it is attacked by your opponent's monster, it doesn't count as a Flip Summon, so be careful.

PGD-031 Fushioh Richie

Card Type: Effect Monster
Monster Type: Zombie
Type: Dark
Level: 7
ATK: 2600
DEF: 2900
Rarity: Ultra Rare

Once per turn, you can switch this card to face-down Defense Position. However, every time it is flipped face-up, you can Special Summon a Zombie-Type monster from your Graveyard.

PGD-032 Cobraman Sakuzy

Card Type: Effect Monster
Monster Type: Reptile
Type: Earth
Level: 3
ATK: 800
DEF: 1400
Rarity: Common

When this card flips, you can look at all the Spell and Trap Cards your opponent has Set. After checking, destroy the ones you don't like using cards like "Mystical Space Typhoon."

PGD-033 Book of Life

Card Type: Spell
Monster Type: —
Type: Spell
Level: —
ATK: —
DEF: —
Rarity: Super Rare

Only Zombie-Type monsters in your Graveyard can be Special Summoned. If your opponent has no Monster Cards in his or her Graveyard, then you cannot use this card.

PGD-034 Book of Taiyou

Card Type: Spell
Monster Type: —
Type: Spell
Level: —
ATK: —
DEF: —
Rarity: Common

This Spell Card switches a face-down Defense Position monster to face-up Attack Position. If you use this on a face-down Flip Effect Monster, you can activate its Flip Effect.

PGD-035 Book of Moon

Card Type: Spell
Monster Type: —
Type: Spell
Level: —
ATK: —
DEF: —
Rarity: Rare

This Spell Card switches a face-up Attack Position monster to face-down Defense Position. Use this card so that you use the effects of Flip Effect Monsters again. Also notice that this is a Quick-Play Spell Card.

PGD-036 Mirage of Nightmare

Card Type: Spell
Monster Type: —
Type: Spell
Level: —
ATK: —
DEF: —
Rarity: Super Rare

You draw on your opponent's turn and discard on your own turn. If you destroy this card during your opponent's turn, then you do not have to discard.

PGD-037 Secret Pass to the Treasures

Card Type: Spell
Monster Type: —
Type: Spell
Level: —
ATK: —
DEF: —
Rarity: Common

This Spell Card allows your monster with 1000 ATK or below to attack your opponent's Life Points directly. Use this card on "Dark Scorpion Burglars" or "Decayed Commander."

PGD-038 Call of the Mummy

Card Type: Spell
Monster Type: —
Type: Spell
Level: —
ATK: —
DEF: —
Rarity: Common

You can Special Summon a Zombie-Type monster, regardless of its Level. You can use this to unleash a big attack on your first turn or rebuild your army if it has been destroyed.

PGD-039 Timidity

Card Type: Spell
Monster Type: —
Type: Spell
Level: —
ATK: —
DEF: —
Rarity: Common

Set Spell and Trap Cards can no longer be destroyed. Use this if there are Spell and Trap Cards that you definitely have to protect.

PGD-040 Pyramid Energy

Card Type: Spell
Monster Type: —
Type: Spell
Level: —
ATK: —
DEF: —
Rarity: Common

You can either increase the ATK of all the monsters on your field, or you can increase its DEF. Notice that it's a Quick-Play Spell Card, so you can use it even on your opponent's turn.

PGD-041 Tutan Mask

Card Type: Trap
Monster Type: —
Type: Trap
Level: —
ATK: —
DEF: —
Rarity: Common

This Counter Trap Card works against Spell and Trap Cards that target Zombie-Type monsters. If you only play with Zombie-Type monsters in your Deck, this card is an excellent addition.

PGD-042 Ordeal of a Traveler

Card Type: Trap
Monster Type: —
Type: Trap
Level: —
ATK: —
DEF: —
Rarity: Common

It's unfortunate that your opponent gets to see a card in your hand, but this powerful Trap Card can force your opponent's monster back into his or her hand. If possible, use this card when you have many cards in your hand.

PGD-043 Bottomless Shifting Sand

Card Type: Trap
Monster Type: —
Type: Trap
Level: —
ATK: —
DEF: —
Rarity: Common

This Continuous Trap Card destroys the monster with the highest ATK on the field. While this card is active, be careful not to use too many cards in your hand.

PGD-044 Curse of Royal

Card Type: Trap
Monster Type: —
Type: Trap
Level: —
ATK: —
DEF: —
Rarity: Rare

You can protect your Spell and Trap Cards from "Mystical Space Typhoon" and "Dust Tornado." However, it can't stop "Harpie's Feather Duster" or "Heavy Storm," so be careful.

PGD-045 Needle Ceiling

Card Type: Trap
Monster Type: —
Type: Trap
Level: —
ATK: —
DEF: —
Rarity: Common

There are only few instances when there are four or more monsters on the field, but if you use "Scapegoat," then you can activate "Needle Ceiling" easily.

PGD-046 Statue of the Wicked

Card Type: Trap
Monster Type: —
Type: Trap
Level: —
ATK: —
DEF: —
Rarity: Super Rare

When this card has been Set and then destroyed, you can Special Summon a token. Combo this card with "Magical Hats."

PGD-047 Dark Coffin

Card Type: Trap
Monster Type: —
Type: Trap
Level: —
ATK: —
DEF: —
Rarity: Common

The effect of this Trap Card activates when this card is sent from the field to the Graveyard. You can activate "Heavy Storm" on your own in order to activate the effect.

PGD-048 Needle Wall

Card Type: Trap
Monster Type: —
Type: Trap
Level: —
ATK: —
DEF: —
Rarity: Common

This is pretty powerful because you may be able destroy your opponent's monster with no risk. Also, since this is a Continuous Trap Card, this card remains on the field.

PGD-049 Trap Dustshoot

Card Type: Trap
Monster Type: —
Type: Trap
Level: —
ATK: —
DEF: —
Rarity: Common

This card is similar to "The Forceful Sentry" but in Trap Card form. Use this card after your opponent used "Witch of the Black Forest" or "Sangan" to search his or her Deck for a Monster Card.

PGD-050 Pyro Clock of Destiny

Card Type: Trap
Monster Type: —
Type: Trap
Level: —
ATK: —
DEF: —
Rarity: Common

You can move the turn count forward of one card on the field by one turn. Think of different combos that take advantage of this.

PGD-051 Reckless Greed

Card Type: Trap
Monster Type: —
Type: Trap
Level: —
ATK: —
DEF: —
Rarity: Rare

You lose two Draw Phases, but you can draw two cards now. This is ideal in combo Decks that require many cards.

PGD-052 Pharaoh's Treasure

Card Type: Trap
Monster Type: —
Type: Trap
Level: —
ATK: —
DEF: —
Rarity: Rare

You can choose a card from your own Graveyard and add it to your hand. Since you choose any card you desire (except this "Pharaoh's Treasure" card), look at the situation of the Duel and decide.

PGD-053 Master Kyonshee

Card Type: Normal Monster
Monster Type: Zombie
Type: Earth
Level: 4
ATK: 1750
DEF: 1000
Rarity: Common

"Master Kyonshee" has very high ATK for a Level 4 Zombie-Type monster. This card will be a featured card in a Zombie-Type Deck.

PGD-054 Kabazauls

Card Type: Normal Monster
Monster Type: Dinosaur
Type: Water
Level: 4
ATK: 1700
DEF: 1500
Rarity: Common

This unique monster is both WATER and Dinosaur-Type. With its 1700 ATK, it can be decently useful in battle.

PGD-055 Inpachi

Card Type: Normal Monster
Monster Type: Machine
Type: Earth
Level: 4
ATK: 1600
DEF: 1900
Rarity: Common

For a monster that doesn't require another monster to be offered as a Tribute, 1900 DEF is not bad. This is a good card if you want to increase the defensive strength of your Deck.

PGD-056 Dark Jeroid

Card Type: Effect Monster
Monster Type: Fiend
Type: Dark
Level: 4
ATK: 1200
DEF: 1500
Rarity: Rare

When this monster is summoned, decrease the ATK of one of the monsters on the field by 800. Make sure you don't summon this monster when there are no other monsters on the field.

PGD-057 Newdoria

Card Type: Effect Monster
Monster Type: Fiend
Type: Dark
Level: 4
ATK: 1200
DEF: 800
Rarity: Rare

This is one of the Effect Monsters that Marik uses. When this monster is sent to the Graveyard in battle, then it will drag another monster down with it.

PGD-058 Helpoemer

Card Type: Effect Monster
Monster Type: Fiend
Type: Dark
Level: 5
ATK: 2000
DEF: 1400
Rarity: Ultra Rare

One of Marik's cards, when this card is sent to the Graveyard in battle, its effect destroys the cards in your opponent's hand.

PGD-059 Gravekeeper's Spy

Card Type: Effect Monster
Monster Type: Spellcaster
Type: Dark
Level: 4
ATK: 1200
DEF: 2000
Rarity: Common

You can Special Summon a monster from your Deck with 1500 ATK or below that have "Gravekeeper's" in its card name. "Gravekeeper's Assailant" is recommended.

PGD-060 Gravekeeper's Curse

Card Type: Effect Monster
Monster Type: Spellcaster
Type: Dark
Level: 3
ATK: 800
DEF: 800
Rarity: Common

When this monster is summoned, it deals 500 points of damage to your opponent's Life Points. Special Summon this monster using "Gravekeeper's Spy," and use it to finish off your opponent's final Life Points.

Pharaonic Guardian

PGD-061 Gravekeeper's Guard

Card Type: Effect Monster
Monster Type: Spellcaster
Type: Dark
Level: 4
ATK: 1000
DEF: 1900
Rarity: Common

When this card flips, one of your opponent's monsters on the field is sent back to the hand. With 1900 DEF, it's no slouch in the defense department.

PGD-062 Gravekeeper's Spear Soldier

Card Type: Effect Monster
Monster Type: Spellcaster
Type: Dark
Level: 4
ATK: 1500
DEF: 1000
Rarity: Common

This Gravekeeper has the ability of "Fairy Meteor Crush." Since it has 1500 ATK, you can Special Summon this monster using "Gravekeeper's Spy."

PGD-063 Gravekeeper's Vassal

Card Type: Effect Monster
Monster Type: Spellcaster
Type: Dark
Level: 3
ATK: 700
DEF: 500
Rarity: Common

This card's Battle Damage is treated as Effect Damage. You can combo this card with "Dark Room on Nightmare."

PGD-064 Gravekeeper's Watcher

Card Type: Effect Monster
Monster Type: Spellcaster
Type: Dark
Level: 4
ATK: 1000
DEF: 1000
Rarity: Rare

When your opponent activates "Graceful Charity" or "Card Destruction," if this card is in your hand, you can discard it to your Graveyard to stop your opponent's effect.

PGD-065 Gravekeeper's Chief

Card Type: Effect Monster
Monster Type: Spellcaster
Type: Dark
Level: 5
ATK: 1900
DEF: 1200
Rarity: Super Rare

Only when the Tribute Summon is successful can you Special Summon a Gravekeeper monster in your Graveyard to the field. The number of monsters on your field doesn't decrease, so it's great!

PGD-066 Gravekeeper's Cannonholder

Card Type: Effect Monster
Monster Type: Spellcaster
Type: Dark
Level: 4
ATK: 1400
DEF: 1200
Rarity: Common

This is the Gravekeeper version of "Cannon Soldier." Its effect deals 700 points of damage, which is higher than "Cannon Soldier."

PGD-067 Gravekeeper's Assailant

Card Type: Effect Monster
Monster Type: Spellcaster
Type: Dark
Level: 4
ATK: 1500
DEF: 1500
Rarity: Common

If "Necrovalley" is on the field, then you can change the Battle Position of your opponent's monsters. You can even defeat "Jinzo!"

PGD-068 A Man with Wdjat

Card Type: Effect Monster
Monster Type: Spellcaster
Type: Dark
Level: 4
ATK: 1600
DEF: 1600
Rarity: Common

You can check your opponent's face-down Defense Position monster or Set Spell and Trap Cards. This effect activates even during your Standby Phase.

PGD-069 Mystical Knight of Jackal

Card Type: Effect Monster
Monster Type: Beast-Warrior
Type: Light
Level: 7
ATK: 2700
DEF: 1200
Rarity: Ultra Rare

This card's effect lets you place the destroyed monster on top of your opponent's Deck. In other words, your opponent can't draw new cards in the Deck. Also, 2700 ATK is very high.

PGD-070 A Cat of Ill Omen

Card Type: Effect Monster
Monster Type: Beast
Type: Dark
Level: 2
ATK: 500
DEF: 300
Rarity: Common

This monster's Flip Effect lets you search your Deck for a Trap Card. If you have "Necrovalley" on the field, then the Trap Card is added directly to your hand.

PGD-071 Yomi Ship

Card Type: Effect Monster
Monster Type: Aqua
Type: Water
Level: 3
ATK: 800
DEF: 1400
Rarity: Common

Unlike "Newdoria," you cannot chose which card to destroy. However, this card's DEF is greater. Your opponent now has to really think about how to attack.

PGD-072 Winged Sage Falcos

Card Type: Effect Monster
Monster Type: Winged Beast
Type: Wind
Level: 4
ATK: 1700
DEF: 1200
Rarity: Rare

This card has the same ability as "Mystical Knight of Jackal." However, you can summon this monster without offering another monster as a Tribute. With 1700 ATK, this card is an excellent choice to put into your Deck.

PGD-073 An Owl of Luck

Card Type: Effect Monster
Monster Type: Winged Beast
Type: Wind
Level: 2
ATK: 300
DEF: 500
Rarity: Common

This card lets you search your Deck for a Field Spell Card. Unlike "Terraforming," it's great that the effect won't be countered.

PGD-074 Charm of Shabti

Card Type: Effect Monster
Monster Type: Rock
Type: Earth
Level: 1
ATK: 100
DEF: 100
Rarity: Common

When this card is discarded to the Graveyard from the hand, then Gravekeeper monsters receive 0 Battle Damage. Use this when you don't want to lose the monsters on your field.

PGD-075 Cobra Jar

Card Type: Effect Monster
Monster Type: Reptile
Type: Earth
Level: 2
ATK: 600
DEF: 300
Rarity: Common

The Flip Effect creates a token, and when the token is destroyed in battle, your opponent receives 500 points of damage to his or her Life Points. This helps you stall for time.

PGD-076 Spirit Reaper

Card Type: Effect Monster
Monster Type: Zombie
Type: Dark
Level: 3
ATK: 300
DEF: 200
Rarity: Rare

This monster cannot be destroyed in battle. If you Set this monster in Defense Position, then it forms a powerful wall. Also, forcing your opponent to discard cards is a great effect.

PGD-077 Nightmare Horse

Card Type: Effect Monster
Monster Type: Zombie
Type: Dark
Level: 2
ATK: 500
DEF: 400
Rarity: Common

This opponent can attack your opponent's Life Points directly. It can also fuse with "Spirit Reaper." You should also take into account that it is a Zombie-Type monster.

PGD-078 Reaper on the Nightmare

Card Type: Fusion/Effect
Monster Type: Zombie
Type: Dark
Level: 5
ATK: 800
DEF: 600
Rarity: Super Rare

This monster combines the effects of the two Fusion-Material Monsters used to create this monster, but be careful that this card can be destroyed by being the target of an Effect Monster's effect or Spell and Trap Cards.

PGD-079 Dark Designator

Card Type: Spell
Monster Type: —
Type: Spell
Level: —
ATK: —
DEF: —
Rarity: Rare

If you use this card on its own, then it only benefits your opponent. However, if you combo this card with "Card Destruction" or "Confiscation," then it becomes useful.

PGD-080 Card Shuffle

Card Type: Spell
Monster Type: —
Type: Spell
Level: —
ATK: —
DEF: —
Rarity: Common

You can shuffle your opponent's Deck or your own Deck. Use this card when your opponent is about to draw "Pharaoh's Treasure" on his or her next turn.

PGD-081 Reasoning

Card Type: Spell
Monster Type: —
Type: Spell
Level: —
ATK: —
DEF: —
Rarity: Common

If you're successful, then you can Special Summon a powerful monster instantly. When using this card, make sure that your opponent doesn't know the structure of your Deck.

PGD-082 Dark Room of Nightmare

Card Type: Spell
Monster Type: —
Type: Spell
Level: —
ATK: —
DEF: —
Rarity: Super Rare

When you inflict damage to your opponent's Life Points which isn't Battle Damage, then you can deal an additional 300 points of damage. It's a good idea to combo this card with "Dark Snake Syndrome."

PGD-083 Different Dimension Capsule

Card Type: Spell
Monster Type: —
Type: Spell
Level: —
ATK: —
DEF: —
Rarity: Common

Though there is a time lag, this powerful Spell Card lets you search your Deck for any card. Make sure you don't let this card be destroyed until the effect ends.

PGD-084 Necrovalley

Card Type: Spell
Monster Type: —
Type: Spell
Level: —
ATK: —
DEF: —
Rarity: Super Rare

This Field Spell Card powers up Gravekeepers. This puts a lid on the Graveyards. You can stop your opponent's "Monster Reborn!"

Pharaonic Guardian

PGD-085 Buster Rancher

- **Card Type:** Spell
- **Monster Type:** —
- **Type:** Spell
- **Level:** —
- **ATK:** —
- **DEF:** —
- **Rarity:** Common

This Equip Spell Card greatly powers up weak monsters. Even if a monster only has 600 ATK, it can destroy "Blue-Eyes White Dragon!"

PGD-086 Hieroglyph Lithograph

- **Card Type:** Spell
- **Monster Type:** —
- **Type:** Spell
- **Level:** —
- **ATK:** —
- **DEF:** —
- **Rarity:** Common

The limit of the number of cards in your hand becomes seven. If you are planning to win by having all five "Exodia" cards in your hand, then it helps to put several copies of "Hieroglyph Lithograph" in your Deck to increase your chances of drawing this card.

PGD-087 Dark Snake Syndrome

- **Card Type:** Spell
- **Monster Type:** —
- **Type:** Spell
- **Level:** —
- **ATK:** —
- **DEF:** —
- **Rarity:** Common

If you make a mistake in damage calculation, then you and your opponent will end the Duel in a draw. Activate this card when you have more Life Points than your opponent.

PGD-088 Terraforming

- **Card Type:** Spell
- **Monster Type:** —
- **Type:** Spell
- **Level:** —
- **ATK:** —
- **DEF:** —
- **Rarity:** Common

You can add a Field Spell Card from your Deck into your hand. Other than a Gravekeeper Deck, this card is also useful in Decks that have monsters of a particular attribute.

PGD-089 Banner of Courage

- **Card Type:** Spell
- **Monster Type:** —
- **Type:** Spell
- **Level:** —
- **ATK:** —
- **DEF:** —
- **Rarity:** Common

This Continuous Spell Card raises the base ATK of your monsters. Be careful—the increase in ATK is only applied during your own Battle Phase.

PGD-090 Metamorphosis

- **Card Type:** Spell
- **Monster Type:** —
- **Type:** Spell
- **Level:** —
- **ATK:** —
- **DEF:** —
- **Rarity:** Common

You can Special Summon a Fusion Monster without using "Polymerization." It's like Ritual Summoning a Ritual Monster, except it's a Fusion Monster.

PGD-091 Royal Tribute

- **Card Type:** Spell
- **Monster Type:** —
- **Type:** Spell
- **Level:** —
- **ATK:** —
- **DEF:** —
- **Rarity:** Common

This hand destruction card can only be activated when you have "Necrovalley" on the field. If you can activate this card on your first turn, then it is extremely powerful.

PGD-092 Reversal Quiz

- **Card Type:** Spell
- **Monster Type:** —
- **Type:** Spell
- **Level:** —
- **ATK:** —
- **DEF:** —
- **Rarity:** Common

This Spell Card exchanges your Life Points with your opponent's Life Points. If you use this card after the effect of "A Cat of Ill Omen" or "An Owl of Luck" resolves, then you can't miss!

PGD-093 Coffin Seller

- **Card Type:** Trap
- **Monster Type:** —
- **Type:** Trap
- **Level:** —
- **ATK:** —
- **DEF:** —
- **Rarity:** Rare

This card activates irregardless of whether your opponent's monster goes to the Graveyard from the field, hand, or Deck. Your Monster Removal Spell Cards also function as Direct Damage Spell Cards!

PGD-094 Curse of Aging

- **Card Type:** Trap
- **Monster Type:** —
- **Type:** Trap
- **Level:** —
- **ATK:** —
- **DEF:** —
- **Rarity:** Common

All your opponent's monsters' ATK and DEF decrease by 500. A good strategy is to activate this card during your turn to weaken your opponent's monsters and then attack.

PGD-095 Barrel Behind the Door

- **Card Type:** Trap
- **Monster Type:** —
- **Type:** Trap
- **Level:** —
- **ATK:** —
- **DEF:** —
- **Rarity:** Super Rare

This Counter Trap Card lets you direct the damage you would have received back to your opponent. Combo this card with "Ring of Destruction" for extreme punishment.

PGD-096 Raigeki Break

- **Card Type:** Trap
- **Monster Type:** —
- **Type:** Trap
- **Level:** —
- **ATK:** —
- **DEF:** —
- **Rarity:** Common

Discard one card from your hand to destroy one card on the field. Though discarding a card is a big cost, it's excellent that you can destroy any card.

PGD-097 Narrow Pass

Card Type: Trap
Monster Type: —
Type: Trap
Level: —
ATK: —
DEF: —
Rarity: Common

Both players can only have a maximum of two monsters each on the field. This prevents three monsters offered as a Tribute to summon "Moisture Creature."

PGD-098 Disturbance Strategy

Card Type: Trap
Monster Type: —
Type: Trap
Level: —
ATK: —
DEF: —
Rarity: Common

Your opponent puts all the cards in his or her hand back into the Deck, shuffles the Deck, and draws the same number of cards. Use this card after your opponent searched his or her Deck for a specific card.

PGD-099 Trap of Board Eraser

Card Type: Trap
Monster Type: —
Type: Trap
Level: —
ATK: —
DEF: —
Rarity: Super Rare

This Trap Card stops the damage you would have received and destroys your opponent's hand in return. When constructing a Hand Destruction Deck, think about including this card.

PGD-100 Rite of Spirit

Card Type: Trap
Monster Type: —
Type: Trap
Level: —
ATK: —
DEF: —
Rarity: Common

This card is similar to "Monster Reborn," except this is specifically for Gravekeepers. You can activate this card even if you have "Necrovalley" so it's useful when you are running low on monsters you need to offer as a Tribute to Tribute Summon a stronger monster.

PGD-101 Non Aggression Area

Card Type: Trap
Monster Type: —
Type: Trap
Level: —
ATK: —
DEF: —
Rarity: Common

By discarding one card from your hand, you can stop your opponent's Normal Summon or Special Summon. You can slow down your opponent's build-up of his or her monster army.

PGD-102 D. Tribe

Card Type: Trap
Monster Type: —
Type: Trap
Level: —
ATK: —
DEF: —
Rarity: Common

All your monsters become Dragon-Type. If your Deck requires many Dragon-Type monsters, include several copies of this card in your Deck.

PGD-103 Byser Shock

Card Type: Effect Monster
Monster Type: Fiend
Type: Dark
Level: 5
ATK: 800
DEF: 600
Rarity: Ultra Rare

When this monster is summoned, then all Set cards on the field are returned to the hand. Summon this monster when your opponent has many Spell and Trap Cards on his or her field.

PGD-104 Question

Card Type: Spell
Monster Type: —
Type: Spell
Level: —
ATK: —
DEF: —
Rarity: Ultra Rare

Your opponent has to guess the Monster Cards in your Graveyard. Before activating this card, use cards like "Graceful Charity" to secretly discard Monster Cards to your Graveyard.

PGD-105 Rope of Life

Card Type: Trap
Monster Type: —
Type: Trap
Level: —
ATK: —
DEF: —
Rarity: Ultra Rare

Not only do you rescue the monster that was destroyed in battle, but it resurrects with 800 additional ATK. Be very careful about the timing of this card's activation.

PGD-106 Nightmare Wheel

Card Type: Trap
Monster Type: —
Type: Trap
Level: —
ATK: —
DEF: —
Rarity: Ultra Rare

You can completely stop one of your opponent's monsters and deal 500 points of damage to your opponent's Life Points during your Standby Phase.

PGD-107 Lava Golem

Card Type: Effect Monster
Monster Type: Fiend
Type: Fire
Level: 8
ATK: 3000
DEF: 2500
Rarity: Secret Rare

This monster is Special Summoned on your opponent's field and deals 1000 points of damage to your opponent's Life Points every turn. You can stop its attack by using "Nightmare Wheel."

PGD-000 Ring of Destruction

Card Type: Trap
Monster Type: —
Type: Trap
Level: —
ATK: —
DEF: —
Rarity: Secret Rare

If you have more Life Points than your opponent, then destroying a monster with higher ATK than your opponent's Life Points can be the final blow. Also, if you are about to lose the Duel, then destroying a monster that has higher ATK than you and your opponent's Life Points will end the Duel in a draw. It's better to get a draw than a loss!

Magician's Force

MFC-001 People Running About

Card Type: Normal Monster
Monster Type: Pyro
Type: Fire
Level: 2
ATK: 600
DEF: 600
Rarity: Common

This card is required to activate "Huge Revolution." Since it has low ATK and DEF, search for this card using "Sangan" or other similar cards.

MFC-002 Oppressed People

Card Type: Normal Monster
Monster Type: Aqua
Type: Water
Level: 1
ATK: 400
DEF: 2000
Rarity: Common

This card is required to activate "Huge Revolution." Though it's only a Level 1 monster, it has 2000 DEF, so it can easily survive.

MFC-003 United Resistance

Card Type: Normal Monster
Monster Type: Thunder
Type: Wind
Level: 3
ATK: 1000
DEF: 400
Rarity: Common

This card is required to activate "Huge Revolution." Special Summon this monster by using cards like "Flying Kamakiri #1."

MFC-004 X-Head Cannon

Card Type: Normal Monster
Monster Type: Machine
Type: Light
Level: 4
ATK: 1800
DEF: 1500
Rarity: Super Rare

Though this a Normal Monster with 1800 ATK, it can be equipped by the Union Monster "Y-Dragon Head" or "Z-Metal Tank" to increase its strength.

MFC-005 Y-Dragon Head

Card Type: Union Monster
Monster Type: Machine
Type: Light
Level: 4
ATK: 1500
DEF: 1600
Rarity: Super Rare

This Union Monster can equip on to "X-Head Dragon," raising "X-Head Dragon's" power to 2200 ATK and 1900 DEF.

MFC-006 Z-Metal Tank

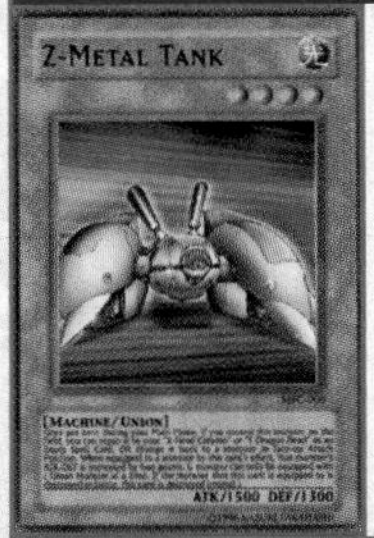

Card Type: Union Monster
Monster Type: Machine
Type: Light
Level: 4
ATK: 1500
DEF: 1300
Rarity: Super Rare

This Union Monster can equip on to "X-Head Dragon" and "Y-Dragon Head." If you get "X-Head Dragon," "Y-Dragon Head," and "Z-Metal Tank" on the field, then you can summon "XYZ-Dragon Cannon."

MFC-007 Dark Blade

Card Type: Normal Monster
Monster Type: Warrior
Type: Dark
Level: 4
ATK: 1800
DEF: 1500
Rarity: Rare

This Normal Monster has 1800 ATK and 1500 DEF. It can be equipped by two powerful Dragon-Type Union Monsters.

MFC-008 Pitch-Dark Dragon

Card Type: Union Monster
Monster Type: Dragon
Type: Dark
Level: 3
ATK: 900
DEF: 600
Rarity: Common

You can equip this Union Monster on to "Dark Blade." If you do so, you can deal damage to your opponent's Life Points even if your opponent's monster is in Defense Position.

MFC-009 Kiryu

Card Type: Union Monster
Monster Type: Dragon
Type: Dark
Level: 5
ATK: 2000
DEF: 1500
Rarity: Common

You can equip this Union Monster on to "Dark Blade." If this card is offered as a Tribute while it is equipped on to "Dark Blade," then you can attack your opponent's Life Points directly!

MFC-010 Decayed Commander

Card Type: Effect Monster
Monster Type: Zombie
Type: Earth
Level: 4
ATK: 1000
DEF: 1500
Rarity: Common

This monster can be equipped by the Union Monster "Zombie Tiger." Even on its own, this useful monster can destroy cards in your opponent's hand.

MFC-011 Zombie Tiger

Card Type: Union Monster
Monster Type: Zombie
Type: Earth
Level: 3
ATK: 1400
DEF: 1600
Rarity: Common

This is the Union Monster for "Decayed Commander." When it is equipped on to "Decayed Commander," it gains the ability to destroy cards in your opponent's hand.

MFC-012 Giant Orc

Card Type: Effect Monster
Monster Type: Fiend
Type: Dark
Level: 4
ATK: 2200
DEF: 0
Rarity: Common

This Level 4 monster has 200 ATK, which is no slouch when compared to "Goblin Attack Force." Equip it with "Second Goblin" and attack!

MFC-013 Second Goblin

Card Type: Union Monster
Monster Type: Fiend
Type: Dark
Level: 1
ATK: 100
DEF: 100
Rarity: Common

This Union Monster can equip on to "Giant Orc." This monster is very weak on its own, so equip it right away.

MFC-014 Vampire Orchis

Card Type: Effect Monster
Monster Type: Plant
Type: Earth
Level: 4
ATK: 1700
DEF: 1000
Rarity: Common

When this monster is summoned, you can Special Summon "Des Dendle" from your hand. With 1700 ATK, this Level 4 monster has decent stats on its own.

MFC-015 Des Dendle

Card Type: Union Monster
Monster Type: Plant
Type: Earth
Level: 4
ATK: 300
DEF: 2000
Rarity: Common

When "Vampire Orchis" is equipped with "Des Dendle," then for every monster it destroys, you can Special Summon a "Wicked Plant Token."

MFC-016 Burning Beast

Card Type: Union Monster
Monster Type: Pyro
Type: Fire
Level: 4
ATK: 1500
DEF: 1000
Rarity: Common

"Burning Beast" can be equipped on to "Freezing Beast." When damage is dealt to your opponent's Life Points, you can destroy one face-up Spell or Trap Card.

MFC-017 Freezing Beast

Card Type: Union Monster
Monster Type: Aqua
Type: Water
Level: 4
ATK: 1500
DEF: 1000
Rarity: Common

"Freezing Beast" can be equipped on to "Burning Beast." When damage is dealt to your opponent's Life Points, you can destroy one face-down Spell or Trap Card.

MFC-018 Union Rider

Card Type: Effect Monster
Monster Type: Machine
Type: Wind
Level: 2
ATK: 1000
DEF: 1000
Rarity: Common

This monster can steal your opponent's Union Monster and equip it on itself. This is a must-have card when you're playing against an opponent who uses a Union Deck.

MFC-019 D.D. Crazy Beast

Card Type: Effect Monster
Monster Type: Beast
Type: Earth
Level: 3
ATK: 1400
DEF: 1400
Rarity: Rare

A monster destroyed by this card in battle is removed from play. You can remove "Witch of the Black Forest" or "Sangan" from play without having their effects activate.

MFC-020 Spell Canceller

Card Type: Effect Monster
Monster Type: Machine
Type: Wind
Level: 5
ATK: 1800
DEF: 1600
Rarity: Ultra Rare

This extremely powerful monster can stop all Spell Cards. However, for a Level 5 monster, it has a low 1800 ATK, so be careful!

MFC-021 Neko Mane King

Card Type: Effect Monster
Monster Type: Beast
Type: Earth
Level: 1
ATK: 0
DEF: 0
Rarity: Common

This monster forcibly ends your opponent's turn. You should include this card when your opponent uses a hand destruction Deck.

MFC-022 Helping Robo For Combat

Card Type: Effect Monster
Monster Type: Machine
Type: Light
Level: 4
ATK: 1600
DEF: 0
Rarity: Rare

This card helps you adjust the contents of your hand. When playing with "Helping Robo for Combat," it's best to use Spell Cards that power it up.

MFC-023 Dimension Jar

Card Type: Effect Monster
Monster Type: Machine
Type: Dark
Level: 2
ATK: 200
DEF: 200
Rarity: Common

When this monster is flipped, up to three cards can be removed from the Graveyard. However, you should watch out because your opponent can remove three cards from your Graveyard.

MFC-024 Great Phantom Thief

Card Type: Effect Monster
Monster Type: Spellcaster
Type: Earth
Level: 3
ATK: 1000
DEF: 1000
Rarity: Rare

Even if your opponent doesn't have the card you named in his or her hand, you can still look at your opponent's hand to see what cards he or she has. This comes in handy during a Duel.

Magician's Force

MFC-025 Roulette Barrel

Card Type: Effect Monster
Monster Type: Machine
Type: Light
Level: 4
ATK: 1000
DEF: 2000
Rarity: Common

There's a chance that the card's effect will destroy "Roulette Barrel" itself, but since you choose only one of two dice rolls, you should relax. With 2000 DEF, it serves as a powerful defense.

MFC-026 Paladin of White Dragon

Card Type: Ritual/Effect Monster
Monster Type: Dragon
Type: Light
Level: 4
ATK: 1900
DEF: 1200
Rarity: Ultra Rare

This is a Ritual Monster, but since it's Level 4, it's easy to Ritual Summon. Not only does this card have "Sasuke Samurai's" effect, but you can also Special Summon "Blue-Eyes White Dragon."

MFC-027 White Dragon Ritual

Card Type: Spell
Monster Type: –
Type: Spell
Level: –
ATK: –
DEF: –
Rarity: Common

This Ritual Spell Card is needed to Ritual Summon "Paladin of White Dragon." If you don't have "White Dragon Ritual" in hand, use "Sonic Bird" to search your Deck for this card.

MFC-028 Frontline Base

Card Type: Spell
Monster Type: –
Type: Spell
Level: –
ATK: –
DEF: –
Rarity: Common

This Continuous Spell Card allows you to Special Summon a Level 4 or below Union Monster. Include this card in your Union Deck and amass your monster army.

MFC-029 Demotion

Card Type: Spell
Monster Type: –
Type: Spell
Level: –
ATK: –
DEF: –
Rarity: Common

This Equip Spell Card lowers the Level of a monster by two. Even if "Gravity Bind's" effect is active, you can attack with a high-level monster.

MFC-030 Combination Attack

Card Type: Spell
Monster Type: –
Type: Spell
Level: –
ATK: –
DEF: –
Rarity: Rare

You can attack twice! If you play with Union Monsters, then you should definitely think about using this card.

MFC-031 Kaiser Colosseum

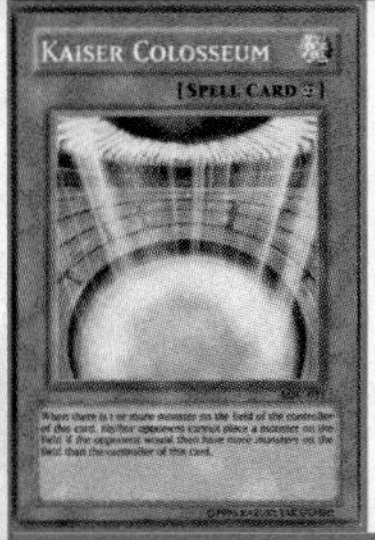

Card Type: Spell
Monster Type: –
Type: Spell
Level: –
ATK: –
DEF: –
Rarity: Common

When this Spell Card activates, your opponent cannot have more monsters on the field than you. This comes in handy if your Deck contains only a few monsters.

MFC-032 Autonomous Action Unit

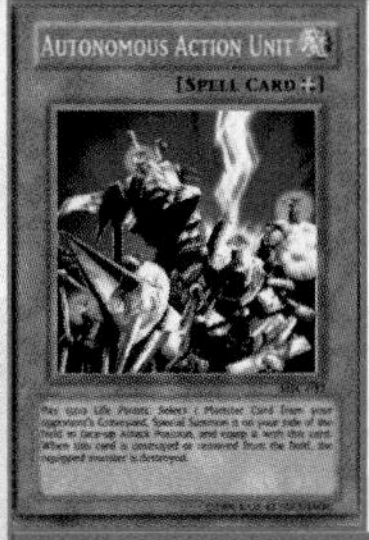

Card Type: Spell
Monster Type: –
Type: Spell
Level: –
ATK: –
DEF: –
Rarity: Common

If you pay 1500 Life Points, then you can Special Summon one of the monsters in your opponent's Graveyard to your field. Use this Spell Card after you check what monsters are in your opponent's Graveyard.

MFC-033 Poison of the Old Man

Card Type: Spell
Monster Type: –
Type: Spell
Level: –
ATK: –
DEF: –
Rarity: Common

This strange Spell Card has both Life Points restoration and Life Points damage on one card. Depending on the status of the Duel, decide which effect to use.

MFC-034 Ante

Card Type: Spell
Monster Type: –
Type: Spell
Level: –
ATK: –
DEF: –
Rarity: Rare

If you definitely want your opponent to discard a card and deal damage to your opponent's Life Points, then only use this card when you have a high-level monster in your hand.

MFC-035 Dark Core

Card Type: Spell
Monster Type: –
Type: Spell
Level: –
ATK: –
DEF: –
Rarity: Rare

This card is useful against an Effect Monster whose effect activates when it's sent to the Graveyard from the field. If a monster is removed from play, then you don't have to worry about it being Special Summoned from the Graveyard.

MFC-036 Raregold Armor

Card Type: Spell
Monster Type: –
Type: Spell
Level: –
ATK: –
DEF: –
Rarity: Common

This is effective when you have a monster that you definitely want to protect. If possible, equip this card on a monster with either high ATK or DEF.

MFC-037 Metalsilver Armor

Card Type: Spell
Monster Type: —
Type: Spell
Level: —
ATK: —
DEF: —
Rarity: Common

When a Spell Card, Trap Card, or Effect Monster's effect targets a specific monster, then the monster equipped with this card has to be the target. Choose wisely which monster to equip with "Metalsilver Armor."

MFC-038 Kishido Spirit

Card Type: Spell
Monster Type: —
Type: Spell
Level: —
ATK: —
DEF: —
Rarity: Common

Instead of you and your opponent's monsters being destroyed, only your opponent's monster is destroyed. This is useful when the Duel has reached a stalemate.

MFC-039 Tribute Doll

Card Type: Spell
Monster Type: —
Type: Spell
Level: —
ATK: —
DEF: —
Rarity: Rare

Usually, you would have to offer two monsters as a Tribute, but with this Spell Card, you only have to offer one monster as a Tribute. Use this to Special Summon a powerful monster.

MFC-040 Wave-Motion Cannon

Card Type: Spell
Monster Type: —
Type: Spell
Level: —
ATK: —
DEF: —
Rarity: Common

After "Wave-Motion Cannon" activates, the more turns that pass, the stronger it gets. If four Standby Phases pass, then you can deal 4000 points of damage!

MFC-041 Huge Revolution

Card Type: Trap
Monster Type: —
Type: Trap
Level: —
ATK: —
DEF: —
Rarity: Common

This ultimate Trap Card destroys all the cards in your opponent's hand and field. If you are successful in activating this Trap Card, then attack and overwhelm your opponent immediately!

MFC-042 Thunder of Ruler

Card Type: Trap
Monster Type: —
Type: Trap
Level: —
ATK: —
DEF: —
Rarity: Common

Your opponent cannot conduct his or her Battle Phase. This is basically a card that helps stall for time, but can you think of using it in a combo!?

MFC-043 Spell Shield Type-8

Card Type: Trap
Monster Type: —
Type: Trap
Level: —
ATK: —
DEF: —
Rarity: Super Rare

This Counter Trap Card has two effects to choose from, so depending on the situation of the Duel, choosing the correct effect will be devastating for your opponent.

MFC-044 Meteorain

Card Type: Trap
Monster Type: —
Type: Trap
Level: —
ATK: —
DEF: —
Rarity: Common

Summon a powerful monster and attack your opponent's monsters in Defense Position. You may be able to deal enough damage to your opponent's Life Points to win the Duel!

MFC-045 Pineapple Blast

Card Type: Trap
Monster Type: —
Type: Trap
Level: —
ATK: —
DEF: —
Rarity: Common

Let your opponent summon monsters, and then use this Trap Card to immediately destroy them. The bigger the difference in the number of monsters, the more painful it will be for your opponent.

MFC-046 Secret Barrel

Card Type: Trap
Monster Type: —
Type: Trap
Level: —
ATK: —
DEF: —
Rarity: Common

Add the number of cards in your opponent's hand with the number of cards on your opponent's field to determine how much damage this card deals to your opponent's Life Points. You can count on this card to deal lots of damage.

MFC-047 Physical Double

Card Type: Trap
Monster Type: —
Type: Trap
Level: —
ATK: —
DEF: —
Rarity: Common

Activate this Trap Card when your opponent attacks with a powerful monster! You can Special Summon a Monster Token with the exact same statistics on your field.

MFC-048 Rivalry of Warlords

Card Type: Trap
Monster Type: —
Type: Trap
Level: —
ATK: —
DEF: —
Rarity: Common

If the monsters in your Deck are all the same type, then you can count on this card's effect. Your opponent will definitely have a hard time.

Magician's Force

MFC-049 Formation Union

Card Type: Trap
Monster Type: —
Type: Trap
Level: —
ATK: —
DEF: —
Rarity: Common

This useful Trap Card freely controls the equipping and removing of Union Monsters. If you are going to play a Union Deck, then definitely consider using this card.

MFC-050 Adhesion Trap Hole

Card Type: Trap
Monster Type: —
Type: Trap
Level: —
ATK: —
DEF: —
Rarity: Common

Immediately after the monster is summoned, its ATK is cut in half. When your opponent summons his or her most powerful monster, don't hesitate in activating this Trap Card.

MFC-051 XY-Dragon Cannon

Card Type: Fusion/Effect Monster
Monster Type: Machine
Type: Light
Level: 6
ATK: 2200
DEF: 1900
Rarity: Ultra Rare

By discarding one card from your hand, you can destroy a face-up Spell or Trap Card on your opponent's field. However, you can't destroy a face-down Spell or Trap Card.

MFC-052 XYZ-Dragon Cannon

Card Type: Fusion/Effect Monster
Monster Type: Machine
Type: Light
Level: 8
ATK: 2800
DEF: 2600
Rarity: Ultra Rare

By discarding one card from your hand, you can destroy any card on your opponent's field. This monster's ATK is also pretty high.

MFC-053 XZ-Tank Cannon

Card Type: Fusion/Effect Monster
Monster Type: Machine
Type: Light
Level: 6
ATK: 2400
DEF: 2100
Rarity: Super Rare

By discarding one card from your hand, you can destroy a face-down Spell or Trap Card on your opponent's field. However, you can't destroy a face-up Spell or Trap Card.

MFC-054 YZ-Tank Dragon

Card Type: Fusion/Effect Monster
Monster Type: Machine
Type: Light
Level: 6
ATK: 2100
DEF: 2200
Rarity: Super Rare

By discarding one card from your hand, you can destroy one face-down Defense Position monster on your opponent's field. However, you can't destroy a face-up monster.

MFC-055 Great Angus

Card Type: Normal Monster
Monster Type: Beast
Type: Fire
Level: 4
ATK: 1800
DEF: 600
Rarity: Common

With Level 4 and 1800 ATK, this monster can play a prominent role in a Deck. When you need a FIRE or Beast-Type monster, this monster will fit the bill.

MFC-056 Aitsu

Card Type: Normal Monster
Monster Type: Fairy
Type: Fire
Level: 5
ATK: 100
DEF: 100
Rarity: Common

For a Level 5 monster, its power is extremely weak. However, when it combines with the Union Monster "Koits," it becomes extremely powerful!

MFC-057 Sonic Duck

Card Type: Normal Monster
Monster Type: Winged Beast
Type: Wind
Level: 3
ATK: 1700
DEF: 700
Rarity: Common

Its power looks relatively low, but it's a Level 3 monster. Depending on the Deck, you can count on this monster to play an excellent role.

MFC-058 Luster Dragon

Card Type: Normal Monster
Monster Type: Dragon
Type: Wind
Level: 4
ATK: 1900
DEF: 1600
Rarity: Ultra Rare

This monster is an excellent Dragon! Even among Level 4 monsters, "Luster Dragon" has top-notch ATK.

MFC-059 Amazoness Paladin

Card Type: Effect Monster
Monster Type: Warrior
Type: Earth
Level: 4
ATK: 1700
DEF: 300
Rarity: Common

If you're creating an Amazoness Deck, then you definitely want this monster in your Deck. If only this card is on your field, it still has 1800 ATK.

MFC-060 Amazoness Fighter

Card Type: Effect Monster
Monster Type: Warrior
Type: Earth
Level: 4
ATK: 1500
DEF: 1300
Rarity: Common

No matter how powerful the DEF of your opponent's Defense Position monster is, you can attack with it without having to worry about taking damage. This also stops you from taking Battle Damage.

MFC-061 Amazoness Swords Woman

Card Type: Effect Monster
Monster Type: Warrior
Type: Earth
Level: 4
ATK: 1500
DEF: 1600
Rarity: Ultra Rare

Even if you choose to attack your opponent's powerful monster, your opponent is going to take the damage! Can this be useful in many different combos!?

MFC-062 Amazoness Blowpiper

Card Type: Effect Monster
Monster Type: Warrior
Type: Earth
Level: 3
ATK: 800
DEF: 1500
Rarity: Common

This skilled monster can shrink the difference in ATK between your opponent's monster and yours. As long as this monster remains on the field, it's nearly impossible to avoid this effect.

MFC-063 Amazoness Tiger

Card Type: Effect Monster
Monster Type: Beast
Type: Earth
Level: 4
ATK: 1100
DEF: 1500
Rarity: Rare

"Amazoness Tiger" has 1500 ATK when it is summoned. If you have one other Amazoness monster, it rises to 1900 ATK. "Amazoness Tiger" also gains the ability to protect other Amazoness monsters.

MFC-064 Skilled White Magician

Card Type: Effect Monster
Monster Type: Spellcaster
Type: Light
Level: 4
ATK: 1700
DEF: 1900
Rarity: Super Rare

The ATK and DEF are both excellent. Not only that, it has the powerful ability to Special Summon "Buster Blader!"

MFC-065 Skilled Dark Magician

Card Type: Effect Monster
Monster Type: Spellcaster
Type: Dark
Level: 4
ATK: 1900
DEF: 1700
Rarity: Super Rare

This monster is even useful on its own because it has high ATK and DEF. Even better, it has the ability to Special Summon the mighty "Dark Magician."

MFC-066 Apprentice Magician

Card Type: Effect Monster
Monster Type: Spellcaster
Type: Dark
Level: 2
ATK: 400
DEF: 800
Rarity: Rare

You want to include this card if your Deck focuses on Spell Counters. When this monster is destroyed in battle, you can Special Summon another monster.

MFC-067 Old Vindictive Magician

Card Type: Effect Monster
Monster Type: Spellcaster
Type: Dark
Level: 2
ATK: 450
DEF: 600
Rarity: Common

If your opponent's monster can be targeted, then you can precisely destroy it with this monster's powerful effect. You can count on "Old Vindictive Magician" to help you out in your Duel.

MFC-068 Chaos Command Magician

Card Type: Effect Monster
Monster Type: Spellcaster
Type: Light
Level: 6
ATK: 2400
DEF: 1900
Rarity: Ultra Rare

Negate the effect of a Monster Card that specifically targets "Chaos Command Magician." Also, with Level 6 and 2400 ATK, this is a top-class monster!

MFC-069 Magical Marionette

Card Type: Effect Monster
Monster Type: Spellcaster
Type: Dark
Level: 5
ATK: 2000
DEF: 1000
Rarity: Common

This Spell Counter Monster has both power-up and Monster Removal effects. Create powerful combos by utilizing Spell Cards.

MFC-070 Pixie Knight

Card Type: Effect Monster
Monster Type: Spellcaster
Type: Light
Level: 2
ATK: 1300
DEF: 200
Rarity: Common

This monster can bring back a Spell Card in your Graveyard back to your Deck. However, this monster is required to battle and be sent to the Graveyard.

MFC-071 Breaker the Magical Warrior

Card Type: Effect Monster
Monster Type: Spellcaster
Type: Dark
Level: 4
ATK: 1600
DEF: 1000
Rarity: Ultra Rare

"Breaker the Magical Warrior" has 1900 ATK just by successfully summoning this monster. By removing its Spell Counter, you can destroy a Spell or Trap Card.

MFC-072 Magical Plant Mandragola

Card Type: Effect Monster
Monster Type: Spellcaster
Type: Dark
Level: 2
ATK: 500
DEF: 200
Rarity: Common

For Decks that require Spell Counters, this monster is indispensable. This one monster has the ability to turn a Duel around!

Magician's Force

MFC-073 Magical Scientist

Card Type: Effect Monster
Monster Type: Spellcaster
Type: Dark
Level: —
ATK: 300
DEF: 300
Rarity: Common

You can only call forth Level 6 or below Fusion Monsters. Therefore, instead of Special Summoning Fusion Monsters based on ATK, you should count on Fusion Monsters that have useful effects.

MFC-074 Royal Magical Library

Card Type: Effect Monster
Monster Type: Spellcaster
Type: Light
Level: 4
ATK: 0
DEF: 2000
Rarity: Common

Since it has high DEF, it can easily survive on the field. Therefore, it's easy to activate this monster's effect. Include this card in your Deck to strengthen your card drawing abilities.

MFC-075 Armor Exe

Card Type: Effect Monster
Monster Type: Rock
Type: Light
Level: 4
ATK: 2400
DEF: 1400
Rarity: Rare

This is the Level 4 monster with the highest ATK! Though there are many limitations on this card, there's no doubt that it's powerful!

MFC-076 Tribe-Infecting Virus

Card Type: Effect Monster
Monster Type: Aqua
Type: Water
Level: 4
ATK: 1600
DEF: 1000
Rarity: Super Rare

Depending on the sitation, this one monster can determine the outcome of the Duel! Use this card's effect to seal away your opponent's useful cards.

MFC-077 Des Koala

Card Type: Effect Monster
Monster Type: Beast
Type: Dark
Level: 3
ATK: 1100
DEF: 1800
Rarity: Rare

Since it has high DEF, it can still be useful even after its Flip Effect activates. Think of combos that can help you to deal lots of damage to your opponent's Life Points.

MFC-078 Cliff the Trap Remover

Card Type: Effect Monster
Monster Type: Warrior
Type: Dark
Level: 3
ATK: 1200
DEF: 1000
Rarity: Common

Though he doesn't have high ATK, his effects are awesome! Do whatever it takes to construct your Deck so that this monster's attack damages your opponent.

MFC-079 Magical Merchant

Card Type: Effect Monster
Monster Type: Insect
Type: Light
Level: —
ATK: 200
DEF: 700
Rarity: Common

If you combine this card with other cards, this is a pretty useful effect. If you can master this card's abilities, it will definitely help you in your Duel.

MFC-080 Koitsu

Card Type: Union Monster
Monster Type: Fairy
Type: Water
Level: 10
ATK: 200
DEF: 100
Rarity: Common

This Union Monser can equip on "Aitsu." Both monsters are useless on their own, but when the two combine, it becomes unbelievably powerful.

MFC-081 Cat's Ear Tribe

Card Type: Effect Monster
Monster Type: Beast-Warrior
Type: Earth
Level: 1
ATK: 200
DEF: 100
Rarity: Rare

When this monster is in Attack Position, your opponent will usually not want to attack it because your opponent's stronger monster will most likely be destroyed. If you use this fact to your advantage, you may be able to make a combo!

MFC-082 Ultimate Obedient Fiend

Card Type: Effect Monster
Monster Type: Fiend
Type: Fire
Level: 10
ATK: 3500
DEF: 3000
Rarity: Common

Not only does "Ultimate Obedient Fiend" have extremely high ATK, but you can attack face-down Defense Position monsters without having to worry about the monsters' effects. However, don't forget the requirements for this monster to attack!

MFC-083 Dark Cat with White Tail

Card Type: Effect Monster
Monster Type: Beast
Type: Earth
Level: 2
ATK: 800
DEF: 500
Rarity: Common

You can return three monsters on the field to the hand. However, more precisely, you have to return two of your opponent's monsters and one of your own monsters to the hand.

MFC-084 Amazoness Spellcaster

Card Type: Spell
Monster Type: —
Type: Spell
Level: —
ATK: —
DEF: —
Rarity: Common

Basically, Amazoness monsters have low ATK. Therefore, if you're going to create an Amazoness Deck, this is an important Spell Card to include.

MFC-085 Continuous Destruction Punch

Card Type: Spell
Monster Type: —
Type: Spell
Level: —
ATK: —
DEF: —
Rarity: Rare

This is the best card to use when your Deck is filled with wall monsters that have high DEF. Include this card in your Deck to use for Monster Removal.

MFC-086 Big Bang Shot

Card Type: Spell
Monster Type: —
Type: Spell
Level: —
ATK: —
DEF: —
Rarity: Rare

Not only does ATK increase, but you can also deal Battle Damage to your opponent's Life Points. Combine this card with Effect Monsters to create an awesome combo!

MFC-087 Gather Your Mind

Card Type: Spell
Monster Type: —
Type: Spell
Level: —
ATK: —
DEF: —
Rarity: Common

This card is used to thin out your Deck. Though this card doesn't have any other effect, you can use it to build up the amount of Spell Counters!

MFC-088 Mass Driver

Card Type: Spell
Monster Type: —
Type: Spell
Level: —
ATK: —
DEF: —
Rarity: Common

Offer your monster as a Tribute to deal Direct Damage to your opponent's Life Points. When your opponent has few Life Points remaining, use this card to finish him or her off!

MFC-089 Senri Eye

Card Type: Spell
Monster Type: —
Type: Spell
Level: —
ATK: —
DEF: —
Rarity: Common

You can check the card your opponent will be drawing before your opponent does. If you use this effect for many turns, you will know exactly what's in your opponent's hand.

MFC-090 Emblem of Dragon Destroyer

Card Type: Spell
Monster Type: —
Type: Spell
Level: —
ATK: —
DEF: —
Rarity: Common

Not only can you get a "Buster Blader" in your Deck to your hand, but you are also thinning out your Deck. Aim for Special Summoning "Buster Blader" from your hand.

MFC-091 Jar Robber

Card Type: Spell
Monster Type: —
Type: Spell
Level: —
ATK: —
DEF: —
Rarity: Common

Almost everyone uses "Pot of Greed" in his or her Deck. You can precisely hurt your opponent's drawing abilities while increasing your own.

MFC-092 My Body As A Shield

Card Type: Spell
Monster Type: —
Type: Spell
Level: —
ATK: —
DEF: —
Rarity: Common

No matter how powerful your opponent's Monster Removal card is, it's powerless against "My Body As A Shield." You can mess up your opponent's calculations and turn the Duel in your favor!

MFC-093 Pigeonholing Books of Spell

Card Type: Spell
Monster Type: —
Type: Spell
Level: —
ATK: —
DEF: —
Rarity: Common

You can freely manipulate the cards at the top of the Deck.

MFC-094 Mega Ton Magical Cannon

Card Type: Spell
Monster Type: —
Type: Spell
Level: —
ATK: —
DEF: —
Rarity: Rare

Gather ten Spell Counters and activate this card! There will be nothing left on your opponent's field. Use this card's effect to crush your opponent instantly!

MFC-095 Pitch-Black Power Stone

Card Type: Trap
Monster Type: —
Type: Trap
Level: —
ATK: —
DEF: —
Rarity: Common

If your Deck is built around Spell Counters, then definitely include this card. Even if you put three copies of this card in your Deck, they'll come in handy.

MFC-096 Amazoness Archers

Card Type: Trap
Monster Type: —
Type: Trap
Level: —
ATK: —
DEF: —
Rarity: Super Rare

This one card switches your opponent's Battle Position, weakens monsters, and also blocks Effect Monsters' effects. This powerful Trap Card with a multitude of effects is geared towards Amazoness Decks.

Magician's Force

MFC-097 Dramatic Rescue

Card Type: Trap
Monster Type: —
Type: Trap
Level: —
ATK: —
DEF: —
Rarity: Rare

The rescued monster must be an Amazoness. However, the monster that is Special Summoned can be any monster.

MFC-098 Exhausting Spell

Card Type: Trap
Monster Type: —
Type: Trap
Level: —
ATK: —
DEF: —
Rarity: Common

This card seals away Spell Counters. If your opponent's Deck focuses on Spell Counters, then this card will work effectively.

MFC-099 Hidden Book of Spell

Card Type: Trap
Monster Type: —
Type: Trap
Level: —
ATK: —
DEF: —
Rarity: Common

You can reuse two Spell Cards that are in your Graveyard. If you can use powerful Spell Cards, like Monster Removal Spell Cards, twice, then it's double the advantage!

MFC-100 Miracle Restoring

Card Type: Trap
Monster Type: —
Type: Trap
Level: —
ATK: —
DEF: —
Rarity: Common

By simply removing two Spell Counters, you can Special Summon a powerful monster from your Graveyard! Activate this card at the right moment to deal the final blow!

MFC-101 Remove Brainwashing

Card Type: Trap
Monster Type: —
Type: Trap
Level: —
ATK: —
DEF: —
Rarity: Common

If your monsters have been taken by your opponent's Spell Cards or effects, you can get them back. If you have this Trap Card, you don't have to worry about your monsters being taken.

MFC-102 Disarmament

Card Type: Trap
Monster Type: —
Type: Trap
Level: —
ATK: —
DEF: —
Rarity: Common

All Equip Spell Cards on the field are destroyed. If your opponent's monster that is powered up with Equip Spell Cards attacks, don't hesitate to activate this Trap.

MFC-103 Anti-Spell

Card Type: Trap
Monster Type: —
Type: Trap
Level: —
ATK: —
DEF: —
Rarity: Common

By removing two Spell Counters, you can stop Spell Cards. Use this card if your Deck is built around Spell Counters.

MFC-104 The Spell Absorbing Life

Card Type: Trap
Monster Type: —
Type: Trap
Level: —
ATK: —
DEF: —
Rarity: Common

Flip face-down Flip Effect Monsters face-up without having to worry about their Flip Effects activating. In addition, this card restores your Life Points.

MFC-105 Dark Paladin

Card Type: Fusion/Effect Monster
Monster Type: Spellcaster
Type: Dark
Level: 8
ATK: 2900
DEF: 2400
Rarity: Ultra Rare

Use your Spell Counters wisely and Fusion Summon "Dark Paladin." With just this one monster, you can change the flow of the Duel.

MFC-106 Double Spell

Card Type: Spell
Monster Type: —
Type: Spell
Level: —
ATK: —
DEF: —
Rarity: Ultra Rare

You can use your opponent's excellent Spell Card in his or her Graveyard as if it were your own by just discarding a Spell Card in your hand. Check your opponent's Graveyard before using this card.

MFC-107 Diffusion Wave-Motion

Card Type: Spell
Monster Type: —
Type: Spell
Level: —
ATK: —
DEF: —
Rarity: Secret Rare

This unbelievably powerful Spell Card may help you deal a lot of Battle Damage to your opponent, depending on the situation. In addition, it stops the effects of Effect Monsters.

MFC-000 Dark Magician Girl

Card Type: Effect Monster
Monster Type: Spellcaster
Type: Dark
Level: 6
ATK: 2000
DEF: 1700
Rarity: Secret Rare

The extremely popular "Dark Magician Girl" has an effect that surpasses even "Dark Magician!"

Dark Crisis

DCR-001 Battle Footballer

Card Type: Normal Monster
Monster Type: Machine
Type: Fire
Level: 4
ATK: 1000
DEF: 2100
Rarity: Common

A cyborg with high defense power. Originally it was invented for a football machine.

DCR-002 Nin-Ken Dog

Card Type: Normal Monster
Monster Type: Beast-Warrior
Type: Wind
Level: 4
ATK: 1800
DEF: 1000
Rarity: Common

A Ninja dog who has mastered extreme Ninjutsu. Through hard training, it learned the technique to metamorphose into a human being.

DCR-003 Acrobat Monkey

Card Type: Normal Monster
Monster Type: Machine
Type: Earth
Level: 3
ATK: 1000
DEF: 1800
Rarity: Common

An autonomous monkey-type robot which was developed with cutting-edge technology. It moves very acrobatically.

DCR-004 Arsenal Summoner

Card Type: Effect Monster
Monster Type: Spellcaster
Type: Wind
Level: 4
ATK: 1600
DEF: 1600
Rarity: Common

FLIP: Select 1 card that includes "Guardian" in its card name from your Deck and add it to your hand. You cannot select "Celtic Guardian," "Winged Dragon, Guardian of the Fortress #1," "Winged Dragon, Guardian of the Fortress #2," "Guardian of the Labyrinth," or "The Reliable Guardian."

DCR-005 Guardian Elma

Card Type: Effect Monster
Monster Type: Fairy
Type: Wind
Level: 3
ATK: 1300
DEF: 1200
Rarity: Common

This card can only be Normal Summoned, Flip Summoned, or Special Summoned when there is a "Butterfly Dagger - Elma" on your side of the field. When this card is summoned successfully, you can select 1 appropriate Equip Spell Card in your Graveyard and equip it to this card.

DCR-006 Guardian Ceal

Card Type: Effect Monster
Monster Type: Pyro
Type: Fire
Level: 4
ATK: 1700
DEF: 1400
Rarity: Ultra Rare

This card can only be Normal Summoned, Flip Summoned, or Special Summoned when there is a "Shooting Star Bow - Ceal" on your side of the field. Send an Equip Spell Card on your side of the field equipped to this card to the Graveyard to destroy 1 monster on your opponent's side of the field.

DCR-007 Guardian Grarl

Card Type: Effect Monster
Monster Type: Dinosaur
Type: Earth
Level: 5
ATK: 2500
DEF: 1000
Rarity: Ultra Rare

This card can only be Normal Summoned, Flip Summoned, or Special Summoned when there is a "Gravity Axe - Grarl" on your side of the field. If this is the only card in your hand, you can Special Summon it without offering a Tribute.

DCR-008 Guardian Baou

Card Type: Effect Monster
Monster Type: Fiend
Type: Dark
Level: 4
ATK: 800
DEF: 400
Rarity: Rare

This card can only be Normal Summoned, Flip Summoned, or Special Summoned when there is a "Wicked-Breaking Flamberge - Baou" on your side of the field. Each time 1 of your opponent's monsters is destroyed and sent to the Graveyard in battle by this monster, increase the ATK of this card by 1000 points. Also negate the effect of an Effect Monster that is destroyed by this monster in battle.

DCR-009 Guardian Kay'est

Card Type: Effect Monster
Monster Type: Sea Serpent
Type: Water
Level: 4
ATK: 1000
DEF: 1800
Rarity: Common

This card can only be Normal Summoned, Flip Summoned, or Special Summoned when there is a "Rod of Silence - Kay'est" on your side of the field. This card is unaffected by any Spell Cards and cannot be attacked by your opponent's monsters.

DCR-010 Guardian Tryce

Card Type: Effect Monster
Monster Type: Thunder
Type: Light
Level: 5
ATK: 1900
DEF: 1700
Rarity: Rare

This card can only be Normal Summoned, Flip Summoned, or Special Summoned when there is a "Twin Swords of Flashing Light - Tryce" on your side of the field. When this card is destroyed and sent to the Graveyard, Special Summon the monster that was offered as a Tribute for this card.

DCR-011 Cyber Raider

Card Type: Effect Monster
Monster Type: Machine
Type: Dark
Level: 4
ATK: 1400
DEF: 1000
Rarity: Common

When this card is Normal Summoned, Flip Summoned, or Special Summoned successfully, select and activate 1 of the following effects:

* Select 1 equipped Equip Spell Card and destroy it.
* Select 1 equipped Equip Spell Card and equip it to this card.

DCR-012 Reflect Bounder

Card Type: Effect Monster
Monster Type: Machine
Type: Light
Level: 4
ATK: 1700
DEF: 1000
Rarity: Ultra Rare

When this face-up Attack Position card is attacked by a monster on your opponent's side of the field, before damage calculation is resolved in the Damage Step, this card inflicts damage to your opponent's Life Points equal to the ATK of the attacking monster. Then, after damage calculation is resolved, this card is destroyed.

Dark Crisis

DCR-013 Little-Winguard

Card Type: Effect Monster
Monster Type: Warrior
Type: Wind
Level: 4
ATK: 1400
DEF: 1800
Rarity: Common

Once during each of your End Phases, you can change the Battle Position of this card.

DCR-014 Des Feral Imp

Card Type: Effect Monster
Monster Type: Reptile
Type: Dark
Level: 4
ATK: 1600
DEF: 1800
Rarity: Rare

FLIP: Select 1 card from your Graveyard and add it to your Deck. Then shuffle your Deck.

DCR-015 Different Dimension Dragon

Card Type: Effect Monster
Monster Type: Dragon
Type: Light
Level: 5
ATK: 1200
DEF: 1500
Rarity: Super Rare

The effect of a Spell or Trap Card cannot destroy this card unless the Spell or Trap Card specifically designates a target. This card is not destroyed as a result of battle when this card battles with a monster with an ATK of 1900 or less.

DCR-016 Shinato, King of a Higher Plane

Card Type: Ritual/Effect Monster
Monster Type: Fairy
Type: Light
Level: 8
ATK: 3300
DEF: 3000
Rarity: Ultra Rare

This card can only be Ritual Summoned with the Ritual Spell Card, "Shinato's Ark." You must also offer monsters whose total Level Stars equal 8 or more as a Tribute from the field or your hand. When a Defense Position monster on your opponent's side of the field is destroyed and sent to the Graveyard by this card as a result of battle, inflict damage to your opponent's Life Points equal to the original ATK of the destroyed monster.

DCR-017 Dark Flare Knight

Card Type: Fusion/Effect Monster
Monster Type: Warrior
Type: Dark
Level: 6
ATK: 2200
DEF: 800
Rarity: Super Rare

"Dark Magician" + "Flame Swordsman"

Any damage to the controller of this card from battle involving this monster becomes 0. When this card is destroyed and sent to the Graveyard as a result of battle, Special Summon 1 "Mirage Knight" from your hand or Deck.

DCR-018 Mirage Knight

Card Type: Effect Monster
Monster Type: Warrior
Type: Light
Level: 8
ATK: 2800
DEF: 2000
Rarity: Super Rare

This card can only be Special Summoned by the effect of "Dark Flare Knight." When this card battles another monster, during damage calculation increase the ATK of this card by the original ATK of the opponent's monster. During the End Phase after this card was involved in battle, remove this card from play.

DCR-019 Berserk Dragon

Card Type: Effect Monster
Monster Type: Zombie
Type: Dark
Level: 8
ATK: 3500
DEF: 0
Rarity: Super Rare

This card can only be Special Summoned by the effect of "A Deal with Dark Ruler." This card can attack all monsters on your opponent's side of the field once. You cannot attack your opponent directly if you attack any monsters first. Decrease the ATK of this card by 500 points during each of your End Phases.

DCR-020 Exodia Necross

Card Type: Effect Monster
Monster Type: Spellcaster
Type: Dark
Level: 4
ATK: 1800
DEF: 0
Rarity: Ultra Rare

This card can only be Special Summoned by the effect of "Contract with Exodia." This card is not destroyed as a result of battle at any time or by the effects of Spell or Trap Cards. During each of your Standby Phases, increase the ATK of this card by 500 points. This card is destroyed when you do not have all 5 of these cards in your Graveyard: "Exodia the Forbidden One," "Right Arm of the Forbidden One," "Left Arm of the Forbidden One," "Right Leg of the Forbidden One," "Left Leg of the Forbidden One."

DCR-021 Gyaku-Gire Panda

Card Type: Effect Monster
Monster Type: Beast
Type: Earth
Level: 3
ATK: 800
DEF: 1600
Rarity: Common

The ATK of this card increases by 500 points for every monster on your opponent's side of the field. When this card attacks with an ATK that is higher than the DEF of your opponent's Defense Position monster, inflict the difference as Battle Damage to your opponent's Life Points.

DCR-022 Blindly Loyal Goblin

Card Type: Effect Monster
Monster Type: Warrior
Type: Earth
Level: 4
ATK: 1800
DEF: 1500
Rarity: Common

As long as this card remains face-up on the field, control of this card cannot switch.

DCR-023 Despair from the Dark

Card Type: Effect Monster
Monster Type: Zombie
Type: Dark
Level: 8
ATK: 2800
DEF: 3000
Rarity: Common

When this card is sent directly from your hand or Deck to your Graveyard by your opponent's card effect, Special Summon this card to your side of the field.

DCR-024 Maju Garzett

Card Type: Effect Monster
Monster Type: Fiend
Type: Dark
Level: 7
ATK: –
DEF: 0
Rarity: Common

The ATK of this card becomes equal to the combined original ATK of the 2 monsters you offered as a Tribute to Tribute Summon this card.

DCR-025 Fear from the Dark

Card Type: Effect Monster
Monster Type: Zombie
Type: Dark
Level: 4
ATK: 1700
DEF: 1500
Rarity: Rare

When this card is sent directly from your hand or Deck to your Graveyard by your opponent's card effect, Special Summon this card to your side of the field.

DCR-026 Dark Scorpion - Chick the Yellow

Card Type: Effect Monster
Monster Type: Warrior
Type: Dark
Level: 3
ATK: 1000
DEF: 1000
Rarity: Common

When this card inflicts Battle Damage to your opponent's Life Points, you can select and activate 1 of the following effects:

* Return 1 card on the field to its owner's hand.
* See 1 card on the top of your opponent's Deck. Your opponent does not see the card. Then return it on the top or the bottom of your opponent's Deck.

DCR-027 D. D. Warrior Lady

Card Type: Effect Monster
Monster Type: Warrior
Type: Light
Level: 4
ATK: 1500
DEF: 1600
Rarity: Super Rare

When this card battles another monster, after Damage Calculation you can remove the opponent's monster and this card from play.

DCR-028 Thousand Needles

Card Type: Effect Monster
Monster Type: Beast
Type: Earth
Level: 4
ATK: 1000
DEF: 1800
Rarity: Common

When this Defense Position card is attacked and the ATK of the attacking monster is lower than the DEF of this card, after Damage Calculation destroy the attacking monster.

DCR-029 Shinato's Ark

Card Type: Spell
Monster Type: –
Type: Spell
Level: –
ATK: –
DEF: –
Rarity: Common

This card is used to Ritual Summon "Shinato, King of a Higher Plane." You must also offer monsters whose total Level Stars equal 8 or more as a Tribute from the field or your hand.

DCR-030 A Deal with Dark Ruler

Card Type: Spell
Monster Type: –
Type: Spell
Level: –
ATK: –
DEF: –
Rarity: Common

You can only activate this card during a turn in which a monster with 8 or more Level Stars on your side of the field was sent to the Graveyard. Special Summon 1 "Berserk Dragon" from your hand or Deck.

DCR-031 Contract with Exodia

Card Type: Spell
Monster Type: –
Type: Spell
Level: –
ATK: –
DEF: –
Rarity: Common

You can only activate this card when you have "Exodia the Forbidden One," "Right Arm of the Forbidden One," "Left Arm of the Forbidden One," "Right Leg of the Forbidden One," and "Left Leg of the Forbidden One" in your Graveyard. Special Summon 1 "Exodia Necross"from your hand.

Dark Crisis

DCR-032 Butterfly Dagger - Elma

Card Type: Spell
Monster Type: —
Type: Spell
Level: —
ATK: —
DEF: —
Rarity: Super Rare

A monster equipped with this card increases its ATK by 300 points. When this card is destroyed and sent to the Graveyard while equipped to a monster, this card can be returned to the owner's hand.

DCR-033 Shooting Star Bow - Ceal

Card Type: Spell
Monster Type: —
Type: Spell
Level: —
ATK: —
DEF: —
Rarity: Common

A monster equipped with this card decreases its ATK by 1000 points. A monster equipped with this card can attack your opponent's Life Points directly.

DCR-034 Gravity Axe - Grarl

Card Type: Spell
Monster Type: —
Type: Spell
Level: —
ATK: —
DEF: —
Rarity: Common

A monster equipped with this card increases its ATK by 500 points. As long as this card remains face-up on the field, monsters on your opponent's side of the field cannot change their Battle Position.

DCR-035 Wicked-Breaking Flamberge - Baou

Card Type: Spell
Monster Type: —
Type: Spell
Level: —
ATK: —
DEF: —
Rarity: Rare

You must send 1 card from your hand to your Graveyard when you activate this card. A monster equipped with this card increases its ATK by 500 points. When a monster equipped with this card destroys a monster with an effect on your opponent's side of the field in battle, negate the effect of that monster.

DCR-036 Rod of Silence - Kay'est

Card Type: Spell
Monster Type: —
Type: Spell
Level: —
ATK: —
DEF: —
Rarity: Common

A monster equipped with this card increases its DEF by 500 points. Negate the effect of a Spell Card (excluding this card) that specifically designates a monster equipped with this card as a target and destroy it.

DCR-037 Twin Swords of Flashing Light - Tryce

Card Type: Spell
Monster Type: —
Type: Spell
Level: —
ATK: —
DEF: —
Rarity: Common

You must send 1 card from your hand to your Graveyard when you activate this card. A monster equipped with this card decreases its ATK by 500 points. A monster equipped with this card can attack twice during the same Battle Phase.

DCR-038 Precious Cards from Beyond

Card Type: Spell
Monster Type: —
Type: Spell
Level: —
ATK: —
DEF: —
Rarity: Common

When you successfully Tribute Summon or Set a monster that required 2 or more Tributes, draw 2 cards from your Deck.

DCR-039 Rod of the Mind's Eye

Card Type: Spell
Monster Type: —
Type: Spell
Level: —
ATK: —
DEF: —
Rarity: Common

When a monster equipped with this card inflicts Battle Damage to your opponent, the damage becomes 1000 points.

DCR-040 Fairy of the Spring

Card Type: Spell
Monster Type: —
Type: Spell
Level: —
ATK: —
DEF: —
Rarity: Common

Select 1 Equip Spell Card from your Graveyard and add it to your hand. You cannot activate that Equip Spell Card this turn.

DCR-041 Token Thanksgiving

Card Type: Spell
Monster Type: —
Type: Spell
Level: —
ATK: —
DEF: —
Rarity: Common

Destroy all tokens on the field. Increase your Life Points by the number of tokens destroyed x 800 points.

DCR-042 Morale Boost

Card Type: Spell
Monster Type: —
Type: Spell
Level: —
ATK: —
DEF: —
Rarity: Common

Each time a player equips an Equip Spell Card, that player's Life Points increase by 1000 points. Each time an Equip Spell Card is destroyed or removed from the field, inflict 1000 damage to the Life Points of the controller of that Equip Spell Card.

DCR-043 Non-Spellcasting Area

Card Type: Spell
Monster Type: —
Type: Spell
Level: —
ATK: —
DEF: —
Rarity: Common

All face-up Monster Cards on the field, except for Effect Monsters, are unaffected by any Spell Card (excluding this card).

DCR-044 Different Dimension Gate

Card Type: Spell
Monster Type: —
Type: Spell
Level: —
ATK: —
DEF: —
Rarity: Rare

Select 1 Monster Card each from you and your opponent's sides of the field and remove them from play. When this card is destroyed and sent to the Graveyard, return those monsters to the field in the same Battle Position as when they were removed from play.

DCR-045 Final Attack Orders

Card Type: Trap
Monster Type: —
Type: Trap
Level: —
ATK: —
DEF: —
Rarity: Common

As long as this card remains face-up on the field, all face-up monsters on the field are changed to Attack Position and their Battle Position cannot be changed.

DCR-046 Staunch Defender

Card Type: Trap
Monster Type: —
Type: Trap
Level: —
ATK: —
DEF: —
Rarity: Common

You can only activate this card when your opponent declares an attack. Select 1 face-up monster on your side of the field. During the turn this card is activated, your opponent can only attack the monster you selected. Your opponent must attack the selected monster with all face-up monsters on his/her side of the field.

DCR-047 Ojama Trio

Card Type: Trap
Monster Type: —
Type: Trap
Level: —
ATK: —
DEF: —
Rarity: Common

Special Summon 3 "Ojama Tokens" (Beast-Type/Light/2 Stars/ATK 0/DEF 1000) in Defense Position on your opponent's side of the field. The tokens cannot be used as a Tribute for a Tribute Summon. When an "Ojama Token" is destroyed, inflict 300 points of damage to the controller's Life Points.

DCR-048 Arsenal Robber

Card Type: Trap
Monster Type: —
Type: Trap
Level: —
ATK: —
DEF: —
Rarity: Common

Your opponent selects 1 Equip Spell Card from his/her Deck and sends it to the Graveyard.

DCR-049 Skill Drain

Card Type: Trap
Monster Type: —
Type: Trap
Level: —
ATK: —
DEF: —
Rarity: Rare

Pay 1000 Life Points. As long as this card remains face-up on the field, negate the effects of all face-up Effect Monsters on the field.

DCR-050 Really Eternal Rest

Card Type: Trap
Monster Type: —
Type: Trap
Level: —
ATK: —
DEF: —
Rarity: Common

Destroy all monsters equipped with Equip Cards.

DCR-051 Kaiser Glider

Card Type: Effect Monster
Monster Type: Dragon
Type: Light
Level: 6
ATK: 2400
DEF: 2200
Rarity: Ultra Rare

This card is not destroyed as a result of battle when this card battles with a monster with the same ATK. When this card is destroyed and sent to the Graveyard, return 1 monster on the field to its owner's hand.

DCR-052 Interdimensional Matter Transporter

Card Type: Trap
Monster Type: —
Type: Trap
Level: —
ATK: —
DEF: —
Rarity: Ultra Rare

Select 1 face-up monster on your side of the field and remove it from play until the End Phase of the turn this card is activated in.

DCR-053 Cost Down

Card Type: Spell
Monster Type: —
Type: Spell
Level: —
ATK: —
DEF: —
Rarity: Ultra Rare

Discard 1 card from your hand. Downgrade all Monster Cards in your hand by 2 Levels until the End Phase of the turn this card is activated in.

DCR-054 Gagagigo

Card Type: Normal Monster
Monster Type: Reptile
Type: Water
Level: 4
ATK: 1850
DEF: 1000
Rarity: Common

This young evildoer used to have an evil heart, but by meeting a special person, he discovered justice.

DCR-055 D. D. Trainer

Card Type: Normal Monster
Monster Type: Fiend
Type: Dark
Level: 1
ATK: 100
DEF: 2000
Rarity: Common

A poor goblin that was sucked into a different dimension. However, he's doing his best with his new destiny.

Dark Crisis

DCR-056 Ojama Green

Card Type: Normal Monster
Monster Type: Beast
Type: Light
Level: 2
ATK: 0
DEF: 1000
Rarity: Common

He's one of the Ojama Trio. It's said that he butts in by any means necessary. It's also said that when the three are together, something happens.

DCR-057 Archfiend Soldier

Card Type: Normal Monster
Monster Type: Fiend
Type: Dark
Level: 4
ATK: 1900
DEF: 1500
Rarity: Rare

An expert at battle who belongs to a crack diabolical unit. He's famous because he always gets the job done.

DCR-058 Pandemonium Watchbear

Card Type: Effect Monster
Monster Type: Beast
Type: Dark
Level: 4
ATK: 1300
DEF: 1800
Rarity: Common

As long as this card remains face-up on your side of the field, "Pandemonium" on your side of the field cannot be destroyed by your opponent's card effects.

DCR-059 Sasuke Samurai #2

Card Type: Effect Monster
Monster Type: Warrior
Type: Wind
Level: 1
ATK: 200
DEF: 300
Rarity: Common

Once per turn, during your Main Phase, you can pay 800 Life Points. If you do this, until the End Phase, Spell and Trap Cards cannot be activated.

DCR-060 Dark Scorpion - Gorg the Strong

Card Type: Effect Monster
Monster Type: Warrior
Type: Dark
Level: 5
ATK: 1800
DEF: 1500
Rarity: Common

When this card inflicts Battle Damage to your opponent's Life Points, you can select and activate 1 of the following effects:

* Return 1 Monster Card on your opponent's side of the field to the top of its owner's Deck.
* Send 1 card from the top of your opponent's Deck to the Graveyard.

DCR-061 Dark Scorpion - Meanae the Thorn

Card Type: Effect Monster
Monster Type: Warrior
Type: Dark
Level: 4
ATK: 1000
DEF: 1800
Rarity: Common

When this card inflicts Battle Damage to your opponent's Life Points, you can select and activate 1 of the following effects:

* Select 1 card that includes "Dark Scorpion" in its card name, or is named "Cliff the Trap Remover," from your Deck and add it to your hand.
* Select 1 card that includes "Dark Scorpion" in its card name, or is named "Cliff the Trap Remover," from your Graveyard and add it to your hand.

DCR-062 Outstanding Dog Marron

Card Type: Effect Monster
Monster Type: Beast
Type: Light
Level: 1
ATK: 100
DEF: 100
Rarity: Common

When this card is sent to your Graveyard, it is returned to your Deck. Then shuffle your Deck.

DCR-063 Great Maju Garzett

Card Type: Effect Monster
Monster Type: Fiend
Type: Dark
Level: 6
ATK: 0
DEF: 0
Rarity: Rare

The ATK of this card becomes twice the original ATK of the Tribute Monster you used to Tribute Summon this card.

DCR-064 Iron Blacksmith Kotetsu

Card Type: Effect Monster
Monster Type: Beast-Warrior
Type: Fire
Level: 2
ATK: 500
DEF: 500
Rarity: Common

FLIP: Select 1 Equip Spell Card from your Deck and add it to your hand.

DCR-065 Goblin of Greed

Card Type: Effect Monster
Monster Type: Fiend
Type: Earth
Level: 4
ATK: 1000
DEF: 1800
Rarity: Common

As long as this card remains face-up on your side of the field, neither player can discard from his/her hand as a cost.

DCR-066 Mefist the Infernal General

Card Type: Effect Monster
Monster Type: Fiend
Type: Dark
Level: 5
ATK: 1800
DEF: 1700
Rarity: Rare

When this card attacks with an ATK that is higher than the DEF of your opponent's Defense Position monster, inflict the difference as Battle Damage to your opponent's Life Points. When this card inflicts Battle Damage to your opponent's Life Points, select 1 card from your opponent's hand randomly and discard it.

DCR-067 Vilepawn Archfiend

Card Type: Effect Monster
Monster Type: Fiend
Type: Earth
Level: 2
ATK: 1200
DEF: 200
Rarity: Common

The controller of this card pays 500 Life Points during each of his/her Standby Phases (this is not optional). When this card is specifically designated as a target of the effect of a card controlled by your opponent, when resolving the effect, roll a six-sided die. If the result is 3, negate the effect and destroy the opponent's card. As long as this card remains face-up on the field, your opponent cannot attack another face-up Archfiend Monster Card.

DCR-068 Shadowknight Archfiend

Card Type: Effect Monster
Monster Type: Fiend
Type: Wind
Level: 4
ATK: 2000
DEF: 1600
Rarity: Common

The controller of this card pays 900 Life Points during each of his/her Standby Phases (this is not optional). When this card is specifically designated as a target of the effect of a card controlled by your opponent, when resolving the effect, roll a six-sided die. If the result is 3, negate the effect and destroy the opponent's card. The Battle Damage this card inflicts to your opponent's Life Points is halved.

DCR-069 Darkbishop Archfiend

Card Type: Effect Monster
Monster Type: Fiend
Type: Water
Level: 3
ATK: 300
DEF: 1400
Rarity: Rare

The controller of this card pays 500 Life Points during each of his/her Standby Phases (this is not optional). When an Archfiend Monster Card on your side of the field is specifically designated as a target of the effect of a card controlled by your opponent, when resolving the effect, roll a six-sided die. If the result is 1, 3, or 6, negate the effect and destroy the opponent's card.

DCR-070 Desrook Archfiend

Card Type: Effect Monster
Monster Type: Fiend
Type: Light
Level: 3
ATK: 1100
DEF: 1800
Rarity: Common

The controller of this card pays 500 Life Points during each of his/her Standby Phases (this is not optional). When this card is specifically designated as a target of the effect of a card controlled by your opponent, when resolving the effect, roll a six-sided die. If the result is 3, negate the effect and destroy the opponent's card. When a "Terrorking Archfiend" on your side of the field is destroyed and sent to the Graveyard, you can send this card from your hand to the Graveyard to Special Summon the "Terrorking Archfiend."

DCR-071 Infernalqueen Archfiend

Card Type: Effect Monster
Monster Type: Fiend
Type: Fire
Level: 4
ATK: 900
DEF: 1500
Rarity: Rare

The controller of this card pays 500 Life Points during each of his/her Standby Phases (this is not optional). When this card is specifically designated as a target of the effect of a card controlled by your opponent, when resolving the effect, roll a six-sided die. If the result is 2 or 5, negate the effect and destroy the opponent's card. As long as this card remains on the field, during each Standby Phase increase the ATK of 1 Archfiend monster by 1000 points.

DCR-072 Terrorking Archfiend

Card Type: Effect Monster
Monster Type: Fiend
Type: Dark
Level: 4
ATK: 2000
DEF: 1500
Rarity: Super Rare

You cannot Normal Summon or Flip Summon this card unless you have an Archfiend Monster Card on your side of the field. The controller of this card pays 800 Life Points during each of his/her Standby Phases (this is not optional). When this card is specifically designated as a target of the effect of a card controlled by your opponent, when resolving the effect, roll a six-sided die. If the result is 2 or 5, negate the effect and destroy the opponent's card. Also negate the effect of an Effect Monster that is destroyed by this monster in battle.

DCR-073 Skull Archfiend of Lightning

Card Type: Effect Monster
Monster Type: Fiend
Type: Dark
Level: 6
ATK: 2500
DEF: 1200
Rarity: Ultra Rare

The controller of this card pays 500 Life Points during each of his/her Standby Phases (this is not optional). When this card is specifically designated as a target of the effect of a card controlled by your opponent, when resolving the effect, roll a six-sided die. If the result is 1, 3, or 6, negate the effect and destroy the opponent's card.

Dark Crisis

DCR-074 Metallizing Parasite - Lunatite

Card Type: Union Monster
Monster Type: Aqua
Type: Water
Level: 7
ATK: 1000
DEF: 500
Rarity: Rare

Once per turn, during your Main Phase, if you control this monster on the field, you can equip it to a face-up monster on your side of the field as an Equip Spell Card, OR change it back to a monster in face-up Attack Position. When equipped to a monster by this card's effect, that monster will not be affected by the effects of Spell Cards controlled by your opponent. (1 monster can only be equipped with 1 Union Monster at a time. If the monster that this card is equipped to is destroyed in battle, this card is destroyed instead.)

DCR-075 Tsukuyomi

Card Type: Spirit Monster
Monster Type: Spellcaster
Type: Dark
Level: 4
ATK: 1100
DEF: 1400
Rarity: Rare

This card cannot be Special Summoned. This card returns to the owner's hand during the End Phase of the turn that it is Normal Summoned, Flip Summoned, or flipped face-up. When this card is Normal Summoned, Flip Summoned, or flipped face-up, flip 1 face-up monster on the field into face-down Defense Position.

DCR-076 Mudora

Card Type: Effect Monster
Monster Type: Fairy
Type: Earth
Level: –
ATK: 1500
DEF: 1800
Rarity: Super Rare

The ATK of this card increases by 200 points for every Fairy-Type monster in your Graveyard.

DCR-077 Keldo

Card Type: Effect Monster
Monster Type: Fairy
Type: Earth
Level: 4
ATK: 1200
DEF: 1600
Rarity: Common

When this card is destroyed and sent to the Graveyard as a result of battle, select 2 cards from your opponent's Graveyard and return them to your opponent's Deck. Your opponent then shuffles his/her Deck.

DCR-078 Kelbek

Card Type: Effect Monster
Monster Type: Fairy
Type: Earth
Level: 4
ATK: 1500
DEF: 1800
Rarity: Common

Any monster that attacks this card is returned to its owner's hand. Damage calculation is applied normally.

DCR-079 Zolga

Card Type: Effect Monster
Monster Type: Fairy
Type: Earth
Level: 4
ATK: 1700
DEF: 1200
Rarity: Common

The controller of this card increases his/her Life Points by 2000 points when this monster is offered as a Tribute for a successful Tribute Summon or Set.

DCR-080 Agido

Card Type: Effect Monster
Monster Type: Fairy
Type: Earth
Level: 4
ATK: 1500
DEF: 1300
Rarity: Common

When this card is destroyed and sent to the Graveyard as a result of battle, roll a six-sided die. You can Special Summon 1 Fairy-Type monster from your Graveyard whose Level Stars are equal to the number rolled. If the result is 6, you can Special Summon a Level 6 or higher monster.

DCR-081 Legendary Flame Lord

Card Type: Ritual/Effect Monster
Monster Type: Spellcaster
Type: Fire
Level: 7
ATK: 2400
DEF: 2000
Rarity: Rare

This card can only be Ritual Summoned with the Ritual Spell Card "Incandescent Ordeal." You must also offer monsters whose total Level Stars equal 7 or more as a Tribute from the field or your hand. Each time you or your opponent activates 1 Spell Card, put 1 Spell Counter on this card. Remove 3 Spell Counters from this card to destroy all monsters on the field except this card.

DCR-082 Dark Master - Zorc

Card Type: Ritual/Effect Monster
Monster Type: Fiend
Type: Dark
Level: 8
ATK: 2700
DEF: 1500
Rarity: Super Rare

This card can only be Ritual Summoned with the Ritual Spell Card, "Contract with the Dark Master." You must also offer monsters whose total Level Stars equal 8 or more as a Tribute from the field or your hand. During your turn you can roll 1 six-sided die. If the result is 1 or 2, destroy all monsters on your opponent's side of the field. If the result is 3, 4, or 5, destroy 1 monster on your opponent's side of the field. If the result is 6, destroy all monsters on your side of the field.

DCR-083 Spell Reproduction

Card Type: Spell
Monster Type: –
Type: Spell
Level: –
ATK: –
DEF: –
Rarity: Common

Send 2 Spell Cards from your hand to the Graveyard. Select 1 Spell Card from your Graveyard and add it to your hand.

DCR-084 Dragged Down into the Grave

Card Type: Spell
Monster Type: —
Type: Spell
Level: —
ATK: —
DEF: —
Rarity: Common

You and your opponent look at each other's hands, select 1 card from each other's hands and discard them to the Graveyard, and each draw 1 card.

DCR-085 Incandescent Ordeal

Card Type: Spell
Monster Type: —
Type: Spell
Level: —
ATK: —
DEF: —
Rarity: Common

This card is used to Ritual Summon "Legendary Flame Lord." You must also offer monsters whose total Level Stars equal 7 or more as a Tribute from the field or your hand.

DCR-086 Contract with the Abyss

Card Type: Spell
Monster Type: —
Type: Spell
Level: —
ATK: —
DEF: —
Rarity: Rare

This card is used to Ritual Summon any DARK monster. You must also offer monsters from the field or your hand whose total Level Stars equal the Level Stars of the Ritual Monster you are attempting to Ritual Summon.

DCR-087 Contract with the Dark Master

Card Type: Spell
Monster Type: —
Type: Spell
Level: —
ATK: —
DEF: —
Rarity: Common

This card is used to Ritual Summon "Dark Master - Zorc." You must also offer monsters whose total Level Stars equal 8 or more as a Tribute from the field or your hand.

DCR-088 Falling Down

Card Type: Spell
Monster Type: —
Type: Spell
Level: —
ATK: —
DEF: —
Rarity: Common

Destroy this card if there is no face-up Archfiend card on your side of the field. Take control of 1 of your opponent's face-up monsters. Inflict 800 points of damage to your Life Points during each of your opponent's Standby Phases.

DCR-089 Checkmate

Card Type: Spell
Monster Type: —
Type: Spell
Level: —
ATK: —
DEF: —
Rarity: Common

Offer 1 Archfiend monster on your side of the field as a Tribute. During the turn this card is activated, 1 "Terrorking Archfiend" on your side of the field can attack your opponent's Life Points directly.

DCR-090 Cestus of Dagla

Card Type: Spell
Monster Type: —
Type: Spell
Level: —
ATK: —
DEF: —
Rarity: Common

This card can only be equipped to Fairy-Type monsters. A monster equipped with this card increases its ATK by 500 points. When this card inflicts Battle Damage to your opponent's Life Points, increase your Life Points by an equal amount.

DCR-091 Final Countdown

Card Type: Spell
Monster Type: —
Type: Spell
Level: —
ATK: —
DEF: —
Rarity: Common

Pay 2000 Life Points. After 20 turns have passed after you activate this card (counting the turn you activate this card as the 1st turn), you win the Duel.

DCR-092 Archfiend's Oath

Card Type: Spell
Monster Type: —
Type: Spell
Level: —
ATK: —
DEF: —
Rarity: Common

Once per turn you can pay 500 Life Points to declare 1 card name. Pick up the top card from your Deck and if the card name is the one you declared, add it to your hand. If not, send the card you picked up to the Graveyard.

DCR-093 Mustering of the Dark Scorpions

Card Type: Spell
Monster Type: —
Type: Spell
Level: —
ATK: —
DEF: —
Rarity: Common

You can only activate this card when you have "Don Zaloog" face-up on your side of the field. You can Special Summon any of the cards from your hand that include "Dark Scorpion" in the card name, or are named "Cliff the Trap Remover." You cannot Special Summon 2 cards with the same card name by the effect of this card.

DCR-094 Pandemonium

Card Type: Spell
Monster Type: —
Type: Spell
Level: —
ATK: —
DEF: —
Rarity: Common

Neither player has to pay Life Points during the Standby Phase for Archfiend monsters. Each time a player's Archfiend Monster Card(s) are destroyed and sent to the Graveyard, except as a result of battle, that player can select 1 Archfiend Monster Card from his/her Deck that has fewer Level Stars than the destroyed card and add it to his/her hand.

DCR-095 Altar for Tribute

Card Type: Trap
Monster Type: —
Type: Trap
Level: —
ATK: —
DEF: —
Rarity: Common

Select 1 monster on your side of the field and send it to the Graveyard. Increase your Life Points by an amount equal to the original ATK of the monster.

Dark Crisis

DCR-096 Frozen Soul

Card Type: Trap
Monster Type: —
Type: Trap
Level: —
ATK: —
DEF: —
Rarity: Common

You can only activate this card when your opponent's Life Points are at least 2000 points higher than yours. Your opponent skips his/her next Battle Phase.

DCR-097 Battle-Scarred

Card Type: Trap
Monster Type: —
Type: Trap
Level: —
ATK: —
DEF: —
Rarity: Common

Select 1 Archfiend monster on your side of the field when you activate this card. When the monster's controller pays Life Points during the Standby Phase for the selected monster, that player's opponent also must pay equal Life Points. If this card is destroyed or removed from the field, destroy the selected monster. When the selected monster is destroyed or removed from the field, this card is also destroyed.

DCR-098 Dark Scorpion Combination

Card Type: Trap
Monster Type: —
Type: Trap
Level: —
ATK: —
DEF: —
Rarity: Rare

You can only activate this card when you have "Don Zaloog," "Cliff the Trap Remover," "Dark Scorpion - Chick the Yellow," "Dark Scorpion - Gorg the Strong," and "Dark Scorpion - Meanae the Thorn" face-up on your side of the field. During the turn this card is activated, any of these 5 cards can attack your opponent's Life Points directly. In that case, the Battle Damage inflicted by each of those cards (that attack your opponent's Life Points directly) becomes 400 points.

DCR-099 Archfiend's Roar

Card Type: Trap
Monster Type: —
Type: Trap
Level: —
ATK: —
DEF: —
Rarity: Common

Pay 500 Life Points to activate this card. Special Summon 1 Archfiend Monster Card from your Graveyard. This monster cannot be offered as a Tribute under any conditions and is destroyed during the End Phase of this turn.

DCR-100 Dice Re-Roll

Card Type: Trap
Monster Type: —
Type: Trap
Level: —
ATK: —
DEF: —
Rarity: Common

After this card is activated, for the rest of this turn you can negate 1 six-sided die roll and re-roll it.

DCR-101 Spell Vanishing

Card Type: Trap
Monster Type: —
Type: Trap
Level: —
ATK: —
DEF: —
Rarity: Super Rare

Discard 2 cards from your hand to negate the activation of a Spell Card and destroy it. Also, check your opponent's hand and Deck and if you find any Spell Cards of the same name as the destroyed Spell Card, send all of them to the Graveyard.

DCR-102 Sakuretsu Armor

Card Type: Trap
Monster Type: —
Type: Trap
Level: —
ATK: —
DEF: —
Rarity: Common

You can only activate this card when your opponent declares an attack. Destroy the attacking monster.

DCR-103 Ray of Hope

Card Type: Trap
Monster Type: —
Type: Trap
Level: —
ATK: —
DEF: —
Rarity: Common

Select 2 LIGHT monsters from your Graveyard and add them to your Deck. Then shuffle your Deck.

DCR-104 Blast Held by a Tribute

Card Type: Trap
Monster Type: —
Type: Trap
Level: —
ATK: —
DEF: —
Rarity: Ultra Rare

You can only activate this card when your opponent declares an attack with a monster on his/her side of the field that has been Tribute Summoned or Set. Destroy all face-up Attack Position monsters on your opponent's side of the field and inflict 1000 points of damage to your opponent's Life Points.

DCR-105 Judgment of Anubis

Card Type: Trap
Monster Type: —
Type: Trap
Level: —
ATK: —
DEF: —
Rarity: Secret Rare

Discard 1 card from your hand to negate the activation and the effect of a Spell Card controlled by your opponent that includes the effect of destroying Spell and/or Trap Card(s) on the field and destroy it. Then, you can destroy 1 face-up monster on your opponent's side of the field and inflict damage to your opponent equal to the ATK of the destroyed monster.

DCR-000 Vampire Lord

Card Type: Effect Monster
Monster Type: Zombie
Type: Dark
Level: 5
ATK: 2000
DEF: 1500
Rarity: Secret Rare

Each time this card inflicts Battle Damage to your opponent, declare 1 card type (Monster, Spell, or Trap). Your opponent selects 1 card of that type from his/her Deck and sends it to the Graveyard. Also, when this card is destroyed and sent to your Graveyard by your opponent's card effect, it is Special Summoned to the field during your next Standby Phase.

Dark Duel Stories

DDS-001 Blue-Eyes White Dragon

- **Card Type:** Normal Monster
- **Monster Type:** Dragon
- **Attribute:** Light
- **Level:** 8
- **ATK:** 3000
- **DEF:** 2500
- **Rarity:** Secret Rare

Kaiba's favorite monster is the most powerful Normal Monster Card. Destroying "Blue-Eyes" without a Spell Card will be difficult!

DDS-002 Dark Magician

- **Card Type:** Normal Monster
- **Monster Type:** Spellcaster
- **Attribute:** Dark
- **Level:** 7
- **ATK:** 2500
- **DEF:** 2100
- **Rarity:** Secret Rare

A high-ranking magician of the Spellcaster-Type, the "Dark Magician" is very dangerous unless you destroy him as soon as your opponent places him on the field.

DDS-003 Exodia the Forbidden One

- **Card Type:** Effect Monster
- **Monster Type:** Spellcaster
- **Attribute:** Dark
- **Level:** 3
- **ATK:** 1000
- **DEF:** 1000
- **Rarity:** Secret Rare

This is one of the five parts necessary to resurrect "Exodia the Forbidden One."

DDS-004 Seiyaryu

- **Card Type:** Normal Monster
- **Monster Type:** Dragon
- **Attribute:** Light
- **Level:** 7
- **ATK:** 2500
- **DEF:** 2300
- **Rarity:** Secret Rare

"Seiyaryu" has the same ATK as "Dark Magician." Use this monster when the situation requires!

DDS-005 Acid Trap Hole

- **Card Type:** Trap
- **Monster Type:** —
- **Attribute:** Trap
- **Level:** —
- **ATK:** —
- **DEF:** —
- **Rarity:** Secret Rare

You can use this Trap Card on face-down monsters. Most monsters have low DEF, so this card is very useful!

DDS-006 Salamandra

- **Card Type:** Spell
- **Monster Type:** —
- **Attribute:** Spell
- **Level:** —
- **ATK:** —
- **DEF:** —
- **Rarity:** Secret Rare

Power up your FIRE monsters with "Salamandra!"

Forbidden Memories

FMR-001 Red-Eyes Black Metal Dragon

- **Card Type:** Effect Monster
- **Monster Type:** Machine
- **Attribute:** Dark
- **Level:** 8
- **ATK:** 2800
- **DEF:** 2800
- **Rarity:** Secret Rare

If you offer "Red-Eyes B. Dragon" equipped with "Metalmorph" as a Tribute, then you place this card on the field from the Deck. When "Red-Eyes B. Dragon" is equipped with "Metalmorph," it has 2700 ATK. "Red-Eyes Black Metal Dragon" has only 100 more ATK, and it also loses the effect of "Metalmorph." Maybe it shouldn't be Tribute Summoned....

FMR-002 Harpie's Pet Dragon

- **Card Type:** Effect Monster
- **Monster Type:** Dragon
- **Attribute:** Wind
- **Level:** 7
- **ATK:** 2000
- **DEF:** 2000
- **Rarity:** Secret Rare

For every face-up "Harpie Lady" on the field, its ATK rises by 300. Since it's a Level 7 monster, you would usually not include this card in your Deck. It's more fun to use this card as the key card in your "Harpie Lady" Deck.

FMR-003 Metalmorph

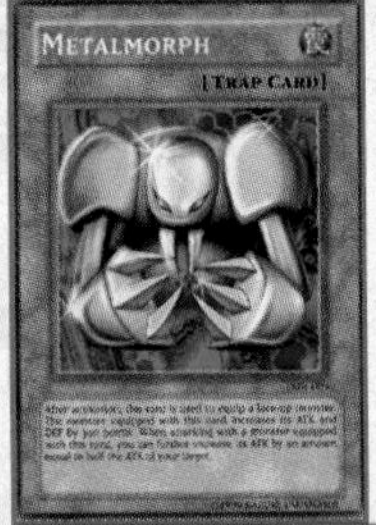

- **Card Type:** Trap
- **Monster Type:** —
- **Attribute:** Trap
- **Level:** —
- **ATK:** —
- **DEF:** —
- **Rarity:** Secret Rare

Increase both ATK and DEF of one monster by 300. When your monster equipped with "Metalmorph" attacks your opponent's monster, then your monster's ATK rises by half your opponent monster's ATK. It's more useful to use this effect than it is to Tribute Summon "Red-Eyes Black Metal Dragon."

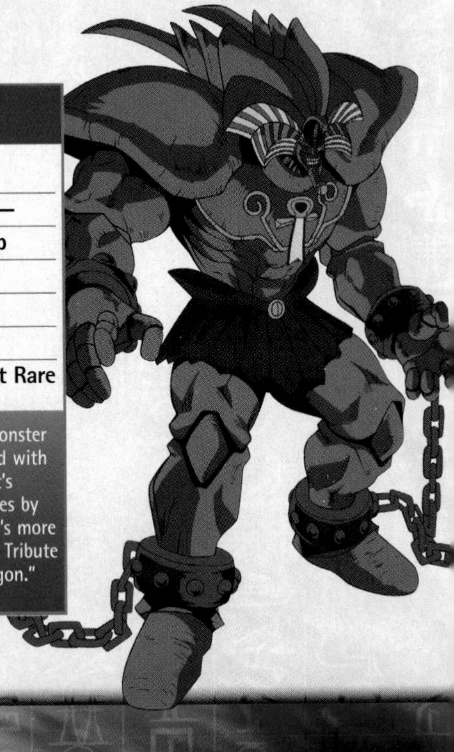

The Eternal Duelist Soul

EDS-001 Exchange

- **Card Type:** Spell
- **Monster Type:** —
- **Attribute:** Spell
- **Level:** —
- **ATK:** —
- **DEF:** —
- **Rarity:** Secret Rare

Take your opponent's powerful Spell Card, such as "Raigeki." Use this card when you have nothing useful in your hand.

EDS-002 Graceful Dice

- **Card Type:** Spell
- **Monster Type:** —
- **Attribute:** Spell
- **Level:** —
- **ATK:** —
- **DEF:** —
- **Rarity:** Secret Rare

The ATK and DEF of all your monsters will increase depending on what you roll.

EDS-003 Skull Dice

- **Card Type:** Trap
- **Monster Type:** —
- **Attribute:** Trap
- **Level:** —
- **ATK:** —
- **DEF:** —
- **Rarity:** Secret Rare

The ATK and DEF of all your opponent's monsters will decrease depending on what you roll.

The Duelists of the Roses

DOR-001 Alpha The Magnet Warrior

- **Card Type:** Normal Monster
- **Monster Type:** Rock
- **Attribute:** Earth
- **Level:** 4
- **ATK:** 1400
- **DEF:** 1700
- **Rarity:** Secret Rare

You need "Alpha the Magnet Warrior," "Beta the Magnet Warrior," and "Gamma the Magnet Warrior" to Special Summon "Valkyrion the Magna Warrior."

DOR-002 Beta The Magnet Warrior

- **Card Type:** Normal Monster
- **Monster Type:** Rock
- **Attribute:** Earth
- **Level:** 4
- **ATK:** 1700
- **DEF:** 1600
- **Rarity:** Secret Rare

You need "Alpha the Magnet Warrior," "Beta the Magnet Warrior," and "Gamma the Magnet Warrior" to Special Summon "Valkyrion the Magna Warrior."

DOR-003 Gamma The Magnet Warrior

- **Card Type:** Normal Monster
- **Monster Type:** Rock
- **Attribute:** Earth
- **Level:** 4
- **ATK:** 1500
- **DEF:** 1800
- **Rarity:** Secret Rare

You need "Alpha the Magnet Warrior," "Beta the Magnet Warrior" and "Gamma the Magnet Warrior" to Special Summon "Valkyrion the Magna Warrior."

Worldwide Edition: Stairway to the Destined Duel

SDD-001 Valkyrion the Magna Warrior

- **Card Type:** Effect Monster
- **Monster Type:** Rock
- **Attribute:** Earth
- **Level:** 8
- **ATK:** 3500
- **DEF:** 3850
- **Rarity:** Secret Rare

This card can only be Special Summoned by offering "Alpha the Magnet Warrior," "Beta the Magnet Warrior," and "Gamma the Magnet Warrior" from your hand or the field as a Tribute. If "Alpha the Magnet Warrior," "Beta the Magnet Warrior," and "Gamma the Magnet Warrior" exist in the Graveyard, you can offer this card as a Tribute to Special Summon these three cards to the field.

SDD-002 Sinister Serpent

- **Card Type:** Effect Monster
- **Monster Type:** Reptile
- **Attribute:** Water
- **Level:** 1
- **ATK:** 300
- **DEF:** 250
- **Rarity:** Secret Rare

During your Standby Phase, if a "Sinister Serpent" exists in your Graveyard, you can return the "Sinister Serpent" to your hand. You can use this monster multiple times!

SDD-003 Harpie's Feather Duster

- **Card Type:** Spell
- **Monster Type:** —
- **Attribute:** Spell
- **Level:** —
- **ATK:** —
- **DEF:** —
- **Rarity:** Secret Rare

This incredibly powerful Spell Card allows you to destroy all your opponent's Spell and Trap Cards, including Field Spell Cards and Equip Spell Cards!

The Falsebound Kingdom

TFK-001 Zoa

Card Type: Normal Monster
Monster Type: Fiend
Attribute: Dark
Level: 7
ATK: 2600
DEF: 1900
Rarity: Secret Rare

Bandit Keith used this powerful Fiend-Type monster. Its true strength is unleashed when it is equipped with "Metalmorph."

TFK-002 Metalzoa

Card Type: Effect Monster
Monster Type: Machine
Attribute: Dark
Level: 8
ATK: 3000
DEF: 2300
Rarity: Secret Rare

If you offer "Zoa" equipped with "Metalmorph" as a Tribute, then you place this card on the field from your Deck. Its ATK and DEF are both excellent. You do not have to have this card in your hand, so it is easy to Special Summon. However, it will lose the effect of "Metalmorph."

TFK-003 Goblin Fan

Card Type: Trap
Monster Type: —
Attribute: Trap
Level: —
ATK: —
DEF: —
Rarity: Secret Rare

As long as this card remains face-up on the field, destroy all Flip Summoned monsters of Level 2 or lower. At that time, their effects are not activated.

The Sacred Cards

TSC-001 Perfectly Ultimate Great Moth

Card Type: Effect Monster
Monster Type: Insect
Attribute: Earth
Level: 8
ATK: 3500
DEF: 3000
Rarity: Secret Rare

Six turns is a lot of time and difficult to maintain, but the end result is well worth it!

TSC-002 Riryoku

Card Type: Spell
Monster Type: —
Attribute: Spell
Level: —
ATK: —
DEF: —
Rarity: Secret Rare

Not only can you weaken your opponent's monster, but you can power up one of your own monsters also!

TSC-003 Negate Attack

Card Type: Trap
Monster Type: —
Attribute: Trap
Level: —
ATK: —
DEF: —
Rarity: Secret Rare

You can immediately stop your opponent's Battle Phase. This not only helps protect your monsters but also your Life Points!

Power of Chaos

PCY-001 Windstorm of Etaqua

Card Type: Spell
Monster Type: —
Attribute: Spell
Level: —
ATK: —
DEF: —
Rarity: Secret Rare

Change the battle positions of all face-up monsters on your opponent's side of the field.

PCY-002 Anti-Spell Fragrance

Card Type: Trap
Monster Type: —
Attribute: Trap
Level: —
ATK: —
DEF: —
Rarity: Secret Rare

As long as this card remains face-up on the field, both players must first Set Spell Cards when they use them and cannot activate them until their next turn.

PCY-003 Thousand Knives

Card Type: Spell
Monster Type: —
Attribute: Spell
Level: —
ATK: —
DEF: —
Rarity: Secret Rare

You can activate this card when you have "Dark Magician" on your side of the field. Destroy 1 monster on your opponent's side of the field.

PCY-004 Dark Magician

Card Type: Normal Monster
Monster Type: Spellcaster
Attribute: Dark
Level: 7
ATK: 2500
DEF: 2100
Rarity: Common

A high-ranking magician of the Spellcaster-Type, the "Dark Magician" is very dangerous unless you destroy him as soon as your opponent places him on the field.

PCY-005 Kuribon

Card Type: Effect Monster
Monster Type: Fiend
Attribute: Dark
Level: 1
ATK: 300
DEF: 200
Rarity: Super Rare

This card acts as a shield for your Life Points. When you're in a difficult situation, add this card to your hand using "Witch of the Black Forest" or "Sangan."

Collectible Tin #1 and #2

Collectible Tin #1

BPT-001 Dark Magician

Card Type: Normal Monster
Monster Type: Spellcaster
Attribute: Dark
Level: 7
ATK: 2500
DEF: 2100
Rarity: Common

A high-ranking magician of the Spellcaster-Type, the "Dark Magician" is very dangerous unless you destroy him as soon as your opponent places him on the field.

BPT-002 Summoned Skull

Card Type: Normal Monster
Monster Type: Fiend
Attribute: Dark
Level: 6
ATK: 2500
DEF: 1200
Rarity: Common

Though "Summoned Skull" is a high-level Fiend, it's easy to summon and extremely useful.

BPT-003 Blue-Eyes White Dragon

Card Type: Normal Monster
Monster Type: Dragon
Attribute: Light
Level: 8
ATK: 3000
DEF: 2500
Rarity: Common

Kaiba's favorite monster is the most powerful Normal Monster Card. Destroying "Blue-Eyes" without a Spell Card will be difficult!

BPT-004 Lord of D.

Card Type: Effect Monster
Monster Type: Spellcaster
Attribute: Dark
Level: 4
ATK: 1200
DEF: 1100
Rarity: Common

"Lord of D." can protect all Dragons, but that's not all! Using "Lord of D." with "The Flute of Summoning Dragon" forms a devastating combo!

BPT-005 Red-Eyes B. Dragon

Card Type: Normal Monster
Monster Type: Dragon
Attribute: Dark
Level: 7
ATK: 2400
DEF: 2000
Rarity: Common

Joey received this rare card by defeating "Rex Raptor." This monster can become even stronger if it fused with another monster by "Polymerization!"

BPT-006 B. Skull Dragon

Card Type: Fusion Monster
Monster Type: Dragon
Attribute: Dark
Level: 9
ATK: 3200
DEF: 2500
Rarity: Common

Create one of the fiercest monsters in action by fusing "Summoned Skull" and "Red-Eyes B. Dragon" with "Polymerization." This must-have card has capabilities for powerful combos.

Collectible Tin #2

BPT-007 Dark Magician

Card Type: Normal Monster
Monster Type: Spellcaster
Attribute: Dark
Level: 7
ATK: 2500
DEF: 2100
Rarity: Common

A high-ranking magician of the Spellcaster-Type, the "Dark Magician" is very dangerous unless you destroy him as soon as your opponent places him on the field.

BPT-008 Buster Blader

Card Type: Effect Monster
Monster Type: Warrior
Attribute: Earth
Level: 7
ATK: 2600
DEF: 2300
Rarity: Ultra Rare

If your opponent plays with many Dragon-Type monsters, then "Buster Blader" is a must-have for your Deck.

BPT-009 Blue-Eyes White Dragon

Card Type: Normal Monster
Monster Type: Dragon
Attribute: Light
Level: 8
ATK: 3000
DEF: 2500
Rarity: Common

Kaiba's favorite monster is the most powerful Normal Monster Card. Destroying "Blue-Eyes" without a Spell Card will be difficult!

BPT-010 XYZ-Dragon Cannon

Card Type: Fusion/Effect Monster
Monster Type: Machine
Type: Light
Level: 6
ATK: 2200
DEF: 1900
Rarity: Ultra Rare

By discarding one card from your hand, you can destroy a face-up Spell or Trap Card on your opponent's field. However, you can't destroy a face-down Spell or Trap Card.

BPT-011 Jinzo

Card Type: Effect Monster
Monster Type: Machine
Attribute: Dark
Level: 6
ATK: 2400
DEF: 1500
Rarity: Secret Rare

"Jinzo" prevents Trap Cards from activating, which can seriously cripple your opponent's strategy if he or she relies on Trap Cards.

BPT-012 Gearfried the Iron Knight

Card Type: Effect Monster
Monster Type: Warrior
Attribute: Earth
Level: 4
ATK: 1800
DEF: 1600
Rarity: Super Rare

"Gearfried the Iron Knight" has high ATK for a Level 4 monster. Though you can't use Equip Spell Cards on "Gearfried the Iron Knight," neither can your opponent!

Tournament Pack #1

TP1-001 Mechanicalchaser

Card Type: Normal Monster
Monster Type: Machine
Attribute: Dark
Level: 4
ATK: 1850
DEF: 800
Rarity: Ultra Rare

This Machine was created with only offense in mind. Don't think about defending; just attack!

TP1-002 Axe Raider

Card Type: Normal Monster
Monster Type: Warrior
Attribute: Earth
Level: 4
ATK: 1700
DEF: 1150
Rarity: Super Rare

With greater ATK than "Beautiful Headhuntress," this Warrior can change the course of battle.

TP1-003 Kwagar Hercules

Card Type: Fusion Monster
Monster Type: Insect
Attribute: Earth
Level: 6
ATK: 1900
DEF: 1700
Rarity: Super Rare

It has lower DEF than "Hercules Bettle," but it has higher ATK.

TP1-004 Patrol Robo

Card Type: Effect Monster
Monster Type: Machine
Attribute: Earth
Level: 3
ATK: 1100
DEF: 900
Rarity: Super Rare

Even if the face-down card is an Effect Monster, since you are only looking at it, the effect doesn't activate.

TP1-005 White Hole

Card Type: Trap
Monster Type: —
Attribute: Trap
Level: —
ATK: —
DEF: —
Rarity: Super Rare

If you have this Trap Card, you don't have to be afraid of "Dark Hole!"

TP1-006 Elf's Light

Card Type: Spell
Monster Type: —
Attribute: Spell
Level: —
ATK: —
DEF: —
Rarity: Rare

If you use this card with "Rogue Doll," its low DEF will become even lower. Use this card wisely.

TP1-007 Steel Shell

Card Type: Spell
Monster Type: —
Attribute: Spell
Level: —
ATK: —
DEF: —
Rarity: Rare

WATER monsters generally have high DEF, so you can use this card without worry.

TP1-008 Blue Medicine

Card Type: Spell
Monster Type: —
Attribute: Spell
Level: —
ATK: —
DEF: —
Rarity: Rare

After drinking this blue liquid, you can taste its power in your mouth, and you gain 400 Life Points.

TP1-009 Raimei

Card Type: Spell
Monster Type: —
Attribute: Spell
Level: —
ATK: —
DEF: —
Rarity: Rare

Lightning falls from the sky and strikes your opponent for 300 Life Points of damage.

Tournament Pack #1

TP1-010 Burning Spear

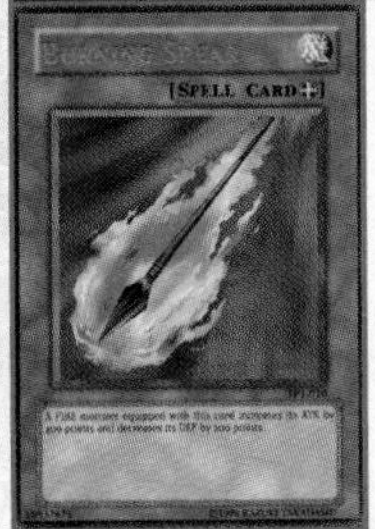

Card Type: Spell
Monster Type: —
Attribute: Spell
Level: —
ATK: —
DEF: —
Rarity: Rare

This Spell Card is important for FIRE monsters.

TP1-011 Gust Fan

Card Type: Spell
Monster Type: —
Attribute: Spell
Level: —
ATK: —
DEF: —
Rarity: Rare

This mysterious fan strengthens WIND monsters, which is useful because there are many monsters that counteract Winged Beasts.

TP1-012 Tiger Axe

Card Type: Normal Monster
Monster Type: Beast-Warrior
Attribute: Earth
Level: 4
ATK: 1300
DEF: 1100
Rarity: Rare

This strong Beast-Warrior's trademark is its huge axe in its hand.

TP1-013 Goddess with the Third Eye

Card Type: Effect Monster
Monster Type: Fairy
Attribute: Light
Level: 4
ATK: 1200
DEF: 1000
Rarity: Rare

They say her third eye can see the truth. Out of monsters that can substitute as Fusion-Material Monsters, this card has very high ATK. When the Fusion-Material Monsters you need have low Attack and DEF, use this card instead. "Goddess with the Third Eye" is also decent in battle.

TP1-014 Beastking of the Swamps

Card Type: Effect Monster
Monster Type: Aqua
Attribute: Water
Level: 4
ATK: 1000
DEF: 1100
Rarity: Rare

This monster lives in bottomless swamps. Out of monsters that can substitute as Fusion-Material Monsters, this card has very high DEF. However, 1100 DEF is still low, so you'll need other cards to power it up or use "Umi" Field Spell Card.

TP1-015 Versago the Destroyer

Card Type: Effect Monster
Monster Type: Fiend
Attribute: Dark
Level: 3
ATK: 1100
DEF: 900
Rarity: Rare

"Versago the Destroyer" materializes in a spooky light and destroys everything around it. Fiend-Type or DARK monsters are very useful. It's easy to create a Deck that is full of DARK monsters, so include this card as a Fusion-Material Monster.

TP1-016 Oscillo Hero #2

Card Type: Normal Monster
Monster Type: Thunder
Attribute: Light
Level: 3
ATK: 1000
DEF: 500
Rarity: Common

This strange electric child does a weird dance to shoot out lightning bolts.

TP1-017 Giant Flea

Card Type: Normal Monster
Monster Type: Insect
Attribute: Earth
Level: 4
ATK: 1500
DEF: 1200
Rarity: Common

"Giant Flea" has high Attack Power, but sometimes, it jumps too high and hits its head.

TP1-018 Bean Soldier

Card Type: Normal Monster
Monster Type: Plant
Attribute: Earth
Level: 4
ATK: 1400
DEF: 1300
Rarity: Common

This useful Plant becomes very flavorful when it takes a shower.

TP1-019 The Statue of Easter Island

Card Type: Normal Monster
Monster Type: Rock
Attribute: Earth
Level: 4
ATK: 1100
DEF: 1400
Rarity: Common

When these statues were created is a source of great discussion. Its thin eyes glow blue-white.

TP1-020 Corroding Shark

Card Type: Normal Monster
Monster Type: Zombie
Attribute: Dark
Level: 3
ATK: 1100
DEF: 700
Rarity: Common

This monster doesn't realize that it has passed away. Many different animals live inside its stomach.

TP1-021 Wow Warrior

Card Type: Normal Monster
Monster Type: Fish
Attribute: Water
Level: 4
ATK: 1250
DEF: 900
Rarity: Common

This Warrior can also fight on land, though its scales aren't very protective.

TP1-022 Winged Dragon, Guardian of the Fortress #2

Card Type: Normal Monster
Monster Type: Winged Beast
Attribute: Wind
Level: 4
ATK: 1200
DEF: 1000
Rarity: Common

This secondary Winged-Beast becomes more useful when combined with "Mountain."

TP1-023 Oscillo Hero

Card Type: Normal Monster
Monster Type: Warrior
Attribute: Earth
Level: 3
ATK: 1250
DEF: 700
Rarity: Common

When it meets a lady, for some reason, it shows off its cape.

TP1-024 Shining Friendship

Card Type: Normal Monster
Monster Type: Fairy
Attribute: Light
Level: 4
ATK: 1300
DEF: 1100
Rarity: Common

When it sees anything big and round, "Shining Friendship" approaches it, thinking that it's a friend. When it realizes its mistake, it flees.

TP1-025 Hercules Beetle

Card Type: Normal Monster
Monster Type: Insect
Attribute: Earth
Level: 5
ATK: 1500
DEF: 2000
Rarity: Common

This beetle has high ATK and DEF. Decide whether to Tribute Summon this monster or use it for Fusion.

TP1-026 The Judgment Hand

Card Type: Normal Monster
Monster Type: Warrior
Attribute: Earth
Level: 3
ATK: 1400
DEF: 700
Rarity: Common

With its powerful fist, it can knock out a weakling in a single blow! However, it's weak at defense.

TP1-027 Wodan the Resident of the Forest

Card Type: Effect Monster
Monster Type: Warrior
Attribute: Earth
Level: 3
ATK: 900
DEF: 1200
Rarity: Common

This card is effective in a Plant-Type Deck, but its basic ATK and DEF are low, so it is not very useful.

TP1-028 Cyber Soldier of Darkworld

Card Type: Normal Monster
Monster Type: Machine
Attribute: Dark
Level: 4
ATK: 1400
DEF: 1200
Rarity: Common

Though this Machine moves using shadow energy, it's not as strong as Fiends and Spellcasters who can truly harness the power of the shadows.

TP1-029 Cockroach Knight

Card Type: Effect Monster
Monster Type: Insect
Attribute: Earth
Level: 3
ATK: 800
DEF: 900
Rarity: Common

This card will always be in your Deck or hand.

TP1-030 Kuwagata

Card Type: Normal Monster
Monster Type: Insect
Attribute: Earth
Level: 4
ATK: 1250
DEF: 1000
Rarity: Common

This powerful Insect is Fusion-Material for summoning "Kwagar Hercules."

Tournament Pack #2

Tournament Pack #2

TP2-001 Morphing Jar

Card Type: Effect Monster
Monster Type: Rock
Attribute: Earth
Level: 2
ATK: 700
DEF: 600
Rarity: Ultra Rare

You can create Decks that focus on this card as its centerpiece. This card is very useful when you have no useful cards in your hand while your opponent has powerful cards in hand.

TP2-002 Dragon Seeker

Card Type: Effect Monster
Monster Type: Fiend
Attribute: Dark
Level: 6
ATK: 2000
DEF: 2100
Rarity: Super Rare

Not only is "Dragon Seeker's" effect somewhat useful, but its ATK and DEF are high. If everything goes according to plan, you can use its effect to destroy a powerful Dragon, then you can attack your opponent.

TP2-003 Giant Red Seasnake

Card Type: Normal Monster
Monster Type: Aqua
Attribute: Water
Level: 4
ATK: 1800
DEF: 800
Rarity: Super Rare

This sea snake is one of the most powerful Aqua-Type monsters. If you power this card up with Spell Cards, then it will be unstoppable!

TP2-004 Exile of the Wicked

Card Type: Spell
Monster Type: –
Attribute: Spell
Level: –
ATK: –
DEF: –
Rarity: Super Rare

Having lost his wife and children to Fiends, he discovered a Spell to counteract Fiends. This eerie Spell scares everyone. Fiend-Type monsters are generally very powerful, especially "Summoned Skull." However, if your opponent does not play Fiend monsters, then this card is useless.

TP2-005 Call of the Grave

Card Type: Trap
Monster Type: –
Attribute: Trap
Level: –
ATK: –
DEF: –
Rarity: Super Rare

Use this card when your opponent is about to revive a powerful monster. Timing is essential.

TP2-006 Mikazukinoyaiba

Card Type: Normal Monster
Monster Type: Dragon
Attribute: Dark
Level: 7
ATK: 2200
DEF: 2350
Rarity: Rare

This high-level monster has high defense points. It is a DARK monster, just like "Red-Eyes B. Dragon."

TP2-007 Skull Guardian

Card Type: Ritual Monster
Monster Type: Warrior
Attribute: Light
Level: 7
ATK: 2050
DEF: 2500
Rarity: Rare

"Skull Guardian" can be counted on to protect the king. With 2500 DEF, ordinary attacks won't hurt it!

TP2-008 Novox's Prayer

Card Type: Spell
Monster Type: –
Attribute: Spell
Level: –
ATK: –
DEF: –
Rarity: Rare

You need this card to summon the Ritual Monster "Skull Guardian." This card is useless by itself, so make sure to get both cards!

TP2-009 Dokurorider

Card Type: Ritual Monster
Monster Type: Zombie
Attribute: Dark
Level: 6
ATK: 1900
DEF: 1850
Rarity: Rare

This legendary monster is a Special Summon, so it cannot be destroyed by "Trap Hole." Also, you can Normal Summon another monster on the same turn "Dokurorider" is summoned, increasing the monsters on your field.

TP2-010 Revival of Dokurorider

- **Card Type:** Spell
- **Monster Type:** —
- **Attribute:** Spell
- **Level:** —
- **ATK:** —
- **DEF:** —
- **Rarity:** Rare

You need this card to summon the Ritual Monster "Dokurorider." This card is useless by itself, so make sure to get both cards!

TP2-011 Beautiful Headhuntress

- **Card Type:** Normal Monster
- **Monster Type:** Warrior
- **Attribute:** Earth
- **Level:** 4
- **ATK:** 1600
- **DEF:** 800
- **Rarity:** Rare

This beautiful woman sharpens her blade everyday. However, she is weak at defending.

TP2-012 Sonic Maid

- **Card Type:** Normal Monster
- **Monster Type:** Warrior
- **Attribute:** Earth
- **Level:** 3
- **ATK:** 1200
- **DEF:** 900
- **Rarity:** Rare

"Sonic Maid" isn't very strong on her own, but when fused, she becomes "Warrior of Tradition!"

TP2-013 Mystical Sheep #1

- **Card Type:** Effect Monster
- **Monster Type:** Beast
- **Attribute:** Earth
- **Level:** 3
- **ATK:** 1150
- **DEF:** 900
- **Rarity:** Rare

The coin on the tip of its tail puts its enemies to sleep. This card is more useful as a Fusion-Material Monster if it is protected by using "Sogen" to power it up.

TP2-014 Warrior of Tradition

- **Card Type:** Fusion Monster
- **Monster Type:** Warrior
- **Attribute:** Earth
- **Level:** 6
- **ATK:** 1900
- **DEF:** 1700
- **Rarity:** Rare

Though this kimono beauty can be rough, her ATK are high to be useful in battle.

TP2-015 Soul of the Pure

- **Card Type:** Spell
- **Monster Type:** —
- **Attribute:** Spell
- **Level:** —
- **ATK:** —
- **DEF:** —
- **Rarity:** Common

A fairy uses her own life essence to heal people.

TP2-016 Dancing Elf

- **Card Type:** Normal Monster
- **Monster Type:** Fairy
- **Attribute:** Wind
- **Level:** 1
- **ATK:** 300
- **DEF:** 200
- **Rarity:** Common

Though this elf is beautiful, she has low ATK and DEF, so she may be only useful in Fairy-Type Decks.

TP2-017 Turu-Purun

- **Card Type:** Normal Monster
- **Monster Type:** Aqua
- **Attribute:** Water
- **Level:** 2
- **ATK:** 450
- **DEF:** 500
- **Rarity:** Common

"Turu-Purun's" large stomach is cool to the touch, so if you rest your face against it, it feels refreshing!

TP2-018 Dharma Cannon

- **Card Type:** Normal Monster
- **Monster Type:** Machine
- **Attribute:** Dark
- **Level:** 2
- **ATK:** 900
- **DEF:** 500
- **Rarity:** Common

"Dharma Cannon" has various weapons all over its body, but it still has low ATK....

TP2-019 Stuffed Animal

- **Card Type:** Normal Monster
- **Monster Type:** Warrior
- **Attribute:** Earth
- **Level:** 3
- **ATK:** 1200
- **DEF:** 900
- **Rarity:** Common

This monster never attacks people who really love stuffed animals.

TP2-020 Spirit of the Books

- **Card Type:** Normal Monster
- **Monster Type:** Winged Beast
- **Attribute:** Wind
- **Level:** 4
- **ATK:** 1400
- **DEF:** 1200
- **Rarity:** Common

"Spirit of the Books" has no strengths of weaknesses. It attacks using different battle strategies, but its lack of firsthand knowledge is its downfall.

TP2-021 Faith Bird

- **Card Type:** Normal Monster
- **Monster Type:** Winged Beast
- **Attribute:** Wind
- **Level:** 4
- **ATK:** 1500
- **DEF:** 1100
- **Rarity:** Common

If you're lost in the mountains at night, "Faith Bird" comes to your rescue as long as you're human.

Tournament Pack #2

TP2-022 Takuhee

Card Type: Normal Monster
Monster Type: Winged Beast
Attribute: Wind
Level: 4
ATK: 1450
DEF: 1000
Rarity: Common

This bird can be useful in various situations due to its decent ATK.

TP2-023 Maiden of the Moonlight

Card Type: Normal Monster
Monster Type: Spellcaster
Attribute: Light
Level: 4
ATK: 1500
DEF: 1300
Rarity: Common

If you take a moonlight swim in the forest, you have a chance to meet this maiden. If you whistle, she will smile.

TP2-024 Queen of Autumn Leaves

Card Type: Normal Monster
Monster Type: Plant
Attribute: Earth
Level: 5
ATK: 1800
DEF: 1500
Rarity: Common

In the calm late afternoon, she relaxes by drinking tea with her husband "Green Phantom King."

TP2-025 Two-Headed King Rex

Card Type: Normal Monster
Monster Type: Dinosaur
Attribute: Earth
Level: 4
ATK: 1600
DEF: 1200
Rarity: Common

This Dinosaur attacks with its two heads simultaneously.

TP2-026 Garoozis

Card Type: Normal Monster
Monster Type: Beast-Warrior
Attribute: Fire
Level: 5
ATK: 1800
DEF: 1500
Rarity: Common

"Garoozis" has the head of a dragon and swings an axe with tremendous strength. However, he cannot defend as well.

TP2-027 Crawling Dragon #2

Card Type: Normal Monster
Monster Type: Dinosaur
Attribute: Earth
Level: 4
ATK: 1600
DEF: 1200
Rarity: Common

Its jaws are so powerful that there's nothing in existence that cannot be torn to shreds by its fangs.

TP2-028 Parrot Dragon

Card Type: Normal Monster
Monster Type: Dragon
Attribute: Wind
Level: 5
ATK: 2000
DEF: 1300
Rarity: Common

This cute and comical Dragon actually thirsts for the taste of destruction.

TP2-029 Sky Dragon

Card Type: Normal Monster
Monster Type: Dragon
Attribute: Wind
Level: 6
ATK: 1900
DEF: 1800
Rarity: Common

With four wings, this Dragon looks more like a bird. Its sharp wings can even cut through diamonds!

TP2-030 Water Magician

Card Type: Normal Monster
Monster Type: Aqua
Attribute: Water
Level: 4
ATK: 1400
DEF: 1000
Rarity: Common

"Water Magician" can control water and drown her enemies.

Tournament Pack #3

TP3-001 Needle Worm

Card Type: Effect Monster
Monster Type: Insect
Attribute: Earth
Level: 2
ATK: 750
DEF: 600
Rarity: Ultra Rare

This card is useful in destroying your opponent's Deck. If your opponent discards key cards, such as Ritual Spell Cards or combo cards, to the Graveyard, then your opponent's strategy will be hindered.

TP3-002 Anti Raigeki

Card Type: Trap
Monster Type: —
Attribute: Trap
Level: —
ATK: —
DEF: —
Rarity: Super Rare

This card not only stops your monsters from being destroyed by "Raigeki," but it destroys all your opponent's monsters instead! There's no way your opponent is going to expect his or her own monsters are going to be destroyed by his or her own Spell Card!

TP3-003 Mechanicalchaser

Card Type: Normal Monster
Monster Type: Machine
Attribute: Dark
Level: 4
ATK: 1850
DEF: 800
Rarity: Super Rare

This Machine was created with only offense in mind. Don't think about defending; just attack!

TP3-004 B. Skull Dragon

Card Type: Fusion Monster
Monster Type: Dragon
Attribute: Dark
Level: 9
ATK: 3200
DEF: 2500
Rarity: Super Rare

Create one of the fiercest monsters in action by fusing "Summoned Skull" and "Red-Eyes B. Dragon" with "Polymerization." This must-have card has capabilities for powerful combos.

TP3-005 Horn of Heaven

Card Type: Trap
Monster Type: —
Attribute: Trap
Level: —
ATK: —
DEF: —
Rarity: Super Rare

You can negate the summon and destroy your opponent's monster no matter how powerful it is. Also notice that you can destroy an Effect Monster without triggering its effect. However, you cannot use "Horn of Heaven" against Fusion and Ritual Monsters.

TP3-006 Axe Raider

Card Type: Normal Monster
Monster Type: Warrior
Attribute: Earth
Level: 4
ATK: 1700
DEF: 1150
Rarity: Rare

With greater ATK than "Beautiful Headhuntress," this Warrior can change the course of battle.

TP3-007 Kwagar Hercules

Card Type: Fusion Monster
Monster Type: Insect
Attribute: Earth
Level: 6
ATK: 1900
DEF: 1700
Rarity: Rare

It has lower DEF than "Hercules Beetle," but it has higher ATK.

TP3-008 Patrol Robo

Card Type: Effect Monster
Monster Type: Machine
Attribute: Earth
Level: 3
ATK: 1100
DEF: 900
Rarity: Rare

Even if the face-down card is an Effect Monster, since you are only looking at it, the effect doesn't activate.

Tournament Pack #3

TP3-009 White Hole

Card Type: Trap
Monster Type: —
Attribute: Trap
Level: —
ATK: —
DEF: —
Rarity: Rare

If you have this Trap Card, you don't have to be afraid of "Dark Hole!"

TP3-010 Dragon Capture Jar

Card Type: Trap
Monster Type: —
Attribute: Trap
Level: —
ATK: —
DEF: —
Rarity: Common

Dragon-Types should be wary of this Trap Card. Even the "Stop Defense" Spell Card can't affect "Dragon Capture Jar!"

TP3-011 Goblin's Secret Remedy

Card Type: Spell
Monster Type: —
Attribute: Spell
Level: —
ATK: —
DEF: —
Rarity: Common

After you bite into this secret remedy cherished by goblin fairies, the bitterness will spread throughout your mouth.

TP3-012 Final Flame

Card Type: Spell
Monster Type: —
Attribute: Spell
Level: —
ATK: —
DEF: —
Rarity: Common

This glowing card does a whopping 800 points of damage to your opponent's Life Points! Save it for the final stroke.

TP3-013 Spirit of the Harp

Card Type: Normal Monster
Monster Type: Fairy
Attribute: Light
Level: 4
ATK: 800
DEF: 2000
Rarity: Common

This female monster has very high DEF. If you use Yami Field Spell Card, "Spirit of the Harp" will power down.

TP3-014 Pot of Greed

Card Type: Spell
Monster Type: —
Attribute: Spell
Level: —
ATK: —
DEF: —
Rarity: Common

Draw 2 cards from your Deck.

TP3-015 Karbonala Warrior

Card Type: Fusion Monster
Monster Type: Warrior
Attribute: Earth
Level: 4
ATK: 1500
DEF: 1200
Rarity: Common

"Karbonala Warrior" is created when the close-knit "M-Warrior" brothers fuse. However, "Karbonala Warrior's" personality is quite different than before.

TP3-016 Darkfire Dragon

Card Type: Fusion Monster
Monster Type: Dragon
Attribute: Dark
Level: 4
ATK: 1500
DEF: 1250
Rarity: Common

"Petit Dragon" has wrapped itself in flames and evolved to "Darkfire Dragon." This Fusion Monster has higher ATK than before.

TP3-017 Elegant Egotist

Card Type: Spell
Monster Type: —
Attribute: Spell
Level: —
ATK: —
DEF: —
Rarity: Common

After Special Summoning "Harpie Lady Sisters," don't forget to shuffle your Deck.

TP3-018 Dark Elf

Card Type: Effect Monster
Monster Type: Spellcaster
Attribute: Dark
Level: 4
ATK: 2000
DEF: 800
Rarity: Common

Finally, here's a Level 4 monster that has 2000 ATK. However, it functions as a wall in Attack Position. Paying 1000 Life Points to attack is usually only useful when your opponent has no monsters on the field.

TP3-019 Little Chimera

Card Type: Effect Monster
Monster Type: Beast
Attribute: Fire
Level: 2
ATK: 600
DEF: 550
Rarity: Common

Use "Little Chimera" in your Deck if you can easily summon FIRE monsters or if your opponent is using WATER monsters.

TP3-020 Bladefly

Card Type: Effect Monster
Monster Type: Insect
Attribute: Wind
Level: 2
ATK: 600
DEF: 700
Rarity: Common

Use "Bladefly" when your Deck is centered on WIND monsters. "Bladefly's" effect also affects itself, so this card's ATK is already 500 points higher.

Tournament Pack #4

TP4-001 Royal Decree

- **Card Type:** Trap
- **Monster Type:** —
- **Attribute:** Trap
- **Level:** —
- **ATK:** —
- **DEF:** —
- **Rarity:** Ultra Rare

This card stops all Trap Cards' effects, other than itself. As long as this card is on the field, neither player can use Trap Cards. If your opponent creates a Deck loaded with Trap Cards, he or she is in big trouble!

TP4-002 Morphing Jar

- **Card Type:** Effect Monster
- **Monster Type:** Rock
- **Attribute:** Earth
- **Level:** 2
- **ATK:** 700
- **DEF:** 600
- **Rarity:** Super Rare

You can create Decks that focus on this card as its centerpiece. This card is very useful when you have no useful cards in your hand while your opponent has powerful cards in hand.

TP4-003 Megamorph

- **Card Type:** Spell
- **Monster Type:** —
- **Attribute:** Spell
- **Level:** —
- **ATK:** —
- **DEF:** —
- **Rarity:** Super Rare

This is a powerful Equip Spell Card. If you have less Life Points than your opponent, equip this card on one of your monsters. If you have more Life Points than your opponent, equip this card on one of your opponent's monsters.

TP4-004 Chain Destruction

- **Card Type:** Trap
- **Monster Type:** —
- **Attribute:** Trap
- **Level:** —
- **ATK:** —
- **DEF:** —
- **Rarity:** Super Rare

If you destroy all the monsters necessary in a combo, then the combo can never take place!

TP4-005 The Fiend Megacyber

- **Card Type:** Effect Monster
- **Monster Type:** Warrior
- **Attribute:** Dark
- **Level:** 6
- **ATK:** 2200
- **DEF:** 1200
- **Rarity:** Super Rare

Summoning a monster with 2200 ATK without having to offer another monster as a Tribute is incredible! You may want to hold off summoning your own monsters until your opponent has two or more than you on the field.

TP4-006 Dragon Seeker

- **Card Type:** Effect Monster
- **Monster Type:** Fiend
- **Attribute:** Dark
- **Level:** 6
- **ATK:** 2000
- **DEF:** 2100
- **Rarity:** Rare

Not only is "Dragon Seeker's" effect somewhat useful, but its ATK and DEF are high. If everything goes according to plan, you can use its effect to destroy a powerful Dragon, and then you can attack your opponent.

TP4-007 Giant Red Seasnake

- **Card Type:** Normal Monster
- **Monster Type:** Aqua
- **Attribute:** Water
- **Level:** 4
- **ATK:** 1800
- **DEF:** 800
- **Rarity:** Rare

This sea snake is one of the most powerful Aqua-Type monsters. If you power this card up with Spell Cards, then it will be unstoppable!

TP4-008 Exile of the Wicked

- **Card Type:** Spell
- **Monster Type:** —
- **Attribute:** Spell
- **Level:** —
- **ATK:** —
- **DEF:** —
- **Rarity:** Rare

Having lost his wife and children to Fiends, he discovered a Spell to counteract Fiends. This eerie Spell scares everyone. Fiend-Type monsters are generally very powerful, especially "Summoned Skull." However, if your opponent does not play Fiend monsters, then his card is useless.

Tournament Pack #4

TP4-009 Call of the Grave

Card Type: Trap
Monster Type: —
Attribute: Trap
Level: —
ATK: —
DEF: —
Rarity: Rare

Use this card when your opponent is about to revive a powerful monster. Timing is essential.

TP4-010 Rush Recklessly

Card Type: Spell
Monster Type: —
Attribute: Spell
Level: —
ATK: —
DEF: —
Rarity: Common

Your opponent may think his or her monster is destroying one of your weak monsters, but with this Spell Card, your opponent is in for a surprise! Your opponent will worry about attacking if his or her Monster's ATK is only 700 more than yours.

TP4-011 Giant Rat

Card Type: Effect Monster
Monster Type: Beast
Attribute: Earth
Level: 4
ATK: 1400
DEF: 1450
Rarity: Common

When "Giant Rat" is destroyed, you can Special Summon another monster to the field!

TP4-012 Senju of the Thousand Hands

Card Type: Effect Monster
Monster Type: Fairy
Attribute: Light
Level: 4
ATK: 1400
DEF: 1000
Rarity: Common

This card allows you to search your Deck for the Ritual Monster Card that you need.

TP4-013 Karate Man

Card Type: Effect Monster
Monster Type: Warrior
Attribute: Earth
Level: 3
ATK: 1000
DEF: 1000
Rarity: Common

You can double the ATK of "Karate Man" for one turn, but it will be destroyed at the end of the turn. Know when to use this effect. Remember, this is NOT a Multi-Trigger Effect.

TP4-014 Nimble Momonga

Card Type: Effect Monster
Monster Type: Beast
Attribute: Earth
Level: 2
ATK: 1000
DEF: 100
Rarity: Common

Not only do you regain Life Points, you can Special Summon another "Nimble Momonga" and repeat the process again!

TP4-015 Mystic Tomato

Card Type: Effect Monster
Monster Type: Plant
Attribute: Dark
Level: 4
ATK: 1400
DEF: 1100
Rarity: Common

When "Mystic Tomato" is destroyed, you can Special Summon another monster to the field!

TP4-016 Nobleman of Extermination

Card Type: Spell
Monster Type: —
Attribute: Spell
Level: —
ATK: —
DEF: —
Rarity: Common

Not only can you destroy one of your opponent's Spell and Trap Cards, but if you're lucky, you may remove a particularly nasty Trap Card from the Duel!

TP4-017 Magic Drain

Card Type: Trap
Monster Type: —
Attribute: Trap
Level: —
ATK: —
DEF: —
Rarity: Common

"Magic Drain" can either negate your opponent's Spell Card or force him or her to lose an additional Spell Card. Whichever your opponent chooses, it's a bonus for you!

TP4-018 Gravity Bind

Card Type: Trap
Monster Type: —
Attribute: Trap
Level: —
ATK: —
DEF: —
Rarity: Common

"Gravity Bind" will stop all your opponent's monsters cold! If you play many low-level monsters, "Gravity Bind" will not affect you at all. This card also helps stall your opponent if you're playing an Exodia Deck.

TP4-019 Hayabusa Knight

Card Type: Effect Monster
Monster Type: Warrior
Attribute: Earth
Level: 3
ATK: 1000
DEF: 700
Rarity: Common

"Hayabusa Knight" can attack twice, but it has low ATK. However, if you power up "Hayabusa Knight," then attacking twice is double the trouble for your opponent!

TP4-020 Mad Sword Beast

Card Type: Effect Monster
Monster Type: Dinosaur
Attribute: Earth
Level: 4
ATK: 1400
DEF: 1200
Rarity: Common

"Mad Sword Beast" can deal damage to your opponent's Life Points even if your opponent's monster is in Defense Position! Find ways to power up "Mad Sword Beast" to deal even more damage!

McDonald's Promotion

MP1-001 Millennium Shield

Card Type: Normal Monster
Monster Type: Warrior
Attribute: Earth
Level: 5
ATK: 0
DEF: 3000
Rarity: Ultra Rare

Even "Blue-Eyes White Dragon" cannot destroy "Millennium Shield" in Defense Position. Use this card to buy yourself some time.

MP1-002 Cosmo Queen

Card Type: Normal Monster
Monster Type: Spellcaster
Attribute: Dark
Level: 8
ATK: 2900
DEF: 2450
Rarity: Ultra Rare

This Spellcaster has higher ATK than "Dark Magician!"

MP1-003 Goddess of Whim

Card Type: Effect Monster
Monster Type: Fairy
Attribute: Light
Level: 3
ATK: 950
DEF: 700
Rarity: Super Rare

Not many Effect Monster cards utilize a coin flip. If you're successful, "Goddess of Whim" has 1900 ATK!

MP1-004 Frog the Jam

Card Type: Normal Monster
Monster Type: Aqua
Attribute: Water
Level: 2
ATK: 700
DEF: 500
Rarity: Common

Though it has low ATK and DEF, it's useful for offering as a Tribute.

MP1-005 Yaranzo

Card Type: Normal Monster
Monster Type: Zombie
Attribute: Dark
Level: 4
ATK: 1300
DEF: 1500
Rarity: Common

"Yaranzo" usually hides inside a treasure chest and waits for its next victim.

MP1-006 Takriminos

Card Type: Normal Monster
Monster Type: Sea Serpent
Attribute: Water
Level: 4
ATK: 1500
DEF: 1200
Rarity: Super Rare

It has high ATK and DEF for a monster that is very easy to summon.

MP1-007 Stuffed Animal

Card Type: Normal Monster
Monster Type: Warrior
Attribute: Earth
Level: 3
ATK: 1200
DEF: 900
Rarity: Common

This monster never attacks people who really love stuffed animals.

MP1-008 Megasonic Eye

Card Type: Normal Monster
Monster Type: Machine
Attribute: Dark
Level: 5
ATK: 1500
DEF: 1800
Rarity: Common

A strange Machine with high DEF, this card is hard to use because you need to offer another monster as a Tribute to summon "Megasonic Eye."

McDonald's Promotion

MP1-009 Yamadron

Card Type: Normal Monster
Monster Type: Dragon
Attribute: Fire
Level: 5
ATK: 1600
DEF: 1800
Rarity: Common

"Yamadron" is a FIRE Dragon that has higher ATK than "Megasonic Eye." Its three heads get along great.

MP1-010 Three-Legged Zombies

Card Type: Normal Monster
Monster Type: Zombie
Attribute: Dark
Level: 3
ATK: 1100
DEF: 800
Rarity: Common

Two strange Zombies only have the strength of one. Since it can't move around easily, it has low DEF....

MP1-011 Flying Penguin

Card Type: Normal Monster
Monster Type: Aqua
Attribute: Water
Level: 4
ATK: 1200
DEF: 1000
Rarity: Common

Not many have ever seen "Flying Penguin." It is usually calm, but when angered, watch out!

MP1-012 Fairy's Gift

Card Type: Normal Monster
Monster Type: Spellcaster
Attribute: Light
Level: 4
ATK: 1400
DEF: 1000
Rarity: Common

If you power up "Fairy's Gift" with Spell Cards, then it can be very useful.

MP1-013 Ushi Oni

Card Type: Normal Monster
Monster Type: Fiend
Attribute: Dark
Level: 6
ATK: 2150
DEF: 1950
Rarity: Common

Dark magic resurrected this cow Fiend, but for some reason, it comes out of a pot. "Ushi Oni" is quite useful for a monster that needs only one monster as a Tribute.

MP1-014 Turtle Bird

Card Type: Normal Monster
Monster Type: Aqua
Attribute: Water
Level: 6
ATK: 1900
DEF: 1700
Rarity: Common

In the air, hunters aim for "Turtle Bird." In the sea, fisherman hunt "Turtle Bird." Isn't there a place in the world safe for this creature?

MP1-015 Dark-Piercing Light

Card Type: Spell
Monster Type: –
Attribute: Spell
Level: –
ATK: –
DEF: –
Rarity: Super Rare

Use this card when you think your opponent is Setting Flip Effect Monsters to force them to activate before you summon a key monster.

Shonen Jump

JMP-001 Blue-Eyes White Dragon

Card Type: Normal Monster
Monster Type: Dragon
Attribute: Light
Level: 8
ATK: 3000
DEF: 2500
Rarity: Common

Kaiba's favorite monster is the most powerful Normal Monster Card. Destroying "Blue-Eyes" without a Spell Card will be difficult!

Top 24 Level 4 and Under Monsters with Highest ATK

Rank: 1

Name: Armor Exe

ATK: 2400

Effect: This card cannot attack in the same turn it is Normal Summoned, Flip Summoned, or Special Summoned. During each of your and your opponent's Standby Phases, remove 1 Spell Counter on your side of the field. If you do not do so, this card is destroyed.

Rank: 2

Name: Goblin Attack Force

ATK: 2300

Effect: When this card attacks, it is changed to Defense Position at the end of the Battle Phase. This position cannot be changed during your next turn.

Rank: 3

Name: Giant Orc

ATK: 2200

Effect: When this card attacks, it is changed to Defense Position at the end of the Battle Phase. This position cannot be changed until the end of your next turn.

Rank: 3

Name: Jirai Gumo

ATK: 2200

Effect: When you attack with this card, toss a coin and call it. If you call it right, attack normally. If you call it wrong, reduce your Life Points by half before attacking.

Rank: 5

Name: Zombyra the Dark

ATK: 2100

Effect: This card cannot attack a player directly. Each time this card destroys a monster in battle, decrease the ATK of this card by 200 points.

Rank: 6

Name: Arsenal Bug

ATK: 2000

Effect: If there are no face-up Insect-Type monsters (except this monster) on your side of the field, both the ATK and DEF of this monster become 1000 points.

Rank: 6

Name: Boar Soldier

ATK: 2000

Effect: This card can only be summoned by a Flip Summon. If summoned by a Normal Summon, the card is destroyed. If your opponent has 1 or more monsters under his/her control, the ATK of this card is decreased by 1000 points.

Rank: 6

Name: Cave Dragon

ATK: 2000

Effect: If there is a monster on your side of the field, you cannot Normal Summon this monster. In addition, if there are no Dragon-Type monsters except this card on your side of the field, this monster cannot attack.

Rank: 6

Name: Dark Elf

ATK: 2000

Effect: This card requires a cost of 1000 of your own Life Points to attack.

Rank: 6

Name: Flash Assailant

ATK: 2000

Effect: Decrease the ATK and DEF of this card by 400 points for every card in your hand.

Rank: 6

Name: Nuvia the Wicked

ATK: 2000

Effect: If this monster is summoned by a Normal Summon, it is destroyed. The ATK of this card is decreased by 200 points for each monster on your opponent's side of the field.

Rank: 6

Name: Shadowknight Archfiend

ATK: 2000

Effect: The controller of this card pays 900 Life Points during each of his/her Standby Phases (this is not optional). When this card is specifically designated as a target of the effect of a card controlled by your opponent, when resolving the effect, roll a six-sided die. If the result is 3, negate the effect and destroy the opponent's card. The Battle Damage this card inflicts to your opponent's Life Points is halved.

Top Monsters in the Yu-Gi-Oh!™ TRADING CARD GAME

Rank: 6

Name: Susa Soldier

ATK: 2000

Effect:
This card cannot be Special Summoned. This card returns to the owner's hand during the End Phase of the turn that this card is Normal Summoned, Flip Summoned, or flipped face-up. The Battle Damage this card inflicts to your opponent's Life Points is halved.

Rank: 6

Name: Terrorking Archfiend

ATK: 2000

Effect:
You cannot Normal Summon or Flip Summon this card unless you have an Archfiend Monster Card on your side of the field. The controller of this card pays 800 Life Points during each of his/her Standby Phases (this is not optional). When this card is specifically designated as a target of the effect of a card controlled by your opponent, when resolving the effect, roll a six-sided die. If the result is 2 or 5, negate the effect and destroy the opponent's card. Also negate the effect of an Effect Monster that is destroyed by this monster in battle.

Rank: 6

Name: The Unfriendly Amazon

ATK: 2000

Effect:
Offer 1 of your monsters on the field as a Tribute (excluding this monster) during each of your Standby Phases. If you cannot, this card is destroyed. Monsters used for a Tribute Summon or that are offered as Tributes due to other cards' effects are excluded.

Rank: 16

Name: Archfiend Soldier

ATK: 1900

Effect:
None

Rank: 16

Name: Gemini Elf

ATK: 1900

Effect:
None

Rank: 16

Name: Luster Dragon

ATK: 1900

Effect:
None

Rank: 16

Name: Paladin of White Dragon

ATK: 1900

Effect:
This monster can only be Ritual Summoned with the Ritual Spell Card, "White Dragon Ritual." You must also offer monsters whose total Level Stars equal 4 or more as a Tribute from the field or your hand. When this monster attacks a face-down Defense Position monster, destroy the face-down monster immediately with this card's effect without flipping it face-up or damage calculation. You can Special Summon 1 "Blue-Eyes White Dragon" from your hand or your Deck by offering this card as a Tribute during your Main Phase. (Blue-Eyes White Dragon cannot attack during that turn.)

Rank: 16

Name: Skilled Dark Magician

ATK: 1900

Effect:
Each time you or your opponent activates 1 Spell Card, put 1 Spell Counter on this card (max. 3). You can Special Summon 1 "Dark Magician" from your hand, Deck, or Graveyard in face-up Attack or Defense Position by offering this monster with 3 Spell Counters as a Tribute during your Main Phase.

Rank: 16

Name: Spear Dragon

ATK: 1900

Effect:
If this card attacks with an ATK that is higher than the DEF of your opponent's Defense Position monster, inflict the difference as Battle Damage to your opponent's Life Points. When this card attacks, it is changed to Defense Position at the end of the Damage Step.

Rank: 16

Name: Thunder Nyan Nyan

ATK: 1900

Effect:
If there is a non-LIGHT monster on your side of the field, this face-up card is immediately destroyed.

Rank: 23

Name: Gagagigo

ATK: 1850

Effect:
None

Rank: 23

Name: Mechanicalchaser

ATK: 1850

Effect:
None

Top 25 Level 4 and Under Monsters with Highest DEF

Rank: 1

Name: Battle Footballer

DEF: 2100

Effect: None

Rank: 2

Name: Aqua Madoor

DEF: 2000

Effect: None

Rank: 2

Name: Arsenal Bug

DEF: 2000

Effect: If there are no face-up Insect-Type monsters (except this monster) on your side of the field, both the ATK and DEF of this monster become 1000 points.

Rank: 2

Name: Banisher of the Light

DEF: 2000

Effect: As long as this card remains face-up on the field, any card sent to the Graveyard is removed from play.

Rank: 2

Name: Cocoon of Evolution

DEF: 2000

Effect: You may treat this card as an Equip Magic Card on a face-up "Petit Moth" on the field. When equipped, the ATK and DEF of "Petit Moth" becomes the same as "Cocoon of Evolution."

Rank: 2

Name: D. D. Trainer

DEF: 2000

Effect: None

Rank: 2

Name: Des Dendle

DEF: 2000

Effect: Once per turn, during your Main Phase, if you control this monster on the field, you can equip it to your "Vampire Orchis" as an Equip Spell Card, OR change it back to a monster in face-up Attack Position. When equipped to a monster by this card's effect, each time that monster destroys 1 of your opponent's monsters, Special Summon 1 "Wicked Plant Token" (Plant-Type/EARTH/1 Star/ATK 800/DEF 800) in Attack or Defense Position. (1 monster can only be equipped with 1 Union Monster at a time. If the monster that this card is equipped to is destroyed in battle, this card is destroyed instead.)

Rank: 2

Name: Earthbound Spirit

DEF: 2000

Effect: None

Rank: 2

Name: Flash Assailant

DEF: 2000

Effect: Decrease the ATK and DEF of this card by 400 points for every card in your hand.

Rank: 2

Name: Giant Soldier of Stone

DEF: 2000

Effect: None

Rank: 2

Name: Gravekeeper's Spy

DEF: 2000

Effect: FLIP: Select 1 monster that includes "Gravekeeper's" in its card name with an ATK of 1500 or less from your Deck and Special Summon it in face-up Attack or Defense Position. The Deck is then shuffled.

Rank: 2

Name: Humanoid Slime

DEF: 2000

Effect: None

Rank: 2

Name: Island Turtle

DEF: 2000

Effect: None

Rank: 2

Name: Maiden of the Aqua

DEF: 2000

Effect: As long as this card remains face-up on the field, the field is treated as "Umi" (however there is no increasing or decreasing of ATK/DEF due to "Umi's" effect). If there is an active Field Spell Card on the field, this effect is not applied.

Rank: 2

Name: Mystical Elf

DEF: 2000

Effect: None

Rank: 2

Name: Oppressed People

DEF: 2000

Effect: None

Rank: 2

Name: Prevent Rat

DEF: 2000

Effect: None

Rank: 2

Name: Roulette Barrel

DEF: 2000

Effect: Once per turn, during your Main Phase, you can roll a six-sided die twice. Select one result and destroy 1 face-up monster on the field whose level is equal to the result.

Rank: 2

Name: Royal Magical Library

DEF: 2000

Effect: Each time you or your opponent activates 1 Spell Card, put 1 Spell Counter on this card (max. 3). You can remove 3 Spell Counters from this card to draw 1 card from your Deck.

Rank: 2

Name: Serpentine Princess

DEF: 2000

Effect: If this face-up card is returned directly from the field to your Deck, Special Summon 1 Level 3 or lower monster from your Deck.

Rank: 2

Name: Spirit of the Harp

DEF: 2000

Effect: None

Rank: 2

Name: The Dragon Dwelling in the Cave

DEF: 2000

Effect: None

Rank: 2

Name: The Forgiving Maiden

DEF: 2000

Effect: Offer this face-up card as a Tribute to return 1 of your monsters destroyed in battle during this turn to your hand.

Top 21 Monsters with Highest ATK

Rank: 2

Name: Throwstone Unit

DEF: 2000

Effect:
Offer 1 Warrior-Type monster on your side of the field as a Tribute to destroy 1 face-up monster on the field whose DEF is equal to or lower than the ATK of this monster.

Rank: 25

Name: Castle of Dark Illusions

DEF: 1930

Effect:
FLIP: Increases the ATK and DEF of all Zombie-Type monsters by 200 points. As long as this card remains face-up on the field, the ATK and DEF of Zombie-Type monsters continues to increase by 200 points during each of your Standby Phases. This effect continues until your 4th turn after the card is activated.

Rank: 1

Name: Gate Guardian

ATK: 3750

Effect:
This card can only be Special Summoned by offering "Sanga of the Thunder," "Kazejin," and "Suijin" on your side of the field as a Tribute.

Rank: 2

Name: Berserk Dragon

ATK: 3500

Effect:
This card can only be Special Summoned by the effect of "A Deal with Dark Ruler." This card can attack all monsters on your opponent's side of the field once. You cannot attack your opponent directly if you attack any monsters first. Decrease the ATK of this card by 500 points during each of your End Phases.

Rank: 2

Name: Perfectly Ultimate Great Moth

ATK: 3500

Effect:
This monster can only be Special Summoned by offering "Petit Moth" as a Tribute on the 6th of your turns after "Petit Moth" has been equipped with "Cocoon of Evolution."

Rank: 2

Name: Ultimate Obedient Fiend

ATK: 3500

Effect:
This card can only attack when there are no other cards on your side of the field, and you also have no hand. Negate the effects of Effect Monsters destroyed by this card.

Rank: 5

Name: Shinato, King of a Higher Plane

ATK: 3300

Effect:
When a Defense Position monster on your opponent's side of the field is destroyed and sent to the Graveyard by this card as a result of battle, inflict damage to your opponent's Life Points equal to the original ATK of the destroyed monster.

Rank: 6

Name: B. Skull Dragon

ATK: 3200

Effect:
None

Rank: 6

Name: The Masked Beast

ATK: 3200

Effect:
None

Rank: 8

Name: Blue-Eyes Toon Dragon

ATK: 3000

Effect:
This card cannot be summoned unless "Toon World" is on the field. This card cannot attack in the same turn that it is summoned. Pay 500 Life Points each time this monster attacks. When "Toon World" is destroyed, this card is also destroyed. If your opponent doesn't control a Toon monster on the field, this card may inflict Direct Damage to your opponent's Life Points. If a Toon monster is on your opponent's side of the field, your attacks must target the Toon monster.

Rank: 8

Name: Blue-Eyes White Dragon

ATK: 3000

Effect:
None

Top Monsters in the Yu-Gi-Oh!™ TRADING CARD GAME

Rank: 8

Name: Lava Golem

ATK: 3000

Effect:

This monster must be Special Summoned on your opponent's side of the field by offering 2 monsters on your opponent's side of the field as a Tribute. This card inflicts 1000 points of Direct Damage to the Life Points of this card's controller during each of his/her Standby Phases. When you Special Summon this monster, you cannot Normal Summon or Set a monster during the same turn.

Rank: 11

Name: Cosmo Queen

ATK: 2900

Effect:

None

Rank: 11

Name: Dark Paladin the Ultimate Magical Swordsman

ATK: 2900

Effect:

This monster can only be Special Summoned by Fusion Summon. As long as this card remains face-up on the field, you can negate the activation of 1 Spell Card and destroy the Spell Card by discarding 1 card from your hand. The ATK of this card increases by 500 points for each Dragon-Type monster on the field and in either player's Graveyard.

Rank: 11

Name: Tyrant Dragon

ATK: 2900

Effect:

When there is a monster on your opponent's side of the field after the first attack of your Battle Phase, this monster can attack once again during the same Battle Phase. In addition, negate the effect of a Trap Card that specifically designates this card as a target and destroy it. If this monster is Special Summoned from the Graveyard, you must offer 1 Dragon-Type monster on your side of the field as a Tribute.

Rank: 14

Name: Tri-Horned Dragon

ATK: 2850

Effect:

None

Rank: 15

Name: Despair from the Dark

ATK: 2800

Effect:

When this card is sent directly from your hand or Deck to your Graveyard by your opponent's card effect, Special Summon this card to your side of the field.

Rank: 15

Name: Mirage Knight

ATK: 2800

Effect:

This card can only be Special Summoned by the effect of "Dark Flare Knight." When this card battles another monster, during damage calculation increase the ATK of this card by the original ATK of the opponent's monster. During the End Phase after this card was involved in battle, remove this card from play.

Rank: 15

Name: Hino-Kagu-Tsuchi

ATK: 2800

Effect:

This card cannot be Special Summoned. This card returns to the owner's hand during the End Phase of the turn that this card is Normal Summoned, Flip Summoned, or flipped face-up. If this card inflicts Battle Damage to your opponent's Life Points, your opponent must discard all cards in his/her hand during the next Draw Phase before he/she draws.

Rank: 15

Name: Moisture Creature

ATK: 2800

Effect:

If you Tribute Summon this monster by offering 3 monsters on the field as a Tribute, destroy all Magic and Trap Cards on your opponent's side of the field.

Rank: 15

Name: St. Joan

ATK: 2800

Effect:

None

Rank: 15

Name: Twin-Headed Thunder Dragon

ATK: 2800

Effect:

None

Rank: 15

Name: XYZ-Dragon Cannon

ATK: 2800

Effect:

Discard 1 card from your hand to destroy 1 card on your opponent's side of the field.

Top 17 Monsters with Highest DEF

Rank: 1

Name: Gate Guardian

DEF: 3400

Effect: This card can only be Special Summoned by offering "Sanga of the Thunder," "Kazejin," and "Suijin" on your side of the field as a Tribute.

Rank: 2

Name: Yamata Dragon

DEF: 3100

Effect: This card cannot be Special Summoned. This card returns to the owner's hand during the End Phase of the turn that this card is Normal Summoned, Flip Summoned or flipped face-up. When this card inflicts Battle Damage to your opponent's Life Points, draw cards from your Deck until you have 5 cards in your hand.

Rank: 3

Name: Despair from the Dark

DEF: 3000

Effect: When this card is sent directly from your hand or Deck to your Graveyard by your opponent's card effect, Special Summon this card to your side of the field.

Rank: 3

Name: Labyrinth Wall

DEF: 3000

Effect: None

Rank: 3

Name: Millennium Shield

DEF: 3000

Effect: None

Rank: 3

Name: Perfectly Ultimate Great Moth

DEF: 3000

Effect: This monster can only be Special Summoned by offering "Petit Moth" as a Tribute on the 6th of your turns after "Petit Moth" has been equipped with "Cocoon of Evolution."

Rank: 3

Name: Shinato, King of a Higher Plane

DEF: 3000

Effect: When a Defense Position monster on your opponent's side of the field is destroyed and sent to the Graveyard by this card as a result of battle, inflict damage to your opponent's Life Points equal to the original ATK of the destroyed monster.

Rank: 3

Name: Ultimate Obedient Fiend

DEF: 3000

Effect: This card can only attack when there are no other cards on your side of the field, and you also have no hand. Negate the effects of Effect Monsters destroyed by this card.

Rank: 3

Name: Wall Shadow

DEF: 3000

Effect: You cannot Normal Summon this monster. This card can only be Special Summoned by offering "Labyrinth Wall" equipped with "Magical Labyrinth" as a Tribute. No other Tribute monsters are necessary.

Rank: 10

Name: Fushioh Richie

DEF: 2900

Effect: This card can only be Special Summoned from your hand or your Deck by offering 1 "Great Dezard" that has fulfilled the condition as a Tribute. You can flip this card into face-down Defense Position once per turn during your Main Phase. As long as this monster remains face-up on the field, negate the activation and effects of all Spell or Trap Cards that specifically designate this card as a target and destroy them. When this card is flipped face-up, you can Special Summon 1 Zombie-Type monster from your Graveyard in face-up Attack or Defense Position.

Rank: 10

Name: Hino-Kagu-Tsuchi

DEF: 2900

Effect: This card cannot be Special Summoned. This card returns to the owner's hand during the End Phase of the turn that this card is Normal Summoned, Flip Summoned, or flipped face-up. If this card inflicts Battle Damage to your opponent's Life Points, your opponent must discard all cards in his/her hand during the next Draw Phase before he/she draws.

Top Monsters in the Yu-Gi-Oh!™ TRADING CARD GAME

Rank: 10

Name: Moisture Creature

DEF: 2900

Effect:

If you Tribute Summon this monster by offering 3 monsters on the field as a Tribute, destroy all Magic and Trap Cards on your opponent's side of the field.

Rank: 13

Name: Dark Necrofear

DEF: 2800

Effect:

This card can only be Special Summoned by removing 3 Fiend-Type monsters in your Graveyard from play. When this card is destroyed in battle or by your opponent's card effect, it is treated as an Equip Spell Card at the end of the turn. Equip 1 of your opponent's monsters with this card. As long as it is equipped with this card, you control the equipped monster.

Rank: 13

Name: Hyozanryu

DEF: 2800

Effect:

None

Rank: 15

Name: Manga Ryu-Ran

DEF: 2600

Effect:

This card cannot be summoned unless "Toon World" is on the field. This card cannot attack in the same turn that it is summoned. Pay 500 Life Points each time this monster attacks. When "Toon World" is destroyed, this card is also destroyed. If your opponent doesn't control a Toon monster on the field, this card may inflict Direct Damage to your opponent's Life Points. If a Toon monster is on your opponent's side of the field, your attacks must target the Toon monster.

Rank: 15

Name: Ryu-Ran

DEF: 2600

Effect:

None

Rank: 15

Name: XYZ-Dragon Cannon

DEF: 2600

Effect:

Discard 1 card from your hand to destroy 1 card on your opponent's side of the field.

Top 10 Fusion Monsters with Highest ATK

Rank: 1

Name: B. Skull Dragon

ATK: 3200

Fusion-Material Monsters: "Summoned Skull" + "Red-Eyes B. Dragon"

Rank: 2

Name: Dark Paladin

ATK: 2900

Fusion-Material Monsters: "Dark Magician" + "Buster Blader"

Rank: 3

Name: St. Joan

ATK: 2800

Fusion-Material Monsters: "The Forgiving Maiden" + "Marie the Fallen One"

Rank: 3

Name: Twin-Headed Thunder Dragon

ATK: 2800

Fusion-Material Monsters: "Thunder Dragon" + "Thunder Dragon"

Rank: 3

Name: XYZ-Dragon Cannon

ATK: 2800

Fusion-Material Monsters: "X-Head Cannon" + "Y-Dragon Head" + "Z-Metal Tank"

Rank: 6

Name: Skull Knight

ATK: 2650

Fusion-Material Monsters: "Tainted Wisdom" + "Ancient Brain"

Rank: 7

Name: Gaia the Dragon Champion

ATK: 2600

Fusion-Material Monsters: "Gaia the Fierce Knight" + "Curse of Dragon"

Rank: 8

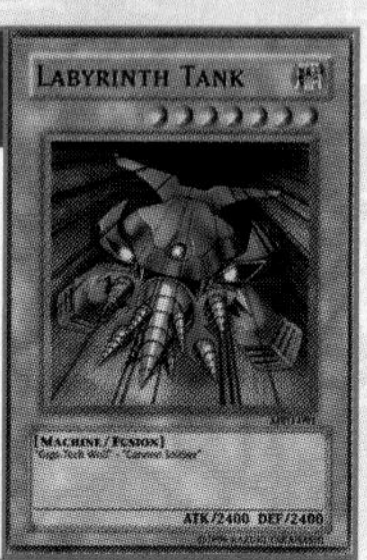

Name: Labyrinth Tank

ATK: 2400

Fusion-Material Monsters: "Giga-Tech Wolf" + "Cannon Soldier"

Rank: 8

Name: Thousand Dragon

ATK: 2400

Fusion-Material Monsters: "Time Wizard" + "Baby Dragon"

Rank: 8

Name: XZ-Tank Cannon

ATK: 2400

Fusion-Material Monsters: "X-Head Cannon" + "Z-Metal Tank"

Top 10 Fusion Monsters with Highest DEF

Rank: 1

Name: XYZ-Dragon Cannon

DEF: 2600

Fusion-Material Monsters:

"X-Head Cannon" + "Y-Dragon Head" + "Z-Metal Tank"

Rank: 2

Name: B. Skull Dragon

DEF: 2500

Fusion-Material Monsters:

"Summoned Skull" + "Red-Eyes B. Dragon"

Rank: 3

Name: Dark Paladin

DEF: 2400

Fusion-Material Monsters:

"Dark Magician" + "Buster Blader"

Rank: 3

Name: Labyrinth Tank

DEF: 2400

Fusion-Material Monsters:

"Giga-Tech Wolf" + "Cannon Soldier"

Rank: 5

Name: The Last Warrior from Another Planet

DEF: 2300

Fusion-Material Monsters:

"Zombyra the Dark" + "Maryokutai"

Rank: 6

Name: Skull Knight

DEF: 2250

Fusion-Material Monsters:

"Tainted Wisdom" + "Ancient Brain"

Rank: 7

Name: YZ-Tank Dragon

DEF: 2200

Fusion-Material Monsters:

"Y-Dragon Head" + "Z-Metal Tank"

Rank: 8

Name: Gaia the Dragon Champion

DEF: 2100

Fusion-Material Monsters:

"Gaia the Fierce Knight" + "Curse of Dragon"

Rank: 8

Name: Twin-Headed Thunder Dragon

DEF: 2100

Fusion-Material Monsters:

"Thunder Dragon" + "Thunder Dragon"

Rank: 8

Name: XZ-Tank Cannon

DEF: 2100

Fusion-Material Monsters:

"X-Head Cannon" + "Z-Metal Tank"

Sample Deck Collection

Deck Construction is the first step on your way to becoming a champion Duelist! No matter how excellent your skills are, you can't win a Duel if your Deck isn't constructed properly. Check out the following Decks to give you an idea of the variety of strategies you can utilize. Remember, you can always tweak a Deck to your liking to create your own powerful Deck!

Basic Search Deck

This Deck relies on using "Witch of the Black Forest" or "Sangan" to search your Deck for cards that will help you, depending on the situation of the Duel. If you activate "Swords of Revealing Light" and won't be attacked, then you want "Goblin Attack Force." If you want to remove your opponent's key monster from play, then you want "Kycoo the Ghost Destroyer." If you want to stop your opponent's Trap Cards, then you can get "Jinzo." The key to this Deck is that you have to think about what cards are in your opponent's and your hands and field, and choose the appropriate card to retrieve.

Monster Cards (14 Cards)

Cannon Soldier x 2
Cyber Jar x 1
Gemini Elf x 3
Goblin Attack Force x 2
Kycoo the Ghost Destroyer x 2
Jinzo x 1
Magician of Faith x 1
Sangan x 1
Witch of the Black Forest x 1

Spell Cards (21 Cards)

Change of Heart x 1
Confiscation x 1
Dark Hole x 1
Graceful Charity x 1
Harpie's Feather Duster x 1
Heavy Storm x 1
Monster Reborn x 1
Mystical Space Typhoon x 2
Nobleman of Crossout x 2
Nobleman of Extermination x 1
Pot of Greed x 1
Premature Burial x 1
Raigeki x 1
Scapegoat x 2
Snatch Steal x 1
Swords of Revealing Light x 1
Tribute to the Doomed x 1
The Forceful Sentry x 1

Trap Cards (5 Cards)

Call of the Haunted x 1
Dust Tornado x 1
Imperial Order x 1
Mirror Force x 1
Ring of Destruction x 1

Countering This Deck

The key to stopping this Deck is to prevent your opponent from searching his or her Deck using "Witch of the Black Forest" or "Sangan." If your opponent Sets either monster in face-down Defense Position, then you can stop their effects using "Nobleman of Crossout."

Sample Deck Collection

One Turn Victory Deck

Keep drawing cards to get "Catapult Turtle" and powerful monsters on the field, and demolish your opponent's Life Points in one fell swoop. If everything goes perfect, you can win in one turn, but it depends on your opening hand and using your cards expertly. The key to this Deck is not wasting the cards in your hand so that you can use "Card Destruction" until you draw "Card of Safe Return." If you succeed, your opponent is in for a huge shock!

Monster Cards (15 Cards)

- Barrel Dragon x 2
- Blue-Eyes White Dragon x 3
- Catapult Turtle x 2
- Cosmo Queen x 3
- Gilasaurus x 2
- Thunder Dragon x 3

Spell Cards (23 Cards)

- Card Destruction x 3
- Card of Safe Return x 3
- Change of Heart x 1
- Dark Hole x 1
- Graceful Charity x 1
- Harpie's Feather Duster x 1
- Megamorph x 3
- Monster Reborn x 1
- Monster Recovery x 3
- Pot of Greed x 1
- Premature Burial x 1
- Raigeki x 1
- The Shallow Grave x 3

Trap Cards (2 Cards)

- Mirror Force x 1
- Ring of Destruction x 1

Countering This Deck

This Deck doesn't work well if your opponent cannot summon monsters. However, in case your opponent does summon monsters, your best defense is "Kuriboh." This is the only card that can stop damage to your Life Points even on your first turn. Your opponent will be frustrated after he or she worked so hard to unleash the combo!

Attack/Defense Swap Deck

Have monsters with high DEF on your field in Defense Position to protect yourself from your opponent's attacks. Once you have all the monsters you need, use "Shield & Sword" to inflict huge damage to your opponent instantly.

This is the exact opposite of the "One Turn Victory Deck" because this Deck takes much more time to gather all the key cards. This Deck will frustrate your opponent because it's very difficult to get rid of high DEF Defense Position monsters.

Monster Cards (20 Cards)

- Catapult Turtle x 2
- Cyber Jar x 1
- Dreamsprite x 1
- Giant Rat x 2
- Giant Soldier of Stone x 3
- Jinzo x 1
- Man-Eater Bug x 2
- Millennium Shield x 2
- Mystical Elf x 3
- Prevent Rat x 3

Spell Cards (13 Cards)

- Change of Heart x 1
- Dark Hole x 1
- Graceful Charity x 1
- Harpie's Feather Duster x 1
- Heavy Storm x 1
- Monster Reborn x 1
- Mystical Space Typhoon x 1
- Pot of Greed x 1
- Raigeki x 1
- Shield & Sword x 3
- Swords of Revealing Light x 1

Trap Cards (7 Cards)

- Call of the Haunted x 1
- Destruction Punch x 2
- Imperial Order x 1
- Magic Jammer x 1
- Mirror Force x 1
- Solemn Judgment x 1

Countering This Deck

In order to prevent your opponent from getting the key cards, use Hand Destruction cards, such as "Delinquent Duo." Use Monster Removal cards on your opponent's high DEF monsters. You will still need monsters with more than 2000 ATK in order to destroy your opponent's defense monsters. Use cards like "Monster Reborn" that will revive your powerful monsters from the Graveyard so that you can keep attacking.

Fire Princess Deck

Use various methods to increase your Life Points and deal Direct Damage to your opponent's Life Points using "Fire Princess." The key points are to send "Marie the Fallen One" to the Graveyard quickly and to protect "Fire Princess." If "Marie the Fallen One" is in the Graveyard, you are going to gain Life Points every turn. Use cards like "Graceful Charity" to put "Marie the Fallen One" in your Graveyard. Also, with the Life Points you gain, activate "Injection Fairy Lily's" effect. That will totally turn the tide of battle!

Monster Cards (17 Cards)

Cyber Jar x 1
Fire Princess x 3
Fushi no Tori x 2
Gemini Elf x 3
Goblin Attack Force x 1
Injection Fairy Lily x 1
Marie the Fallen One x 3
UFO Turtle x 2
Witch of the Black Forest x 1

Spell Cards (14 Cards)

Change of Heart x 1
Dark Hole x 1
Graceful Charity x 1
Harpie's Feather Duster x 1
Heart of Clear Water x 2
Heavy Storm x 1
Monster Reborn x 1
Mystical Space Typhoon x 2
Pot of Greed x 1
Premature Burial x 1
Raigeki x 1
Swords of Revealing Light x 1

Trap Cards (9 Cards)

Call of the Haunted x 1
Imperial Order x 1
Magic Jammer x 2
Mirror Force x 1
Ring of Destruction x 1
Solemn Wishes x 3

Countering This Deck

"Bad Reaction to Simochi" is the main card that stops this Deck because when your opponent tries to gain Life Points, he or she loses Life Points instead. This Deck is geared toward long Duels, so if your opponent is losing Life Points instead of gaining them, then it's fatal!

Sheep Attack Deck

The concept of this Deck is to use "Scapegoat" and "Sheep Tokens" as your attacking force. Power up your 0 ATK "Sheep Tokens" with "Milus Radiant." Their combined ATK will be a formidable 2800, and if you also activate "Robbin' Goblin," then your opponent will lose five cards in his or her hand! In order for this combo to work, the timing of when "Torrential Tribute" and "Scapegoat" activate is crucial. They're both key cards that help stall for time, so use them wisely.

Monster Cards (13 Cards)

Cannon Soldier x 2
Giant Soldier of Stone x 2
Hayabusa Knight x 1
Jinzo x 1
Milus Radiant x 2
Sangan x 1
Spear Dragon x 3
Witch of the Black Forest x 1

Spell Cards (12 Cards)

Change of Heart x 1
Dark Hole x 1
Graceful Charity x 1
Harpie's Feather Duster x 1
Monster Reborn x 1
Pot of Greed x 1
Premature Burial x 1
Raigeki x 1
Scapegoat x 3
Swords of Revealing Light x 1

Trap Cards (15 Cards)

Dust Tornado x 3
Imperial Order x 1
Jar of Greed x 2
Magic Jammer x 2
Mirror Force x 1
Robbin' Goblin x 3
Torrential Tribute x 3

Countering This Deck

Aim to stop "Torrential Tribute" because this card is the key card for combos in this Deck. This annoying card wipes out all the monsters you summoned. Even if your opponent doesn't use "Torrential Tribute" in a combo, it still can be used to stall for time. Use "Imperial Order" to stop it!

Shining Power Deck

This powerful monster Deck focuses on Special Summoning "Soul of Purity and Light" and reviving "Blue-Eyes White Dragon." A feature of this Deck is that "Thunder Dragon" cards are included solely for the purpose of sending them to the Graveyard. Not only does this thin the Deck, but it also allows you to Special Summon "Soul of Purity and Light" quicker. Summon and battle using powerful monsters at the beginning of the Duel to gain a quick advantage, and then use your hand to immediately win when victory is in the books. Aim for the final blow!

Monster Cards (19 Cards)

- Blue-Eyes White Dragon x 2
- Cyber Jar x 1
- Helping Robo for Combat x 2
- Hoshiningen x 2
- Pixie Knight x 1
- Roulette Barrel x 1
- Shining Angel x 3
- Soul of Purity and Light x 3
- Thunder Dragon x 3
- Witch of the Black Forest x 1

Spell Cards (13 Cards)

- Change of Heart x 1
- Dark Hole x 1
- Graceful Charity x 1
- Harpie's Feather Duster x 1
- Heavy Storm x 1
- Monster Reborn x 1
- Mystical Space Typhoon x 2
- Nobleman of Crossout x 2
- Pot of Greed x 1
- Premature Burial x 1
- Raigeki x 1

Trap Cards (8 Cards)

- Call of the Haunted x 1
- Dust Tornado x 2
- Imperial Order x 1
- Jar of Greed x 3
- Ring of Destruction x 1

Countering This Deck

If you can remove "Blue-Eyes White Dragon" and "Soul of Purity and Light" in the Graveyard from play, then the Deck is rendered powerless. When your opponent sends monsters to the Graveyard, use "Kycoo the Ghost Destroyer" to remove them from play. Your opponent's army is gone!

Band of Warriors Deck

This all-around Deck searches for Warrior-Type monsters. This is different than the "Basic Search Deck" because instead of waiting for "Witch of the Black Forest" to be destroyed, you can quickly draw a card by using the Spell Card "Reinforcement of the Army." This way, you won't run out of Monster Cards in your hand, and by using Effect Monsters that have Monster Removal effects, you have an advantage in battle.

Monster Cards (17 Cards)

- Axe Raider x 1
- Crimson Sentry x 1
- Exiled Force x 1
- Freed the Matchless General x 1
- Gearfried the Iron Knight x 2
- Giant Rat x 2
- Goblin Attack Force x 2
- Hayabusa Knight x 1
- Marauding Captain x 2
- Throwstone Unit x 1
- Warrior Dai Grepher x 1
- Zombyra the Dark x 2

Spell Cards (20 Cards)

- Change of Heart x 1
- Dark Hole x 1
- Fusion Sword Murasame Blade x 2
- Gaia Power x 2
- Graceful Charity x 1
- Harpie's Feather Duster x 1
- Heavy Storm x 1
- Monster Reborn x 1
- Mystical Space Typhoon x 2
- Nobleman of Crossout x 2
- Pot of Greed x 1
- Raigeki x 1
- Reinforcement of the Army x 2
- Swords of Revealing Light x 1
- The Warrior Returning Alive x 1

Trap Cards (3 Cards)

- Call of the Haunted x 1
- Imperial Order x 1
- Mirror Force x 1

Countering This Deck

Since this Deck has monsters with the same type, use cards that eliminate monsters of a certain type. However, keep the cards in the Side Deck because you don't know if you're facing an opponent who is using a "Band of Warriors" Deck.

Gear Crush Deck

Equip "Gearfried the Iron Knight" with "Smoke Grenade of the Thief" and "Blast with Chain," which are activated when your opponent's card destroys it. Thanks to "Smoke Grenade of the Thief," it strengthens your Hand Destruction ability. "Blast with Chain" is flexible and allows you to destroy Monster, Spell, or Trap Cards. While you are using these cards to destroy your opponent's hand and field, lock your opponent using "Yata-Garasu." If your opponent loses all cards and is unable to draw, then your opponent has to forfeit!

Monster Cards (14 Cards)

Airknight Parshath x 1
Exiled Force x 1
Gearfried the Iron Knight x 3
Gemini Elf x 3
Jinzo x 1
Magician of Faith x 1
Summoned Skull x 1
White Magical Hat x 1
Witch of the Black Forest x 1
Yata-Garasu x 1

Spell Cards (19 Cards)

Change of Heart x 1
Confiscation x 1
Dark Hole x 1
Delinquent Duo x 1
Graceful Charity x 1
Harpie's Feather Duster x 1
Heavy Storm x 1
Monster Reborn x 1
Nobleman of Crossout x 2
Pot of Greed x 1
Raigeki x 1
Reinforcement of the Army x 2
Smoke Grenade of the Thief x 3
Swords of Revealing Light x 1
The Forceful Sentry x 1

Trap Cards (7 Cards)

Blast with Chain x 3
Call of the Haunted x 1
Imperial Order x 1
Magic Drain x 2

Countering This Deck

The key card in this Deck is, of course, "Gearfried the Iron Knight." As long as this card is not on the field, "Smoke Grenade of the Thief" and "Blast with Chain" can't be used effectively, and your opponent will have many useless cards. When your opponent tries to summon "Gearfried the Iron Knight," immediately use "Bottomless Trap Hole" to remove it from play!

Spirit Drain Deck

This is a combo Deck that uses Spirit monsters as key cards. Use the heavy-duty "Hino-Kagu-Tsuchi" to force your opponent to discard his or her entire hand, and then lock your opponent by using "Yata-Garasu" so that your opponent cannot draw a card. Also, combos using "Creature Swap" is also quite powerful. If the two Spirit monsters can attack your opponent even once, then victory is guaranteed. Therefore, you can use "Ultimate Offering" as many times as you need. An excellent strategy is to offer "Sangan" as a Tribute to Tribute Summon "Hino-Kagu-Tsuchi." Use "Sangan's" effect to get "Yata-Garasu" and you're on your way to victory!

Monster Cards (14 Cards)

Asura Priest x 2
Gemini Elf x 3
Goblin Attack Force x 3
Hino-Kagu-Tsuchi x 2
Sangan x 1
Witch of the Black Forest x 1
Yata-Garasu x 1
Change of Heart x 1

Spell Cards (17 Cards)

Change of Heart x 1
Creature Swap x 3
Dark Hole x 1
Graceful Charity x 1
Harpie's Feather Duster x 1
Heavy Storm x 1
Monster Reborn x 1
Mystical Space Typhoon x 2
Nobleman of Crossout x 2
Pot of Greed x 1
Premature Burial x 1
Raigeki x 1
Swords of Revealing Light x 1

Trap Cards (9 Cards)

Call of the Haunted x 1
Dust Tornado x 2
Imperial Order x 1
Mirror Force x 1
Torrential Tribute x 2
Ultimate Offering x 2

Countering This Deck

"Fengsheng Mirror" is highly recommended because it pinpoints Spirit monsters and discards them. Since Spirit monsters cannot be Special Summoned, cards such as "Monster Reborn" cannot be used and become useless. Calculate when your opponent has a Spirit monster in his or her hand and send it to the Graveyard!

Twilight of the Gravekeepers Deck

This Deck relies on summoning Gravekeeper monsters and pounding your opponent into submission. First, Set "Gravekeeper's Spy" in face-down Defense Position. You can use "Gravekeeper's Spy's" Flip Effect to Special Summon Gravekeeper monsters. Use this effect to Special Summon excellent monsters, such as "Gravekeeper's Assailant" and "Gravekeeper's Spear Soldier." When the time is right, activate "Necrovalley" and power up all your Gravekeepers! Overwhelm your opponent with this mighty force! While your opponent's Graveyard is sealed, use "Rite of Spirit" and "Gravekeeper's Chief" to Special Summon your Gravekeepers from the Graveyard.

Monster Cards (15 Cards)

Cyber Jar x 1
Gravekeeper's Assailant x 3
Gravekeeper's Chief x 2
Gravekeeper's Guard x 2
Gravekeeper's Spear Soldier x 2
Gravekeeper's Spy x 3
Gravekeeper's Watcher x 2

Spell Cards (18 Cards)

Change of Heart x 1
Dark Hole x 1
Graceful Charity x 1
Harpie's Feather Duster x 1
Heavy Storm x 1
Monster Reborn x 1
Necrovalley x 3
Nobleman of Crossout x 2
Pot of Greed x 1
Raigeki x 1
Royal Tribute x 2
Snatch Steal x 1
Terraforming x 1
United We Stand x 1

Trap Cards (7 Cards)

Imperial Order x 1
Magic Jammer x 2
Mirror Force x 1
Ring of Destruction x 1
Rite of Spirit x 2

Countering This Deck

"Nobleman of Crossout" not only removes the face-down Defense Position monster from play, but it removes same-named cards from the Deck. If you can remove "Gravekeeper's Spy" from your opponent's Deck, then your Duel will flow more smoothly. "Gravekeeper's Guard" should also be the target of "Nobleman of Crossout."

Rebellion of the Weak Deck

The concept of this Deck is to use "Huge Revolution" to attain victory. Basically, until you can activate "Huge Revolution," you don't attack much. While defending against your opponent's attacks, use "Witch of the Black Forest" and "Sangan" to get the three key cards in your hand. When you're ready, activate "Ultimate Offering" to get all three Monster Cards on the field. However, you can only use "Huge Revolution" during your Main Phase, so don't mess up your timing! After activating "Huge Revolution," your opponent's field is empty, so you can launch a huge attack and win! As long as your opponent's draws aren't very good, it's certain that you will win the Duel.

Monster Cards (16 Cards)

Cyber Jar x 1
Fiber Jar x 1
Flying Kamakiri #1 x 2
Morphing Jar #2 x 1
Oppressed People x 3
People Running About x 3
Sangan x 1
United Resistance x 3
Witch of the Black Forest x 1

Spell Cards (15 Cards)

Change of Heart x 1
Dark Hole x 1
Delinquent Duo x 1
Graceful Charity x 1
Harpie's Feather Duster x 1
Heavy Storm x 1
Monster Reborn x 1
Mystical Space Typhoon x 2
Pot of Greed x 1
Premature Burial x 1
Raigeki x 1
Reinforcement of the Army x 1
Swords of Revealing Light x 1
United We Stand x 1

Trap Cards (9 Cards)

Backup Soldier x 1
Call of the Haunted x 1
Huge Revolution x 3
Imperial Order x 1
Mirror Force x 1
Ultimate Offering x 2

Countering This Deck

"Jinzo" is the best card to counter this Deck. Only Monster Removal Spell Cards in the "Rebellion of the Weak" Deck can counter "Jinzo." If "Jinzo" is on the field, then you don't have to be afraid of "Huge Revolution." Just be careful of Monster Removal cards and summon it!

Revenge of the Union Deck

This Deck showcases Union Monsters with the main monster being "Dark Blade!" "Dark Blade" is a Warrior-Type monster, so you can effectively use "Reinforcement of the Army" and "The Warrior Returning Alive" to Special Summon it. Next, use Union Monsters and attack! Depending on the situation of the Duel, if you can use the two types of Union Monsters effectively, then you can definitely deal lots of damage to your opponent! Support your Union Monsters using "Frontline Base" and "Formation Union." Using this Deck as an example, think of other types of Union Decks you can create!

Monster Cards (16 Cards)

- Cyber Jar x 1
- Dark Blade x 3
- Exiled Force x 1
- Jinzo x 1
- Kiryu x 3
- Marauding Captain x 2
- Pitch-Dark Dragon x 3
- Sangan x 1
- Witch of the Black Forest x 1

Spell Cards (19 Cards)

- Combination Attack x 3
- Dark Hole x 1
- Frontline Base x 2
- Graceful Charity x 1
- Harpie's Feather Duster x 1
- Heavy Storm x 1
- Monster Reborn x 1
- Pot of Greed x 1
- Premature Burial x 1
- Raigeki x 1
- Reinforcement of the Army x 2
- Snatch Steal x 1
- Swords of Revealing Light x 1
- The Warrior Returning Alive x 2

Trap Cards (5 Cards)

- Call of the Haunted x 1
- Formation Union x 2
- Imperial Order x 1
- Mirror Force x 1

Countering This Deck

Use Spell Cards that eliminate the key cards, which are Warrior-Type monsters. If you can use a single card that eliminates monsters that are all the same type, then your opponent's field will be defenseless, and you can strike a powerful blow all in a single stroke!

Trap of the Thieves Deck

The concept of this Deck is to destroy your opponent's hand and not let him or her draw any cards. Use "Delinquent Duo" from the very beginning. Along with that Spell Card, use "Don Zaloog" and "Spirit Reaper" to increase your Hand Destruction capability. If your opponent summons monsters to defend with, it's time for "Airknight Parshath." Activate "Robbin' Goblin," and when you damage your opponent's Life Points, then his or her hand is further destroyed. When your opponent's hand and field are empty, then summon "Yata-Garasu." If you prevent your opponent from drawing cards, then your opponent can't do anything!

Monster Cards (16 Cards)

- Airknight Parshath x 3
- Cyber Jar x 1
- Don Zaloog x 3
- Sangan x 1
- Spear Dragon x 3
- Spirit Reaper x 3
- Witch of the Black Forest x 1
- Yata-Garasu x 1

Spell Cards (12 Cards)

- Confiscation x 1
- Dark Hole x 1
- Delinquent Duo x 1
- Graceful Charity x 1
- Harpie's Feather Duster x 1
- Heavy Storm x 1
- Monster Reborn x 1
- Pot of Greed x 1
- Premature Burial x 1
- Raigeki x 1
- Swords of Revealing Light x 1
- The Forceful Sentry x 1

Trap Cards (12 Cards)

- Call of the Haunted x 1
- Drop Off x 3
- Imperial Order x 1
- Mirror Force x 1
- Robbin' Goblin x 2
- Thunder of Ruler x 2
- Trap Dustshoot x 2

Countering This Deck

Find ways to stop your opponent's key cards, such as stopping his or her Spell and Trap Cards. If you find a way to reverse the effect back to your opponent, you're in even better shape!

Sample Deck Collection

Cast of the Bold Deck

The core of this Deck are Spellcaster-Type Effect Monsters, that are found in "Magician's Force" Booster Packs.

The basic way to achieve victory is to use "Skilled White Magician" to Special Summon "Buster Blader" or use "Skilled Dark Magician" to Special Summon "Dark Magician." In order to Special Summon these two monsters, you need Spell Counters. Therefore, use "Apprentice Magician" and "Magical Plant Mandragola" to quickly increase the amount of Spell Counters. Even if your Special Summoned monster is destroyed, use "Miracle Restoring" to Special Summon it back from the Graveyard. If you're really in trouble, then you can turn the tables with "Mega Ton Magical Cannon."

Monster Cards (20 Cards)

- Apprentice Magician x 2
- Buster Blader x 2
- Cyber Jar x 1
- Dark Magician x 3
- Magical Plant Mandragola x 3
- Royal Magical Library x 3
- Skilled Dark Magician x 3
- Skilled White Magician x 2
- Witch of the Black Forest x 1

Spell Cards (12 Cards)

- Change of Heart x 1
- Dark Hole x 1
- Diffusion Wave-Motion x 2
- Graceful Charity x 1
- Harpie's Feather Duster x 1
- Heavy Storm x 1
- Mega Ton Magical Cannon x 1
- Monster Reborn x 1
- Pot of Greed x 1
- Raigeki x 1
- Swords of Revealing Light x 1

Trap Cards (8 Cards)

- Call of the Haunted x 1
- Imperial Order x 1
- Miracle Restoring x 2
- Mirror Force x 1
- Pitch-Black Power Stone x 3

Countering This Deck

With "Jowgen the Spiritualist," if you discard one card from your hand, all Special Summoned monsters on the field are destroyed. Not only that, as long as "Jowgen the Spiritualist" is face-up on the field, monsters cannot be Special Summoned. Your opponent's "Dark Magician" will most likely have to be Special Summoned, so "Jowgen the Spiritualist" will stop it. However, be careful because "Jowgen the Spiritualist's" ATK is very low.

The Captivating Amazoness Deck

If you only look at attack strength, then this Deck is weak overall. However, this Deck can hold its own! Compensate for low ATK with "Amazoness Blowpiper," "Amazoness Spellcaster" and "Amazoness Archers." If an Amazoness monster goes to the Graveyard, you can return it to your hand using "The Warrior Returning Alive." Since all the monsters are Level 4 or below, "Cyber Jar" and "Reinforcement of the Army" are very easy to use. Also, use the effects of "Giant Rat," "Witch of the Black Forest," and "Sangan" to their maximum potential and battle!

If you want to further tinker with this Deck, remove some cards to make space for "Marauding Captain." Now you have nothing to fear!

Monster Cards (18 Cards)

Amazon Archer x 1
Amazoness Blowpiper x 2
Amazoness Fighter x 2
Amazoness Paladin x 3
Amazoness Swords Woman x 3
Amazoness Tiger x 2
Cyber Jar x 1
Giant Rat x 2
Sangan x 1
Witch of the Black Forest x 1

Spell Cards (14 Cards)

Amazoness Spellcaster x 3
Change of Heart x 1
Dark Hole x 1
Graceful Charity x 1
Harpie's Feather Duster x 1
Heavy Storm x 1
Monster Reborn x 1
Pot of Greed x 1
Raigeki x 1
Reinforcement of the Army x 2
The Warrior Returning Alive x 1

Trap Cards (8 Cards)

Amazoness Archers x 3
Call of the Haunted x 1
Dramatic Rescue x 2
Imperial Order x 1
Mirror Force x 1

Countering This Deck

There aren't many ways to counter this Deck. The best strategy is to defeat the Amazoness monsters in battle because they have low ATK. Use cards that stop your opponent's Spell Cards, such as "Spell Canceller," so that your opponent cannot Special Summon monsters. Specifically target your opponent's strongest Spell Cards, such as "Amazoness Spellcaster," "The Warrior Returning Alive," and "Reinforcement of the Army." It also doesn't hurt to stop your opponent's Trap Cards.

Mark of the Offering Deck

This Deck uses an extravagant amount of combos, but in the end, you seal your opponent's choices with "Thousand-Eyes Restrict" and deal damage to your opponent's Life Points using effects. Combos that deal damage to your opponent's Life Points are "Ameba" + "Creature Swap" and "Marie the Fallen One" + "Fire Princess." After the combos are successful, use "Metamorphosis" on "Sinister Serpent" and Special Summon "Thousand-Eyes Restrict." Now your opponent can't attack. Don't forget to protect "Thousand-Eyes Restrict" using "Maryokutai" and "Spell Canceller."

Monster Cards (19 Cards)

Ameba x 3
Cyber Jar x 1
Fire Princess x 3
Jinzo x 1
Marie the Fallen One x 3
Maryokutai x 2
Morphing Jar x 1
Sinister Serpent x 1
Spell Canceller x 1
Thousand-Eyes Restrict x 3

Spell Cards (17 Cards)

Card Destruction x 1
Creature Swap x 2
Graceful Charity x 1
Harpie's Feather Duster x 1
Heavy Storm x 1
Metamorphosis x 3
Monster Reborn x 1
Mystical Space Typhoon x 2
Nobleman of Crossout x 2
Painful Choice x 1
Pot of Greed x 1
Swords of Revealing Light x 1

Trap Cards (6 Cards)

Call of the Haunted x 1
Imperial Order x 1
Mirror Force x 1
Reckless Greed x 1
Ring of Destruction x 1
Spell Shield Type-8 x 1

Countering This Deck

"Imperial Order" can stop the key card "Metamorphosis" or the combo card "Creature Swap." As long as you don't make a mistake in timing, you can stop your opponent's strategy with this one card. Think about the cost of paying your Life Points and the timing when you activate "Imperial Order!"

Questions and Answers

There are many cards in Yu-Gi-Oh! TRADING CARD GAME, and they all have their own unique powers and abilities. Sometimes, it can be confusing how certain cards work and interact. Check this section out for common questions regarding specific cards! (For more card rulings and gameplay questions, check out Yu-Gi-Oh! TRADING CARD GAME Rule Book—Prima's Official Strategy Guide.)

Monster Card Rulings

Armor Exe

Q: In regards to the Spell Counter I have to remove due to "Armor Exe's" effect, can I remove any Spell Counter on my field?

A: Yes. As long as you remove any Spell Counter on your field from the game, that satisfies "Armor Exe's" cost requirement. This is also the same for "Mega Ton Magical Cannon."

Dark Paladin

Q: Can I discard a card during my opponent's turn to negate and destroy a Spell Card?

A: Yes. The timing of this effect is similar to "Kuriboh." This effect is Spell Speed 2, so it can be used regardless of whose turn it is.

Dark Ruler Ha Des

Q: When "Dark Ruler Ha Des" destroys "Witch of the Black Forest" in battle, what happens to "Witch of the Black Forest's" effect?

A: When a Fiend-Type monster destroys an Effect Monster (such as "Witch of the Black Forest," "Cockroach Knight," or "Sinister Serpent") in battle, then the effect of the Effect Monster does not activate even if it is sent to the Graveyard.

Hino-Kagu-Tsuchi

Q: If my "Hino-Kagu-Tsuchi" deals damage to my opponent, when does my opponent discard his or her hand?

A: Your opponent discards his or her hand at the beginning of your next turn. More specifically, your opponent discards during the Draw Phase before he or she draws a card. This is a special example, so you should memorize it.

Lava Golem

Q: When Special Summoning "Lava Golem," can I offer Monster Tokens?

A: Yes. When Special Summoning "Lava Golem" and other Special Summon monsters, you can offer Monster Tokens. These are not considered Tribute Summons. The Monster Tokens are offered as a Tribute to meet the requirement for a Special Summon. Similarly, Kuriboh Tokens and Sheep Tokens can be offered.

Q: Can I Special Summon "Lava Golem" on to my field using "Monster Reborn?"

A: If "Lava Golem" is sent to the Graveyard after it was brought on to the field in the proper manner, then you can use "Monster Reborn" to Special Summon "Lava Golem." Also in this case, the controller of "Lava Golem" takes 1000 points of damage during your Standby Phase. Also, you cannot Normal Summon or Set for that turn.

Q: Can I Tribute Summon "Lava Golem" on to the field?

A: "Lava Golem" has to be Special Summoned, so it cannot be Normal Summoned. Therefore, it cannot be Tribute Summoned on to your field.

Magical Scientist

Q: After activating "Magical Scientist's" effect, my opponent chains "Ring of Destruction" and destroys "Magical Scientist." Can I Special Summon a Fusion Monster from the Fusion Deck?

A: Yes, you can Special Summon. "Magical Scientist's" effect activates immediately, so even if it is destroyed in a chain, the effect is not negated.

Skilled White Magician

Q: When a Spell Card is activated, when do I put on the Spell Counter? Also, when Special Summoning "Buster Blader," when do I activate the effect?

A: Place the Spell Counter immediately after the Spell Card resolves, even if it's during a chain. When Special Summoning "Buster Blader," you can activate the effect during your Main Phase.

Spirit Reaper

Q: When "Spirit Reaper" or "Reaper on the Nightmare" is the target of an effect, when is it destroyed? Is it destroyed right when it is selected as a target?

A: The monster is destroyed after the targeting card's effect is resolved. For example, if "Magic Cylinder" is used on an attacking "Spirit Reaper," then "Spirit Reaper" is destroyed after it deals damage to the opponent.

Q: When "Spirit Reaper" or "Reaper on the Nightmare" is face-down on the field, if it is the target of a Spell Card, Trap Card or Effect Monster, is it destroyed?

A: Basically, when a monster is face-down, the monster's effect is not applied. Therefore, even if "Spirit Reaper" is the target, it is not destroyed. Even if "Spirit Reaper" is flipped face-up due to "Book of Moon," since it was targeted while it was face-down, it is not destroyed.

Q: What happens when I use "Monster Reborn," "Call of the Haunted," or "Premature Burial" on "Spirit Reaper" in the Graveyard?

A: For Normal Spell Cards, such as "Monster Reborn," "Spirit Reaper" can be Special Summoned from the Graveyard. For Continuous Trap Cards, such as "Call of the Haunted" and "Premature Burial," even after "Spirit Reaper" is Special Summoned, "Spirit Reaper" continues to be the target of Continuous Trap Cards. Therefore, it is destroyed after it is Special Summoned.

Q: Right when a Spell Card, Trap Card, or Monster Effect targets "Spirit Reaper," I activate "Magic Jammer" to negate the activation. What happens to "Spirit Reaper?"

A: If the activation is negated, then it does not target. Therefore, "Spirit Reaper" is not destroyed.

Q: When "Gravekeeper's Assailant" declares its attack, "Spirit Reaper" is the target. Will "Spirit Reaper" be destroyed? If yes, will the Battle Step rewind?

A: "Gravekeeper's Assailant's" effect is a targeting effect, so "Spirit Reaper" will be destroyed after it changes Battle Position. Afterwards, the player receiving the attack will have a change in the number of monsters, so the Battle Step rewinds.

Questions and Answers

Tyrant Dragon

Q: Can I use "Call of the Haunted" on my "Tyrant Dragon" in my Graveyard?

A: Yes. When "Tyrant Dragon" is in the Graveyard, its effect does not activate. Therefore, "Call of the Haunted" activates and can target "Tyrant Dragon." However, in order to Special Summon "Tyrant Dragon" from the Graveyard, a Dragon-Type monster on the field must be offered as a Tribute. Also, after "Tyrant Dragon" is Special Summoned due to "Call of the Haunted's" effect, "Tyrant Dragon's" effect negates "Call of the Haunted's" effect, and "Call of the Haunted" is destroyed. In this case, the Special Summoned "Tyrant Dragon" will not be destroyed.

Union Monsters

Q: Union Monsters can "change back to a monster in face-up Attack Position." If I use this effect, does this count as a Special Summon?

A: Yes, this is a Special Summon. Also, you can only use the "change back to a monster in face-up Attack Position" effect when you have an open space on your Monster Card Zone because you can only Special Summon monsters when you have an open space.

Q: I use "Union Rider's" effect to take control of a Union Monster on my opponent's field and equip it to "Union Rider." What will happen to the Union Monster's "when equipped to a monster by this card's effect..." effect?

A: When you use "Union Rider's" effect to take control of your opponent's Union Monster and equip it to "Union Rider," the Union Monster hasn't become an Equip Spell Card due to its own effect. Therefore, the "when equipped to a monster by this card's effect..." effect cannot be used.

Q: A Union Monster is the target of "Premature Burial" or "Call of the Haunted." If the Union Monster uses its effect to become an Equip Spell Card, is the Union Monster destroyed?

A: No. The Union Monster becomes the Equip Spell Card of its target. "Premature Burial" loses its target, so it is sent to the Graveyard. "Call of the Haunted" loses its target, and it remains on the field.

Q: During the Battle Step, after a monster equipped with a Union Monster attacks, "Formation Union" is activated. The Union Monster is removed and placed on the field in face-up Attack Position. Can the Union Monster attack during this Battle Phase?

A: Yes. Similar to "Call of the Haunted," a monster is Special Summoned during the Battle Phase. Therefore, the Union Monster can attack.

XY-Dragon Cannon

Q: Can I remove from play the Union Monster that is currently an Equip Spell Card in order to Special Summon "XY-Dragon Cannon?" For example, while "Y-Dragon Head" is equipped on "X-Head Cannon," can I offer "X-Head Cannon" and "Y-Dragon Head" (which is currently an Equip Spell Card) to Special Summon "XY-Dragon Cannon?"

A: Yes. As long as it is face-up on the field, even if the Union Monster is an Equip Spell Card, you can remove it from play to Special Summon the Fusion Monster.

Q: It says "Discard 1 card from your hand to destroy 1 face-up Spell Card or Trap Card on your opponent's side of the field." When does this effect activate? Also, once this effect activates, can it be chained?

A: For monster effects that do not have specific instructions regarding timing, they basically activate during your Main Phase and can be chained.

Q: Can "XY-Dragon Cannon" be Special Summoned using "Monster Reborn?" Also, can I use "Goddess with the Third Eye" as a Fusion-Material Monster?

A: No.

XYZ-Dragon Cannon

Q: In one turn, how many times can I discard a card from my hand to activate "XYZ-Dragon Cannon's" effect?

A: As long as you have cards in your hand, you can activate it as many times as you like in one turn.

Y-Dragon Head

Q: "Z-Metal Tank" is equipped on to "Y-Dragon Head." My opponent uses "Snatch Steal" to take control of "Y-Dragon Head." Which player can use "Z-Metal Tank's" effect?

A: Even if your opponent takes control of your monster using "Snatch Steal," your opponent does not take control of the Equip Spell Card. You retain control of the Equip Spell Card. Therefore, your opponent cannot use the Union Monster's effect to remove it from "Y-Dragon Head." During your Standby Phase, you can remove "Z-Metal Tank" and change it back to a monster.

Questions and Answers

Spell Card Rulings

A Legendary Ocean

Q: I am Ritual Summoning a Ritual Monster. How many Level Stars does the WATER monster I am offering as a Tribute have?

A: A Ritual Spell Card's requirement is the total number of Level Stars. If "A Legendary Ocean" is on the field, then the Level of WATER monsters on the field and in the hand are decreased by one. Since the Level (number of stars) is decreased, you are now required to offer more as a Tribute.

Q: Can I include three copies of both "Umi" and "A Legendary Ocean" in my Deck?

A: No. "A Legendary Ocean" has an effect that states "This card's name is treated as 'Umi.'" In your Deck and Side Deck combined, you can only have a maximum of three copies of cards with the same name. Therefore, you can only have a combined total of three "Umi" and "A Legendary Ocean" cards.

Different Dimension Capsule

Q: After "Different Dimension Capsule" activates, does it remain on the field? Also, if it remains on the field, if it is destroyed before my second Standby Phase, does the effect disappear?

A: "Different Dimension Capsule" remains on the field after it is activated. If it is destroyed before the second Standby Phase by another card, then the card removed from play remains removed from play.

Q: During my second Standby Phase after "Different Dimension Capsule" is activated, if "Imperial Order" is on the field, does "Different Dimension Capsule" become destroyed, and can I add the card removed from play to my hand?

A: "Imperial Order" negates the effects of Spell Cards, so "Different Dimension Capsule" is not destroyed and remains on the field without its effect activating. The card removed from play also remains removed from play.

Yata-Garasu

Q: If two "Yata-Garasu" deal damage to my opponent in one turn, does my opponent skip two Draw Phases?

A: No. Let's say you have a "Yata-Garasu" on your field and you take control of your opponent's "Yata-Garasu." You attack with both "Yata-Garasu" cards. Even if both deal damage to your opponent's Life Points, the timing of skipping your opponent's next Draw Phase is the same. This effect does not repeat, so your opponent skips only one Draw Phase.

Q: While "Imperial Order" negates the effect of "Different Dimension Capsule," do the turn counts continue?

A: Though "Different Dimension Capsule's" effect is negated, the Standby Phase count continues.

Double Spell

Q: Does "Double Spell" allow me to take a Spell Card in my opponent's Graveyard and add it to my hand?

A: No. The Spell Card you select in your opponent's Graveyard must be activated from the Graveyard as your Spell Card. You cannot put the chosen Spell Card in your hand.

Q: I use "Double Spell" and activate the Spell Card in my opponent's Graveyard. Can my opponent chain the Spell Card in the Graveyard?

A: No. The Spell Card in your opponent's Graveyard that is activated is being resolved due to the effect of "Double Spell." Therefore, it cannot be chained. If your opponent is going to chain, then he or she must chain "Double Spell."

Heart of Clear Water

Q: What is an "effect of a card that specifically designates a target?"

A: These are effects that specifically target one monster, such as the effects of "Tribute to the Doomed" and "Man-Eater Bug." These cards cannot destroy the monster equipped with "Heart of Clear Water." However, against cards whose effects do not target, such as "Mirror Force" and "Raigeki," "Heart of Clear Water" cannot stop the monster from being destroyed.

Necrovalley

Q: When "Necrovalley" is on the field and "Black Pendant," "Witch of the Black Forest," or "Giant Rat" sent to the Graveyard, are the effects stopped?

A: No. The effects activate from the Graveyard, but the effects themselves are not involved with the Graveyard.

Q: "Imperial Order" is stopping the effect of "Necrovalley." Can I use the effects of "A Cat of Ill Omen" or "Royal Tribute" that require "Necrovalley" to be on the field?

A: Yes. They only require that "Necrovalley" be on the field, so even if "Necrovalley's" effect is stopped, you can use those effects.

Question

Q: During the Duel, though no particular effect has activated, can I change the order of the cards in my Graveyard?

A: No. Also, when using cards like "Monster Reborn" or "Sinister Serpent" that lets you search your Graveyard for a card, make sure to keep the cards in order.

Q: When one card effect sends multiple cards to the Graveyard, such as "Dark Hole" and "Painful Choice," who decides what order the cards go to the Graveyard?

A: The owner of the card decides the order. Also, the card that was used goes to the Gravyard last. For example, if you use "Dark Hole," the monsters are sent to the Graveyard, and after the effect is over, then "Dark Hole" is sent to the Graveyard.

Q: Can I activate "Question" when I only have one Monster Card in my Graveyard? If yes, can I hide the topmost Monster Card so it can't be seen?

A: Yes, you can activate "Question" when you only have one Monster Card in your Graveyard. However, the topmost card in the Graveyard is for everyone to see, so you cannot hide it.

Super Rejuvenation

Q: Since I have more than six cards in my hand, I have to discard cards during my End Phase. Will "Super Rejuvenation" activate if I discard a Dragon-Type Monster Card?

A: No. Regulating the number of cards in hand occurs at the end of the End Phase. Therefore, the Dragon-Type Monster Card you discarded does not activate "Super Rejuvenation."

Wave-Motion Cannon

Q: The card says, "Inflict Direct Damage to your opponent's Life Points equal to the number of your Standby Phases that have passed after this card was activated x 1000 points." When this effect is activated, can my opponent chain it with "Mystical Space Typhoon" to destroy it and stop this effect?

A: No. Sending "Wave-Motion Cannon" to the Graveyard during your Main Phase is a cost. Even if you activate "Mystical Space Typhoon" to chain the effect, "Wave-Motion Cannon" is sent to the Graveyard as a cost for activation, so it cannot be the target of "Mystical Space Typhoon."

Q: While "Imperial Order" is active, can I send "Wave-Motion Cannon" to the Graveyard and deal damage to my opponent?

A: You can activate "Wave-Motion Cannon" and send "Wave-Motion Cannon" to the Graveyard as a cost, but its effect is negated, so you are unable to deal damage.

Q: While "Imperial Order" is active, what happens to the Standby Phase turn count for "Wave-Motion Cannon?"

A: While "Imperial Order" is active, if "Wave-Motion Cannon" is face-up on the field, then count each of the Standby Phases.

Trap Card Rulings

Barrel Behind the Door

Q: When card effects that deal damage to both players, such as "Tremendous Fire" and "Ring of Destruction," activate, can I use "Barrel Behind the Door" or "Trap of Board Eraser" so that only my opponent takes damage?

A: Yes. In the case of "Barrel Behind the Door," your opponent will end up taking twice the damage.

Q: Can I chain "Barrel Behind the Door" to an effect I activated? For example, can I chain "Barrel Behind the Door" after I activate "Ring of Destruction?"

A: Yes. You can chain "Barrel Behind the Door" to an effect you activated.

Remove Brainwashing

Q: If "Remove Brainwashing" is destroyed while it is active, who has control of a monster that has changed control previously due to "Change of Heart?"

A: Cards like "Change of Heart" and "Creature Swap" are not Continuous Spell Cards. Therefore, once "Remove Brainwashing" activates, those effects are negated and control reverts back to their original owner. Even if "Remove Brainwashing" is destroyed, the opponent does not regain control. For cards with Continuous Effects, such as "Snatch Steal," the player who activated "Snatch Steal" regains control.

Rivalry of Warlords

Q: When "Rivalry of Warlords" activates and I can only have one Monster Type on the field, do I take into account my face-down Monster Cards?

A: No. Face-down Monsters have not revealed themselves. When "Rivalry of Warlords" activates, do not include face-down monsters. Only the face-up monsters must now be of one Monster Type. Also, while "Rivalry of Warlords" is active, you can Set monsters that are a different Monster Type.

Q: While "Rivalry of Warlords" is active, multiple monsters on my field are all the same type. However, the type is not a Machine-Type monster. Can I offer one of the monsters as a Tribute to Tribute Summon "Jinzo?"

A: No. While "Rivalry of Warlords" is active, "Each player can only summon or control one type of face-up monster at a time." You cannot summon a monster that is a different type. Even though "Jinzo" has the effect to negate traps, you cannot Tribute Summon "Jinzo." Similarly, you cannot Special Summon "Jinzo" using "Monster Reborn."

Q: While "Rivalry of Warlords" is active, can I Summon, Flip Summon, or Special Summon a monster that is different than the Monster Type on my field?

A: No. You cannot summon, Flip Summon, or Special Summon a monster that is different than the Monster Type on your field. Also, cards that have the ability to Special Summon a monster do not work if the monster that is being Special Summoned is of a different type. If your face-down monster is flipped face-up due to your opponent's attack or card effects, such as "Swords of Revealing Light," and the monster is of a different type, then the monster is destroyed.

Rope of Life

Q: Can I activate "Rope of Life" when I have zero cards in my hand?

A: Yes. Even if you have zero cards in your hand, you can activate "Rope of Life." If you do have cards in your hand, then you discard all the cards in your hand.

Q: After I Special Summon a monster using "Rope of Life," "Book of Moon," or "Ready for Intercepting" flips the monster face-down. Does the monster lose the 800 ATK increase effect?

A: Yes. Basically, a card effect that changes a monster's abilities disappears when the monster becomes face-down or leaves the field.

Q: Can I use "Rope of Life" to Special Summon my "Jinzo" which was sent to the Graveyard in battle?

A: Yes. You can Special Summon "Jinzo." Also, "Jinzo" gains 800 ATK because the effect is resolved by the time "Jinzo" is Special Summoned.

Q: My opponent has taken control of my monster using "Change of Heart." If that monster is destroyed in battle, can I activate "Rope of Life?"

A: If the monster destroyed in battle is sent to your Graveyard, then you can activate "Rope of Life." In the case of "Change of Heart," when your opponent takes control of your monster and the monster is destroyed in battle, the monster is sent to your opponent's Graveyard, so you cannot use "Rope of Life."

CARD NAME — EXPANSION — PAGE NO.

4-Starred Ladybug of Doom *PSV* 68

Alphabetical Card Listing

Alphabetical Card Listing

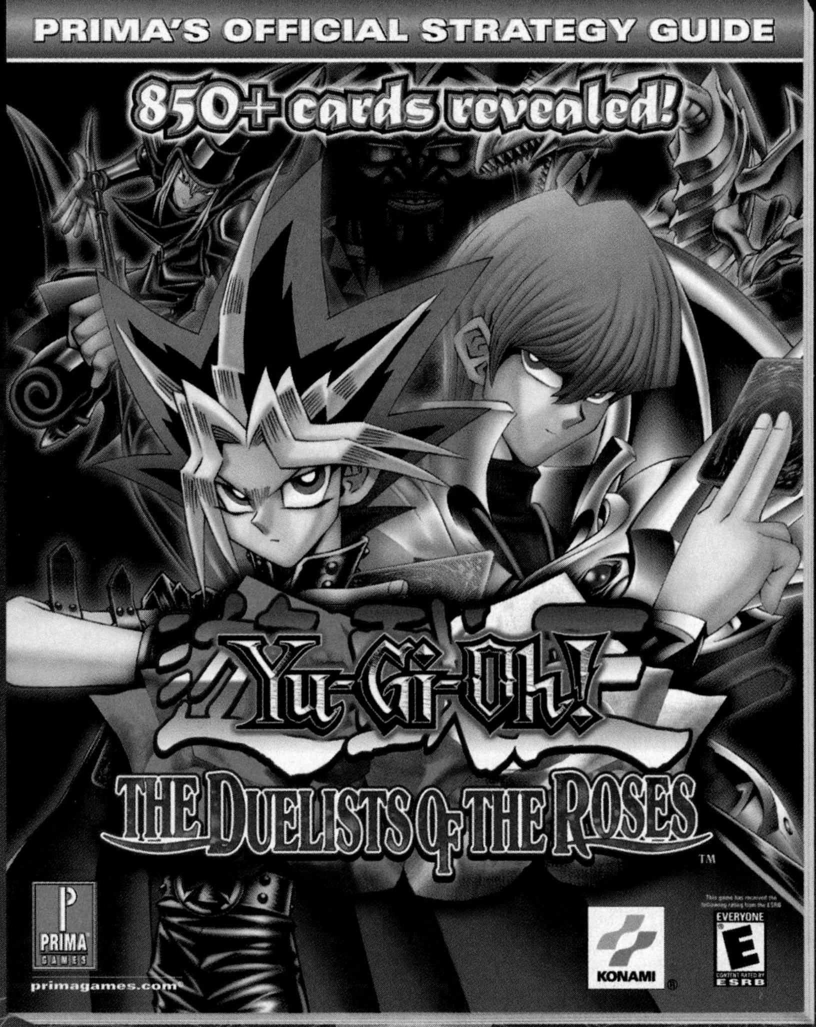
PRIMA'S OFFICIAL STRATEGY GUIDE
850+ cards revealed!
Yu-Gi-Oh!
THE DUELISTS OF THE ROSES
PRIMA GAMES
primagames.com
KONAMI
EVERYONE
E
ESRB